Management for Professionals

More information about this series at http://www.springer.com/series/10101

Chitra Sharma

Business Process Transformation

The Process Tangram Framework

Springer

Chitra Sharma
ICT, Change and Process Management
Professional
Gurgaon, India

ISSN 2192-8096 ISSN 2192-810X (electronic)
Management for Professionals
ISBN 978-81-322-2348-1 ISBN 978-81-322-2349-8 (eBook)
DOI 10.1007/978-81-322-2349-8

Library of Congress Control Number: 2015938916

Springer New Delhi Heidelberg New York Dordrecht London

Printed on acid-free paper

Springer (India) Pvt. Ltd. is part of Springer Science+Business Media (www.springer.com)

To My Parents
For their unconditional faith in me

Foreword

For the last 30 years, I have been fortunate enough to be involved in many diverse industry activities, from fast-moving consumer goods to publishing and, for the most part, the electronic communications explosion, most recently as an executive officer at Qualcomm Inc. The one resounding conclusion that I have made is that you must change or die. My experience ranges from technology start-ups to turnarounds at established major players, and in each case it has been critical to make significant transformations to succeed.

Transformation is complex, vast and at times extremely overwhelming. What one needs to do is to look around, learn from others and yet create one's own unique recipe for success. Critical to success is the development of common goals, language and milestones.

There are many useful books, models and theories that are available and can guide us through transformation. Most of these books are, however, at a strategic level and provide little help on how the goals can be translated into realistic plans – plans that are tangible and yield real results in terms of the top line and the bottom line.

The 'Process Tangram' is a refreshing way to look at business process transformation. With its concept of seven 'tans' of triggers, goals, tools and techniques, culture, communication, success factors and the programme, this framework creates the bridge between strategy and realization. Indeed, each organization has its own emphasis on these 'tans', yet a transformation is unfathomable without them. In varying degrees, every transformation is touched by them. When one knows what to manage and how to manage, they can create their own pattern out of the Tangram puzzle.

The 'tans' have been discussed in a way that they are easy to understand and bring in the result of research of existing material and experience in a lucid manner. Triggers are a comprehensive listing of real scenarios that make an organization start its transformation journey. The possible objectives for such a journey are covered under goals. The extensive coverage of elements in the tools and techniques section enables any professional to get a feel of the possibilities and provides them with an opportunity to choose the relevant ones. As an aid to application, tools and techniques have even been grouped into clusters that enables quick shortlisting based on requirement.

This book can be read as two interleaved parts. One is a thorough textbook bringing together the learnings from many excellent sources as diverse as Mckinsey's 7-step model and Dr. Elisabeth Kubler-Ross' observations of terminally ill patients. The second part is the inclusion of excellent snippets of practical advice such as 'picking out the relevant', 'don't substitute feelings for facts' and my old favourite of always using SMART goals. The combination of these two parts wrapped up in the flexible structure of the 'tans' is most helpful. Finally, there is much emphasis on the human element that is so often missing from the typical process transformation book – we must always remember that at the heart of transformation are the people that transform their environment.

With cases and examples from across the industries, this book is bound to be useful for the executive, the strategist, the change manager, the professional and even for the student who wants to understand and build a career in business process management.

Gildrew Limited
London, England

Andrew Gilbert

Acknowledgments

Many professionals have one thing in common – they secretly nurture the dream of writing a book, however, in the hustle and bustle of life and the corporate, are unable to take to the pen. I am happy that I could pursue mine.

This dream was not the only reason that I wrote this book, the greater reason was the "missing link," between the knowledge banks that exist all around us and the practicality of their application. Business process transformation is like a "Tangram puzzle" where everyone wants to create a different picture with essentially the same pieces.

The immense knowledge that exists in the minds and works related to business process transformation is so scattered that one can easily get lost. For me, this book has been the quest to find how this enormity can be translated into something that is simple, is available at one place, and allows the professional to make informed choice of the elements available in the "tans" of the "Process Tangram."

Naturally, I could not have done it alone and therefore would like to acknowledge the support of the people who helped me.

I would like to thank Prof. (Dr.) Dhruv Nath and Prof. (Dr.) Sangeeta Shah Bharadwaj from MDI Gurgaon and Prof. (Dr.) Amit Mookerjee (IIM Lucknow) for their guidance and help in the development and scoping of the book. I enjoyed the benefits of the wonderful MDI library and therefore extend my appreciation to Dr. Antony Jose, Ms. Priyadarshini, and Mr. Parmeshwar Prasad for creating an environment that was conducive to the flow of thoughts.

I acknowledge the contribution of Mr. Bruno Schenk for collaborating with me on the chapters on change management and managed services. His expert comments and inputs have helped in bringing out very real and practically useful cases that focus on the application of the prevalent models and theories.

This book is about learning, sharing, and synthesizing, which makes me immensely thankful to my friends and colleagues especially in the Netherlands, United States, and India who encouraged and helped me through the development of the book by sharing their experiences.

I am thankful to Ms. Chhaya Kain, my friend and colleague, for helping me in the preparation of the manuscript.

Credit is also due to Ms. Sagarika Ghosh and Ms. Nupoor Singh from Springer for promoting and supporting new authors.

While writing the book, I could always draw energy from my children Dhruv and Utkarsh, who took so much pride in my work and hoped it would inspire others. I must also recognize the contribution of my husband Sudhir, the in-house critic, for his copious supply of comments and suggestions. Besides this, my immediate and extended family always rallied behind me, and I am grateful to God for the same.

1 Nov 2014 Chitra Sharma

Contents

About the Authors

Chitra Sharma is an experienced ICT, Change and Process Management Professional. She has worked in Europe and India for over 17 years, which allows her to uniquely blend the East with the West. She holds a master's degree in Business Process Management and Information Technology from Open University, The Netherlands, and an M.B.A. from FMS Udaipur, India. She is trained on frameworks and methodologies such as CMMI, RUP, ITIL, ASL, Six Sigma, and PRINCE 2. Websites: www.verbeter.biz, www.processtangram.com.

Bruno Schenk is a born change and business leader with the ability to inspire others in making their goals a success. He has travelled and explored more than 55 countries and worked for a long or short period in more than 20 countries to date, and therefore gained a global understanding of cultures, the different ways of working, habits, values, and simply the local people and market developed his global understanding and interest. Bruno Schenk has contributed to various global top-listed companies as President, Managing Director, COO and CTO, Executive Consultant, Analyst and Project Manager. He has transitioned and transformed 10,000+ people around the world with key cornerstones in India, Bulgaria and Switzerland. His education includes an EMBA, diplomas in business, management, economic and information technologies and Harvard Business School's top executive program Advanced Management Program. He is married and lives with his wife Melissa in Remetschwil, near Zurich, Switzerland.

1 Introduction

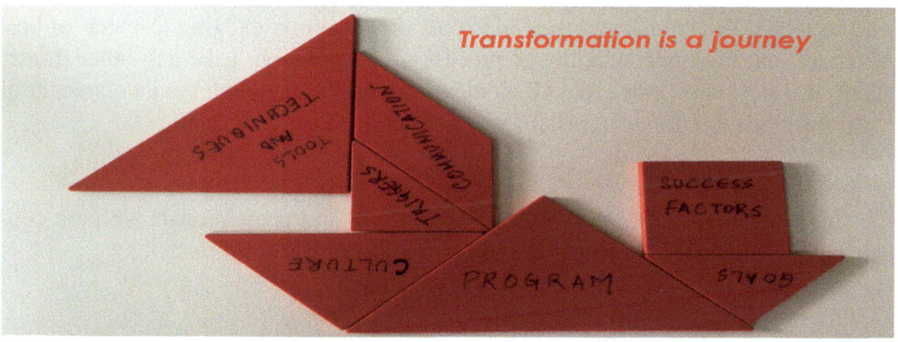

Many of us have been a part of a business process transformation or aspire to participate in one. With so many prevailing definitions of business process transformation, it is, however, difficult to understand what business process transformation really means. It is even more difficult to understand how to undertake one.

For the purpose of this book, I would like to propose business process transformation or process transformation as a change in business processes that involves more than an incremental change and has certain characteristics. It is started by a trigger, which sets the organizational thinking in motion. It is initiated to achieve certain goals. Goals cannot be achieved without involving tools and techniques, culture, and communication. Even with all this, there are success factors that differentiate between one transformation and another. And finally, since it is so complex to understand and undertake, it is advisable to undertake it as a program. This leads to the genesis of the "Process Tangram" Framework which takes its cue from the Chinese puzzle game "Tangram" and **PROCESS** T**r**A**N**sformation pro**GRAM**.

As per the legend of the "Tangram" (http://www.tangram-channel.com/legend-of-the-tangram/), a sage who was carrying a precious glass window for the king

C. Sharma, *Business Process Transformation*, Management for Professionals,
DOI 10.1007/978-81-322-2349-8_1

inadvertently broke it when he stumbled down the side of a mountain. To his luck, the glass broke into seven geometric pieces, which he used to create figures such as mountains to describe the journey to the king. The king liked the glass pieces and the associated figures so much that he ordered to create a wooden version of the 'glass pieces', and the "Tangram" puzzle was born. Each of the glass pieces was called a "tan" and the puzzle was called "Tangram."

Similar is the case of process transformation. It is nothing short of a long journey and there are seven pieces that can hold it together. These seven pieces of Tangram, also called "tans," are thus the triggers, goals, tools and techniques, culture, communication, success factors, and the program itself. Like the Tangram puzzle, these "tans" can be used to create an image that is unique to the organization and suits the organization best.

The "tans" can be used to organize the process transformation at a high level. In order to support the implementation of a Process Tangram, each of the "tans" is divided into elements. These elements help in creating the bridge between the vision and strategy. The "tans" and their elements are based on existing research of best practices and my understanding of process transformation. Like any other framework, it is not prescriptive that all elements are utilized, though the involvement of "tans" is advisable for a successful transformation (Fig. 1.1).

Is this book for you? Why?

This book is intended primarily for executives and professionals who are connected in some way to business processes. This book is useful for:

- Process professionals
- Change managers
- Executives and professionals involved in business process transformation and transition
- Professionals involved with managed services
- Students who want to build a career in business process management

This book is helpful because:

- It is a comprehensive framework covering all aspects of transformation from business case to culture.
- It is easy to understand with practical examples.
- It enables the user to create his or her own transformation program with the help of Process Tangram.
- It starts from the basics, so previous background is not required.

How can you use this book?

This book can be used in many ways. Once the reader has gone through the introduction, one can read each chapter independently. The chapters have been written to be complete in themselves, with lot of examples incorporated in them. There are examples from various industries such as manufacturing, software and IT, semiconductor, health, and telecom. Processes pervade through all organizations; therefore,

TRANSFORMATION PROGRAM	Transformation Charter	Business Case, Milestones & Toll Gates	Team Structure	Risk & Issue Management	Governance	Handover & Closure
TRIGGERS	Business Strategy Change/ Alignment	Compliance Requirements	Voice of Customer & Quality	Mergers and Acquisitions	Implementation of Enterprise Architecture	Failure of existing Process to Deliver
	Alignment with the Customer	Contractual Obligations	Loss in shareholder Value	Outsourcing	SubOptimal Utilization of Infrastructure	Shortage of Resources
GOALS	Dramatic Improvement in Performance	Achieve/ Retain Market Leadership	Customer Delight	New revenue streams	Increase in Competence	Revenue Growth
	Optimal Advantage of Technological Advancements	Virtualization of Enterprise	Enterprise as a Network	Economies of Scale	Increase in Productivity	Cost Reduction
TOOLS & TECHNIQUES	Process Analysis	Functional Analysis	Best Practice Analysis	Lessons Learnt logs	Performance Metrics	Quality Tools
	Productivity Analysis	Business Process Modeling	Competitive analysis	Life Cycle Analysis	Financial Metrics	Data Analytics
	Customer Analysis	Value Stream Mapping	Market Trends	Organization Analysis	Investment Analysis	Cost Analysis
CULTURE	Value System	Organization Structure	Motivation	Change Management	Conflict Management	Capability Development
COMMUNICATION	Engagement Strategy	Stakeholder Analysis	Communication Plan	Identification of barriers to communication	Communication Package	Feedback & Evaluation
SUCCESS FACTORS	Leadership Commitment	Process orientation	Quality	Speed	Adequate funding	Flexible IT Structure
	Clear Strategy & Vision	Value Focus	Innovation	Portfolio Management Approach	Cross Functional Teams	MIS and knowledge assets

Fig. 1.1 Process Tangram

the Process Tangram is not limited to any one industry. Process Tangram can be helpful to anyone who wants to go further in transformation.

Reading the chapters sequentially will facilitate the reader in understanding the concept of Process Tangram and learning about it in a structured way. Due to time constraints, if the reader is unable to go through all the chapters of the book, it is still feasible to get the gist and application possibilities of "Process Tangram" by reading the conclusion along with the introduction.

While going through the book, one experiences the vastness of knowledge required for a transformation. The elements of each "tan" can be utilized to match the specific requirements of an organization. The Process Tangram provides the visualization of how these concepts, tools, and techniques can be held together and utilized for transforming business processes.

It is to be noted that for the purpose of this book, people and employees have been used interchangeably and mean the same. Business process transformation is a change and is used interchangeably, depending on the context with transformation, Process Tangram, and change.

Except where clearly mentioned, all names of companies and the stories covered are hypothetical, based on the author's imagination and experience.

1.1 Chapter Overview

1.1.1 Transformation Program, Triggers, Goals, Tools and Techniques

This chapter proposes the "Process Tangram" derived from process transformation program. It takes its cue from the Chinese game of Tangram where seven pieces are cleverly put together to create the desired picture. The seven pieces (tans) are the transformation program itself, triggers, goals, tools and techniques, culture, communication, and success factors. Within this chapter, the "tans" transformation program, triggers, goals, and tools and techniques are covered.

1.1.1.1 Transformation Program

The transformation program "tan" covers the following elements: transformation charter; business case, milestones, and tollgates; and team structure, risk and issue management, governance, handover, and closure.

The transformation charter has many parts. One of them is the Program Overview which describes the goals that the program intends to achieve along with the desired outcomes and benefits for the organization. The Program Overview is followed by the Program Organization discussing the roles and responsibilities of the involved stakeholders. The Transformation Program Charter sums up the Program Business Case and Milestones which include summary of the costs and associated benefits and the funding and approval mechanisms from sponsor for any deviations in the scope, timeline, quality, or costs.

Business case is the basis for the program sponsor to take the decision to provide approval for going ahead with the envisaged program. Once the detailed business case is worked out and approved, the program can commence. The essential components of business case of the transformation program – executive summary, objective, option evaluation and recommendation, timeline and investment analysis, and supporting material – have been discussed.

Milestones and tollgates are a mechanism for the program/project manager to review the progress of the program/project at predefined moments. If required, besides the core team, key stakeholders may also be invited to a milestone review. This also acts as a test of readiness for program/project to move to a moment of decision making, often referred to as tollgates.

Team structure comprises of a steering committee, process teams, line management and facilitators, and at times super-users.

Risk and issue management is at the program and project levels.

Good governance is not optional, but crucial for the success of the transformation program. It provides the necessary structure and processes to facilitate the delivery of program as per agreed-upon specifications of scope, time, budget, and quality.

Once the transformation program reaches its conclusion, handover and closure come into picture. The deliverables arising out of the program should be handed over and embedded in the organization as the normal ways of working.

1.1.1.2 Triggers and Goals

A trigger in itself is nothing unless it is crystallized into goals. These two "tans" are interlinked; therefore, these have been explained together. Though there can be many triggers, the ones considered under the "triggers" "tan" are business strategy change/alignment, alignment with the customer, compliance requirements, contractual obligations, voice of the customer and quality, loss in shareholder value, mergers and acquisitions, outsourcing, implementation of enterprise architecture, suboptimal utilization of infrastructure, failure of existing process to deliver, and shortage of resources. Interlinked to these triggers, there can be multiple goals that an organization can choose from. The goals covered under the goals "tan" are:

- Dramatic improvement in performance
- Optimal advantage of technological advancements
- Achieve/retain market leadership
- Virtualization of enterprise
- Customer delight
- Enterprise as a network
- New revenue streams
- Economies of scale
- Increase in competence
- Increase in productivity
- Revenue growth
- Cost reduction
- Competitive advantage on the basis of cost or differentiation

- Regulatory compliance
- Plug revenue leakage
- Consolidation
- Standardization
- Improved measurement and control

1.1.1.3 Tools and Techniques

"Tools and techniques" can be used to gain an understanding of the current status and as enablers to define and design new ways of working to achieve breakthrough results. There could be many tools and techniques that can be utilized for the purpose of transformation. The prominent ones are covered as elements of this "tan." These are process analysis, productivity analysis, customer analysis, functional analysis, business process modeling, value stream mapping, best practice analysis, competitive analysis, market trends, lesson learned log, life-cycle analysis, organization analysis, performance metrics, financial metrics, investment analysis, quality tools, data analytics, and cost analysis.

1.1.2 Culture and Communication

This chapter covers two soft "tans," communication and culture, which impact how the organization thinks, feels, and adjusts to the transformed process and makes them vital to the "Process Tangram."

The ideas, customs, and social behavior of people and society form its culture. In a similar way, in an organization, its culture is the ideology, customs, and behavior of the members of the organization. In other words, the visible and invisible elements of an organization that influence the success of a transformation program immensely form its culture. Culture is about people, their relationship with the organization, and how they feel.

Transformation requires people to adapt to the changing environment, and culture helps in achieving the same. From the perspective of the transformation team, knowledge of culture helps in understanding how change can be rolled out, what can be expected, and finally, how transformation can be ingrained in the culture.

Culture is divided into value system, organization structure, motivation, change management, conflict management, and capability development.

Communication connects people with each other, stakeholders, and transformation. There can never be enough of communication, although information overload should not be confused with communication. Communication can range from interpersonal to mass and online communication thus occurs in many forms and can be spread in space. Communication should be precise, should be targeted to the right people, should overcome barriers, and should be improvised through feedback.

Within Process Tangram, communication is divided into the engagement strategy, stakeholder analysis, communication plan, identification of barriers to communication, communication package and feedback, and evaluation.

1.1.3 Success Factors

Success factors are the last "tan" of the Process Tangram. Success factors differentiate one transformation from another. The success factors covered in this "tan" are leadership commitment, clear strategy and vision, process orientation, value focus, quality, innovation, speed, portfolio management approach, adequate funding, cross-functional teams, and MIS and knowledge assets. They are discussed with respect to their implication to the process transformation program.

1.1.4 Process Modeling

Process modeling is an element of the tools and techniques "tan." Process modeling as a technique enables comprehension and conceptualization of complex processes around us which in turn become the basis for discussion, analysis, design, optimization, and documentation. It provides a mechanism to decompose large processes into smaller chunks called sub-processes that are complete in themselves yet are related to the main process.

This chapter covers how the "as is" and "to be" processes can be modeled. Process modeling is explained using BPMN 2.0 (business process modeling notation) in a simplified manner. While this book is not meant to be used as a substitute for advanced books on process modeling, it provides a fair opportunity to learn how to model simple business processes using BPMN2.0.

1.1.5 Change Management

Change management is a part of the culture "tan"; however, it is a complete subject in itself, and therefore, this chapter attempts to cover it in a systematic and structured manner. Managing change is important so that people are not fearful of change but become a part of a successful change initiative that sustains itself. Change disturbs the status quo and makes people uncomfortable due to the associated uncertainties. In order to pull the change through, the role of the change manager assumes significance, which along with the change agents manage and channelize resistance creatively. They manage the implementation of change in such a way that the employees are able to survive the change. A successful change initiative ensures that the change becomes ingrained in the lives of people and sustains itself.

This chapter uses the transformation initiative of a fictitious semiconductor foundry "Semicron" to explain the concepts of change management. The important change models and theories are translated to provide real insight into how Semicron decided to learn from them and deploy them.

1.1.6 Managed Services: A Case of Business Process Transformation?

Managed services is an engagement model for product or service delivery. The current offerings are enumerated to provide a glimpse of the breadth of managed services. With the help of network managed services process of a telecom operator, the process, transition, and the role of IT are explained. It is evaluated if managed services is really a win-win scenario for the provider as well as the client. Finally, it is discussed if managed services can be categorized as a case of business process transformation.

While this chapter has been covered from the perspective of a telecom operator, on how and why a fictitious telecom operator TX (managed services client) chooses vendor Y (managed service provider), it also throws light on how their relationship is envisaged. This chapter is relevant for anyone who wants to understand the aspects that need to be covered before entering into a managed service agreement. It covers the perspectives of the managed service provider (vendor) as well as the managed services client (operator).

1.1.7 Recapitulation and Application of Process Tangram

This chapter provides a summary of the chapters covered in the book. It is a means to not only recapitulate but also to get insight into the application of Process Tangram. While all topics have been covered, tools and techniques have been divided into clusters as an aid to their application. Process transformation is a journey, and this framework is the quest to convert transformation goals into operational reality.

To sum up, this book proposes a framework for business process transformation. This framework is based on best practices, and like any other framework, it provides the building blocks for undertaking a transformation exercise. It is vital to recognize that while all seven "tans" are relevant, all elements of the "tans" may or may not apply. The wisdom lies in picking out the relevant from the elements to chart one's unique path to process transformation. Although the focus of this book is from a process perspective, it is relevant for any organization which plans to undertake a transformation as processes do not exist in vacuum and are a part and parcel of the functioning of any organization.

Reference

http://www.tangram-channel.com/legend-of-the-tangram/. Accessed 1 Oct 2014

Transformation Program, Triggers, Goals, and Tools and Techniques

2

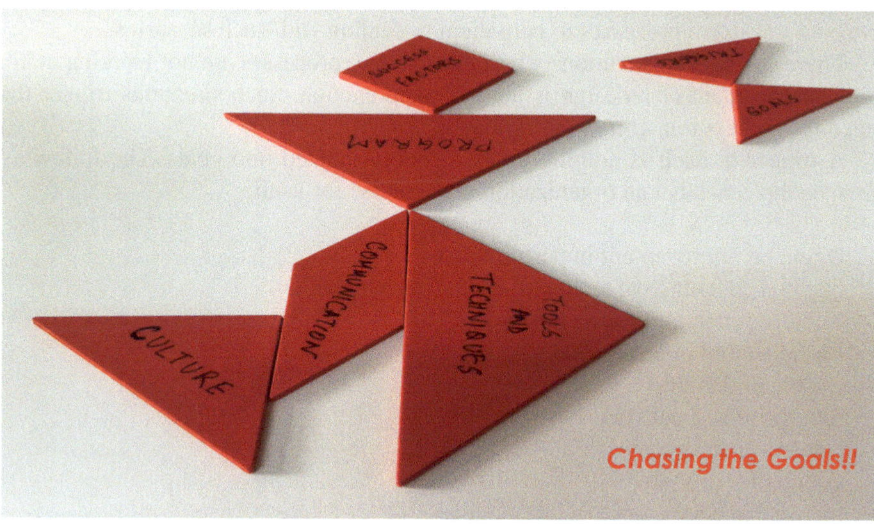

2.1 Transformation Program, Triggers, Goals, and Tools and Techniques

Process transformation can be triggered by many reasons. Sometimes due to changing markets, the strategy of the business undergoes changes and requires realignment. When the realignment begins, often it is not small increments that suffice, rather a complete process transformation is required.

In other cases compliance requirements may call for a transformation of processes. There can also be contractual obligations agreed with a supplier or customer that may trigger process transformation. The end customer may decide to redo its

C. Sharma, *Business Process Transformation*, Management for Professionals,
DOI 10.1007/978-81-322-2349-8_2

processes, and as a result, the downstream processes of the manufacturer may require transformation.

Voice of the customer and voice of quality can be triggers for a transformation initiative as organizations strive for excellence. An organization continuously losing shareholder value may sit up to realize that the processes need to be transformed. On the other hand, there may be an organization which wants to increase the shareholder value and therefore triggers transformation. There could be others who decide to outsource, merge, or acquire to ebb the decline in shareholder value which in turn can lead to transformation.

Implementation of enterprise architecture which applies architecture principles and practices to guide organizations through the business, information, process, and technology changes necessary to execute their strategies often results in a process transformation initiative.

When an organization realizes that its infrastructure such as that of IT and HR is not optimally utilized or faces shortage of resources, it may look out for innovative ways to transform processes to help them in dealing with such scenarios.

There can also be situations where the existing processes are not working at all, and improvement or redesign is not adequate enough. Such situations trigger the need for process transformation.

A trigger in itself is nothing unless it is crystallized into goals. The following may be the goals that an organization may choose for itself:

- Dramatic improvement in performance
- Optimal advantage of technological advancements
- Achieve/retain market leadership
- Virtualization of enterprise
- Customer delight
- Enterprise as a network
- New revenue streams
- Economies of scale
- Increase in competence
- Increase in productivity
- Revenue growth
- Cost reduction
- Competitive advantage on the basis of cost or differentiation
- Regulatory compliance
- Plug revenue leakage
- Consolidation
- Standardization
- Improved measurement and control

There are many *tools and techniques* that can be used through the life of the process transformation program. While there could be many tools and techniques that can be utilized to gain an understanding of the current “as is” process and design of the “to be” process, the prominent ones are process analysis, productivity analysis, customer analysis, functional analysis, business process modeling, value stream mapping, best practice analysis, competitive analysis, market trends, lesson learned log, life-cycle analysis, organization analysis, performance metrics, financial metrics, investment analysis, quality tools, data analytics, and cost analysis. These have been covered in the chapter.

2.1.1 Transformation Program

In order to ensure that a trigger converges into a result that is per expectation, it makes sense to consider *process transformation* (hereafter used interchangeably as transformation) as a program. While any methodology can be followed, the essential components of such a program would be to have a clear charter supported by a business case. The progress can be monitored through the use of milestones and tollgates. Team structure should be clearly established, and governance mechanisms should be put in place. Risk and issue management should be taken up rigorously throughout the program, and handover and closure should be done carefully so that not only the benefits are institutionalized; the lessons learned during the life of the program are available for future reference and use.

The transformation program holds everything together, ensuring that interdependent projects happen in a coordinated manner and achieve the desired business goals within the specified constraints and specifications. The transformation program can be organized in the manner described below.

2.1.1.1 The Transformation Program Charter

Typically the program is divided into multiple interrelated projects with clear scope, timeline, and deliverables with cross-disciplinary project teams along with a core transformation team. The division of the program into multiple projects having a common vision yet having individual deliverables enables allocation of projects to multiple project managers, while the transformation manager provides the overall guidance and holds the program together. These projects are interrelated, so cross-project coordination effort is high. The fact that such programs cut across different departments which have their individual goals, they provide an opportunity to align the department goals to business goals.

The program charter covers at least the following:

Program Overview

Program overview provides objectively stated problem statement/need that the program intends to solve/fulfill. It has a brief description of the program wherein the benefits of the program are identified. The link to the organization's overall strategy is established along with linkages to any other strategic programs that are planned or in progress. Besides this, program goals and outcomes, what is in-scope and what is out-scope, are mentioned. Program assumptions, constraints, initial risks, and issues are also included. At the project level, the project charter can refer to the program charter to establish the link between the project and the program.

Program Organization

This includes the program structure outlining the projects/components and their relationship. A high-level program plan may be included here. The governance structure, stakeholders, communication chart, roles, and responsibilities are listed down in RASCI format.

Program Business Case and Milestones

This includes summary of costs and associated benefits. The funding and approval mechanisms from the sponsor for any deviations in the scope, timeline, quality, or costs are covered as well. A business case should be present at the program level as well as the project level. It is likely that some of the projects may not yield a positive business case but would be required for the overall objective. Some of the costs and benefits will be at the overall program level and would be assigned on pro rata basis to the projects. The important thing is to ensure that the projects deliver what they are expected to deliver and happen in a harmonized manner. Important milestones with timelines (start and end dates) should always be mentioned and subject to version control.

2.1.1.2 Business Case, Milestones, and Tollgates

The business case is the basis for the program sponsor to take the decision to provide approval for going ahead with the envisaged program. The business case is an ongoing document and should be constantly updated through change management process. Usually a preliminary study is conducted to create a very high-level business case to initiate the program. Once the detailed business case is worked out and approved, the program can commence. The budget and planning of the initial study falls outside the scope of the program.

The business case of the transformation program should have at least the following components:

Executive Summary

This covers in short the salient points of the business case, the options investigated, the cost associated with not undertaking transformation, recommendation on the best option, and its associated costs and benefits. The executive summary is very important as this creates the first impression and provides the sponsor an opportunity to quickly get an overview of the proposal. The approved business case serves as a reference baseline and helps in exercising control through the life of the program.

Objective

The objective of the program should clearly specify the benefits that would be achieved. The objectives should be specific, measurable, achievable, relevant, and timely. The benefits to be derived from the program should be clearly stated drawing a comparison between the current and future business states.

Timeline and Investment Analysis

Besides the benefits, a realization plan should also be offered in terms of time required, assignment of responsibility, and accrual of benefits with timeline.

Investment analysis is required to ensure that a relationship exists between the costs and benefits; a clear picture of whether the returns justify and outweigh the costs, return on investment, and time value of money is taken into consideration. The common techniques are covered under the tools and techniques section.

Option Evaluation and Recommendation

In this section all relevant ways to achieve the desired result should be captured for the purpose of option evaluation. This could include the option of not undertaking the program which, when turned around, could highlight the imperative of taking action as the cost of not undertaking an action may be too high.

Option evaluation should be done on the basis of costs and benefits. An objective assessment of all benefits and associated costs should be made. As an example, suppose a bank wants to transform its banking operations and a part of the proposal is workflow automation and digitization of files. Automation through workflow could increase the efficiency of transactions but would necessitate capital and operational expenditure. Digitization of documents could result in logistics savings while having associated costs. Another approach for the bank could be to outsource operations and focus on the core areas.

Once both the options are evaluated, it would result in recommendation based on specified parameters. One way could be to assign weightage to identified parameters and evaluate on the basis of aggregated scores. This allows for a systematic comparison enabling objective evaluation and selection. In cases where the benefits cannot be directly quantified in monetary terms such as increase in motivation or a compliance requirement, they should still be stated and utilized while making a comparison.

Supporting Material

The supporting material for assumptions, calculations, etc. should also be provided to justify the business case. Typically this is an excel sheet embedded in a word document.

2.1.1.3 Milestones and Tollgates

The program can be managed by making use of milestones and tollgates. Milestone reviews are a mechanism for the program/project manager to review the progress of the program/project at predefined moments. If required, besides the core team, key stakeholders may also be invited to a milestone review. This also acts as a test of readiness for program/project to move to a moment of decision making, often referred to as tollgates. A tollgate meeting must have the sponsor of the program who authorizes the project to go ahead. In some cases there may be conditional approval and certain commitments may be required from the program manager before the next tollgate. In some cases the tollgate may lead to early closure of the program.

The number of milestones and tollgates can be customized as per the size of the program; however, a minimum of two, one for start and one for closure, is required to retain the structure in the program. Tollgates are sometimes referred to as stage gates.

In case of early closure due to unforeseen circumstance, the in-between tollgates can be skipped, but the last one should be held.

2.1.1.4 Team Structure

The process transformation team at the minimum should have a steering committee, process teams, line management, and facilitators. Very often a group of super-users also forms a part of the core team.

Steering Committee

It provides overall direction with respect to business vision and the transformation program. Besides the initial approval to go ahead, it is also responsible for reviewing the program through the tollgates and facilitating the sponsor in decision making. The committee champions the change effort and removes barriers to acceptance.

Process Teams

The process team is responsible for actually executing the process transformation. With the help of the steering committee, they finalize the vision for the "to be" process. They undertake a gap analysis between the current state and the desired state often referred to as "as is analysis" and "to be modeling." Since process transformation is not just process improvement, the process teams undertake the crucial task of redefining/redesigning the process. The implementation plan and associated metrics are also created by the process team. It is very important that the process team is cross-functional so that different perspectives and possibilities are available.

Line Management

Process transformation cannot be successful without the involvement of line management. Line management should be committed to and convinced of the benefits of process transformation. Line management involvement ensures that they have an answer for the classic question: "What's in it for me?" They lead the teams, and their involvement right from the beginning ensures that they are able to guide the real people who run the new process and eventually make it work. While this group is very important, it is also often the most impacted by process changes; therefore, it is important to ensure that this group does not hijack objectives of process transformation in order to retain their political/hierarchical status in the organization. Besides the steering committee which ensures the necessary support, the role of facilitators becomes very important to safeguard the objective of process transformation.

Facilitators

Process transformation is complex and is accompanied by changes in technical, political, and cultural paradigm. Facilitators who could be internal, though are mostly external consultants, bring with them the knowledge and know-how of undertaking the process transformation journey. Since they are brought in by the steering committee, they command necessary authority and respect. Facilitators are not necessarily great analytical planners, but they are the people who have a vision and have rich experience in process transformation. They have the capability to create a bridge of trust and confidence by not only providing awareness on alternative paradigm(s) but also in development of the new paradigm and its acceptance.

Super-Users

"Super-users" is a group of people who have good functional knowledge of the process across the value chain and/or have good knowledge of the organizational policies. They should be identified and used as resonating board for the process team. Super-users can help in the review and provide advice at the time of new process development. Subsequently some of them can act as change champions to percolate the changes through the organization.

2.1.1.5 Risk and Issue Management

Risk and issues need to be managed both at the program and project level. Risks can be described as an uncertain event that can have an impact (positive or negative) on the expected outcome. Some project-level risk and issues may qualify to be at program level. The existing templates for risk and issue management can be used.

The risks should be identified right from the start and should be regularly reviewed through the life of the program. Risks can be either internal or external to the organization. There can be various ways of identifying the risks. Existing upstream and downstream processes, people, internal and external data sources, IT landscape of the organization, expert opinion, older risk logs, issue logs, and lesson learned logs are some of the important sources of information for risk identification.

On the basis of the impact and likelihood often called as severity and probability of occurrence, the risks can be plotted as shown below on x and y axes and assigned a priority. Table 2.1 provides a simple way of assessing risk. Frequency of reoccurrence and impact on the critical path are factors that need to be taken into consideration when assigning values. Many a times, risks are correlated and this should be always taken into consideration.

Organizations may sometimes choose for a more detailed risk assessment on a five-point scale as shown in Table 2.2.

Irrespective of the style chosen, it is important to review the risks at regular intervals. The risks should be entered into the risk log which should be maintained through the life of the program and subsequently archived for later use. All the risks should be uniquely numbered. Risks should be closed and not deleted from the risk log. This enables management of repeating risks in a structural manner. Risks that are correlated to each other can be managed collectively.

The common strategies adopted for risk mitigation are acceptance, avoidance, transfer, contingency, and reduction. The time required on risk management will be more towards the start and end of the program.

Table 2.1 Risk assessment

Impact	Impact value (IV)	Likelihood	Likelihood value (LV)	Aggregated value (IV*LV)	
Low	1	Low	1	1	
Low	1	Medium	2	2	
Low	1	High	3	3	
Medium	2	Low	1	2	No action
Medium	2	Medium	2	4	Manage
Medium	2	High	3	6	Esclate
High	3	Low	1	3	
High	3	Medium	2	6	
High	3	High	3	9	

Table 2.2 Detailed risk assessment

Likelihood		Rare	Unlikely	Possible	Likely	Almost certain
Impact	Very high	Mitigation plan	Action plan	Escalate	Escalate	Escalate
	High	Monitor	Mitigation plan	Action plan	Escalate	Escalate
	Medium	Monitor	Monitor	Mitigation plan	Action plan	Escalate
	Low	Routine review	Routine review	Monitor	Mitigation plan	Action plan
	Very low	Routine review	Routine review	Routine review	Monitor	Monitor

When a risk becomes a reality, it is termed as an issue. Issues can simply be defined as hindrances that should be overcome in order to achieve program objectives. Issues need to be identified, analyzed, assigned priority, and acted upon till they reach closure. Issues should be uniquely numbered and should remain in the issue log when they get a closed status as they are useful source of information for future. An issue can occur even if it has not been identified as a risk. In case a risk gets converted into an issue, a reference should be created to the risk.

The description of the risks should be very clear to enable action, for example, "resources not available" is more difficult to act upon compared to "solution architect not available for creation of software architecture document." Issues are often assigned to different stakeholders/team members who are responsible for bringing it to closure on agreed-upon target dates. In case issues are not resolved as per expectation, the escalation mechanism comes into picture. Clear escalation mechanisms for management of risks and issues should be agreed upon and documented right at the beginning of the program.

2.1.1.6 Governance

Governance provides the necessary structure and processes to facilitate the delivery of program as per specified scope, time, budget, and quality. The method of governance is dependent on the structure, strategy, and culture of the organization. For a process transformation program, good governance is not optional, but crucial for its success.

In simple words it is a regular review mechanism which enables sharing of information with the stakeholders on a regular basis and is an opportunity to get decisions on matters such as investment decisions, prioritization of resources, and final approval and ratification of process changes for them to become the new ways of working.

Typically two to three levels of governance are in place in most organizations.

At the first level, a weekly meeting is held between the program manager and the project managers on a one-on-one or collective basis. A status report is presented which can be the specific template being followed in the organization. The risks, issues, opportunities, financials, deliverables, and timelines are the main components that form the status report. The status report also contains a log of action points and decisions taken with target and completion date. Older status reports are archived as reference and closed items removed to keep the status report as short and actual as possible. The program manager can provide necessary direction and facilitation depending on requirement.

It is important to ensure that the status report is short and crisp so that the effort taken in generating the report is not an overkill. In organizations where project and portfolio management tools are in place, these reports can be generated by the system, with the project manager only required to make small updates. Usually the expectation from the project manager is to enter daily update in the tool while the financials are pulled out from the financial system through an interface. This meeting does not substitute the day-to-day interaction between the project managers and the program manager.

The second level of governance is between the program manager and the steering committee. The frequency of this meeting is usually once a month. In this meeting review is done at the overall program level. If needed, there may be representation from the project. Besides the review of the progress against time, money, quality, and scope, time is also devoted on approvals of change requests that need discussion. Regular change requests are cleared on an ongoing basis. It provides an opportunity to the steering committee to provide direction and share information on other ongoing programs.

The help of the steering committee may be sought in adoption of the transformed processes and approval of new policies and standards. Since the steering committee is usually formed by senior members of the organization, their acceptance and approval have a favorable top-down effect on the team. It is a good opportunity to discuss escalations which may have been dealt with on a regular basis but require further deliberation.

The third level of governance happens with strategic business unit. This is meant to be a review on the progress of the program from an organizational perspective. The frequency may be once a month or once in 2 months.

Besides the structured review, it is always possible that a meeting is called for at any of the levels on the basis of requirement. In case of involvement of external customer, additional meetings may be held as per mutual agreement.

2.1.1.7 Handover and Closure

Since the program organization is essentially a temporary organization, the deliverables arising out of the program need to be handed over and be embedded in the organization as the normal way of working. This is the point where the transition actually happens. Open issues/points should be handed over. In case there is a budget allocated to resolve these issues to the program organization, the budget should be handed over as well. Handover should be formally documented, and all the relevant documentation and training should be passed on to the receiving organization.

Some members of the core team may be retained or attached to the line organization for a period of 1–3 months to support the institutionalization of the new processes.

In order to bring the program to closure, the program manager should create and hand over a program closure report to the program management office containing:

- A brief history of the program along with its objectives
- Assessment of the achievement in terms of business case and deliverables
- Status of handover along with acceptance document
- Lesson learned report
- Link to all archived program documents
- In case of early closure, the reasons for closure and relevant information regarding handover
- Formal sign-off from the sponsor after steering committee review
- Link to archived program closure report

2.1.2 Triggers and Goals

Process transformation can be triggered by many reasons and should have clear goal(s). A trigger is an acknowledgment of the need to undertake the action. There can be multiple triggers translating into multiple goals. Triggers and goals for a process transformation are closely linked to each other; therefore, these two "tans" are explained together through the following cases.

2.1.2.1 Case 1

Consider the news brief (http://newsroom.cisco.com/press-release-content?articleId=1240830) on Cisco site:

SAN JOSE, Calif., Aug. 21, 2013 – Cisco today announced the availability of Business Transformation Certifications *(*http://www.cisco.com/web/learning/

certifications/specialist/bus/bus_transformation.html*) and training. The curriculum and exams, previewed at Cisco Partner Summit 2013 earlier this year, are designed to help the direct Cisco® sales force and channel partners satisfy a customer desire to engage in higher-value, structured, business-relevant conversations.*

In response to the shift in Enterprise IT budget planning, combined with the increasing influence of business leaders in the IT spend decision making process, Cisco and its partners are moving from selling hardware to selling solutions that solve business issues. Customer leaders recognize that IT and business architectures, solutions and services play a critical role in efforts ranging from automation and cost reduction to innovation and transformation. They demand that investment business cases clearly outline financial outcomes. To succeed in this competitive global economy, organizations must refine their business models, execute flawlessly and move quickly to seize new opportunities. Cisco partners must therefore be able to work with technology groups as well as business leaders to help overcome complex business challenges.

Jeanne Beliveau-Dunn, vice president and general manager at Learning@Cisco, said: "Customers are making purchase decisions based on integrated business solutions that provide competitive advantage, drive growth and enable their long-term strategic initiatives. To accelerate results, we are shifting our sales approach from an IT hardware emphasis toward one centered on architecture and solutions. Individuals need to understand and develop sales and engagement models with a stronger focus on customer business leadership. At Cisco, we are committed to delivering the certification programs that afford learners with the skills and knowledge to keep up with evolving practices, and their employers with unrivaled value."

Alan Sturgess, Consultancy Practice: Technology Leader, Networking, Security and Unified Communications, Computacenter (UK) Ltd., said: "Cisco Business Transformation training provided a consolidated methodology for understanding business goals and translating them into technology roadmaps. This allowed us to address both the immediate and future business needs of the customer. The techniques covered can be leveraged whenever engineers or consultants are engaged with the customer. Most technology deployments, large or small, are generally driven by an underpinning business outcome. From my perspective, these techniques can only enhance the customer experience and, by association, help develop stronger relationships."

Now let us analyze the following sentences and look for triggers:

'Cisco and its partners are moving from selling hardware to selling solutions that solve business issues.'

This statement indicates a *change in business strategy.*

'Customer leaders recognize that IT and business architectures, solutions and services play a critical role in efforts ranging from automation and cost reduction to innovation and transformation. They demand that investment business cases clearly outline financial outcomes'

'Cisco partners must therefore be able to work with technology groups as well as business leaders to help overcome complex business challenges.'

The above statements indicate the *voice of the customer and quality*. It also indicates *alignment with the customer* because the customer wants to have a better overview of the financial outcomes of the complete solution rather just hardware. The customers require that Cisco partners should be able to support them in complex business challenges.

The goals for the change in business strategy could be *customer delight, new revenue streams* for the learning arm through aspirants of the certification, *increase in competence* by way of deploying trained professionals, and *revenue growth* from existing customers through increased business.

From a process transformation perspective, the service delivery could undergo transformation since there is a change in business strategy from delivery of hardware to delivery of solutions. This would be connected to the recruitment process, sales process, and after-sales process. Since the change is substantial, incremental improvement to existing processes is not the objective. The interrelated processes need to be looked at in a holistic manner.

2.1.2.2 Case 2

Amazon Prime Air in its press release (http://www.amazon.com/b?ie=UTF8&node=8037720011) on delivery of books within 30 min through unmanned drones (Fig. 2.1), declared:

We're excited to share Prime Air – something the team has been working on in our next generation R&D lab.

The goal of this new delivery system is to get packages into customers' hands in 30 minutes or less using unmanned aerial vehicles.

Putting Prime Air into commercial use will take some number of years as we advance the technology and wait for the necessary FAA rules and regulations.

Fig. 2.1 Amazon unmanned aerial vehicles

If we analyze this case and assume that this announcement would become a reality, the triggers are many. It indicates *change in business strategy* to offer a new, quick mode of delivery of books.

It serves the need of customers who still like to read and feel the old-fashioned books despite the availability of e-books and readers. They, however, find it annoying to wait for 2–3 days before the physical copy of the book arrives. In this sense the trigger is the *voice of the customer*.

The goals in this case would be to *retain market leadership* and to take *optimal advantage of technological advancements*.

It would provide Amazon the *competitive advantage* on the basis of differentiation.

The supply chain process will undergo transformation with new vendors (drone suppliers) and new ways of distribution. The sales process being connected to this endeavor would also be impacted. It would be also interesting to consider the impact of this announcement on Amazon's competitors and the changes they may bring in their strategy to ensure that their shareholder value does not take a hit.

2.1.2.3 Case 3

Consider a case of an IT company LionSoft[1] which acquired another IT company TigerSoft. LionSoft has the ambition of being listed on NASDAQ, the American stock exchange. Both the companies have their own set of processes. Some lines of business are common; some are unique to both of them.

TigerSoft was making losses despite an impressive product line. The losses led to the sell-off. The executives of LionSoft were of the opinion that while some of the business lines of TigerSoft were making losses due to their cumbersome processes and mismatch between demand and supply, some lines were in the red due to revenue leakage.

The directors of LionSoft met after the acquisition to decide on the future course of action. They wanted to chalk out a strategy on how to capitalize on the acquisition. They were looking for *consolidation* and *standardization*. They also wanted to get listed on NASDAQ, which implied the need for necessary steps to *ensure compliance to regulations* such as SOX. They were even open to *outsource* certain functions to focus on their core competency.

It was decided to hire a top-notch consultancy firm to guide and implement what the board has called "business process transformation."

After spending a week at various locations, the principal consultant had the following observation after a weeklong interaction with staff and department heads of TigerSoft and LionSoft.

Interaction with the Head of Product Development: TigerSoft

The head of product development keeps the correct delivery dates under his sleeve, i.e., in his own application which is not accessible to others. He was very upset with the pool manager who he claimed was diverting his development resources as on-site consultants without providing timely replacements. This is resulting in

[1] LionSoft and TigerSoft are fictitious companies.

delivery delays. He confided that his team was getting informal feelers from their customers that they were on the lookout for new products owing to the TigerSoft's delayed product deliveries.

Interaction with the Pool Manager: TigerSoft

The pool manager of TigerSoft is responsible for the supply of resources who either are deployed as on-site consultants or work on niche products of TigerSoft. Surprisingly, the sales orders for on-site consultants and product sales are not linked to the application maintained by the pool manager. The pool manager admitted that due to lack of correct forecasts from sales, he has had to resort to simple extrapolation of previously supplied resources to create a forecast for himself. He also told that there have been times that he has had to divert resources from ongoing development of products to outside clients to meet the requirement of on-site consultants. He complained that very often he is not informed of changes in sales orders due to which he is unable to provide the resources on the specified time.

Interaction with the Sales Head: TigerSoft

The sales head complained that TigerSoft is unable to honor the orders in a timely manner. Whenever, with a lot of effort, the sales team has been able to increase the orders corresponding the supply, the resources for on-site consultants have not been made available leading to angry and dissatisfied customer.

Interaction with the CFO: TigerSoft

The only reason that the CFO of TigerSoft finds to be happy is that they have been acquired by LionSoft who is doing very well for themselves. The account receivable situation in TigerSoft is not good. Instead of recovery in the specified period of 30 days, 70 % of the payments are coming in >30 days and 50 % are coming in >45 days. This is leading to a working capital crunch.

He raised the issue of credit limits being ignored while taking orders. Even when the credit limits are being exceeded, the sales team continues to seek more and more orders from such customers. Some customers are now delaying acceptance documents for lame reasons, which is resulting in delay in invoicing.

Interaction with LionSoft Staff

LionSoft is in a comparatively better position and is a profitable company; however, it also struggles with applications running everywhere. There are many hobby applications which are very close to the developers who are proud to demonstrate them. It is costing LionSoft a lot of man-hours and hardware space. The source lines of code (SLOC) are below the industry benchmark. The engineers are bright and their productivity can easily be increased with some effort. The documentation quality is very poor and traceability to requirements is missing. When asked for requirements, the latest are to be found somewhere in the mailbox.

The engineers of LionSoft are very apprehensive of new counterparts from TigerSoft as for some of the product lines they have been competitors.

Both LionSoft and TigerSoft have a setup of finance and HR at all their locations. There are 10 locations where both LionSoft and TigerSoft have offices.

Initial Recommendation

It is suggested that the goals of *compliance to regulation, plug revenue leakage, revenue growth, economies of scale, and increase in productivity* should be considered. Besides this, *improvement of measurement and control* could also be one of the goals of process transformation. The possible candidates for transformation processes could be the sales and delivery process. It would be important to look at them with a portfolio approach so that the visible gaps in exchange of information in TigerSoft and LionSoft can be fixed. They can clearly benefit from an integrated system of forecast, orders, and delivery.

Besides the triggers explained so far, the other triggers for process transformation are *suboptimal utilization of infrastructure, decision to implement enterprise architecture, shortage of resources*, and *failure of existing process to deliver.*

Suboptimal utilization of infrastructure is the trigger when HR and IT are not optimally utilized. Consider the example a telecom organization having two product lines and contractual commitments to support both the lines for level three support. It was, however, facing shortage of resources. There were also complaints from the customer that the SLAs were not being met and they were facing churn of end customer. The company led an HR and IT transformation supported by process transformation. They realized that in order to support the current requirement, cross-training of resources would be required so that the people could handle both the product lines. A front desk was created to prioritize the service request as per the agreed-upon turnaround time (TAT). A workflow facilitated tracking and monitoring of the requests till closure. Repeat complaints could be identified and problem management was also enforced. The end result was a successful fix of resource crunch and process and a happy customer.

For some organizations, the decision to implement enterprise architecture brings about a complete process transformation. The purpose of enterprise architecture is to better align complex and expensive IT systems to business needs. Business processes and functions, technology, information, and data together form the base for enterprise architecture. Whenever this alignment happens, processes also undergo transformation.

An organization may decide to go online (virtualization) and distribute its operations across the world collaborating worldwide. In such a case it functions as enterprise as a network. Such a business transformation is inevitably coupled with a process transformation. Cost reduction is one of the objectives with reduction in overhead activities.

Once the triggers and goals for a process transformation are finalized, the process team needs to systematically approach the process transformation effort. There are many tools and techniques that can be deployed which are covered under the "tan" "tools and techniques."

2.1.3 Tools and Techniques

2.1.3.1 Process Analysis

It offers the process transformation team insight in the current process and the expected end objectives. The result is a clear definition of the scope, boundaries, and documentation of the current process with its performance measures. The current performance is analyzed to come up with inputs for process transformation.

Flow chart is one way of depicting the process by use of symbols. The common symbols are shown in Fig. 2.2.

In cases where documented process is not available, it is best to understand and draw it with the help of people who actually run the process. The technical experts may not be the best people to give the real picture of the current process. In cases where the existing process is already documented, it is advisable to go to the floor to see how far the documented process overlaps with the real situation.

FMEA, the acronym for failure mode and effects analysis, is a technique which identifies the potential failure modes of a process and its severity on the basis of impact on customer, occurrence, and detection. Consider the example in Table 2.3 which illustrates FMEA of a telecom service provider where an incoming call needs to be picked up in time and allocated to a qualified engineer within 2 h.

The scoring of severity, occurrence, and detection has been done on the basis of guideline given in Table 2.4.

The Risk Priority Number (RPN) is arrived at by multiplying the three scores. Not all failure modes require action. Only the ones with a higher score as shown in the example require action to ensure that the RPN comes to acceptable levels.

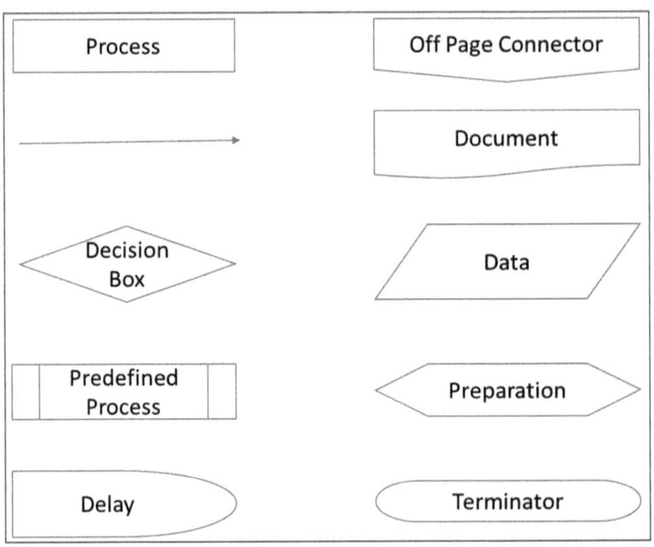

Fig. 2.2 Common flow chart symbols

Table 2.3 FMEA calculation

Process function	Potential failure mode	Potential effect(s) of failure	Severity (Sev)	Potential cause(s)/ mechanism(s) of failure	Occur-rence (Occ)	Current process controls	Detection (Det)	RPN	Recommended action(s)	Responsibility and target completion date	Action results				
											Actions taken	Sev	Occ	Det	RPN
Pick up and answer call in up to three ringtones	Call picked up later than three ringtones	Dissatisfied customer + lower CSAT	7	Inadequate personnel at the call center	2	Call that is not picked up gets diverted to supervisor	2	28							
Allocate engineer within 2 h	Qualified engineer with skill set match not available for allocation	Customer SLA not met. Penalties may be imposed	7	Engineers specialized according to skill sets and allocated accordingly. Even though an engineer may be available, allocation not possible due to skill set mismatch	7	Key responsibility area of resource pool managers expected to provide trained resources	7	343	Analyze the type of incoming calls on monthly basis to ensure there is a match between the requirements. Also ensure that engineers are trained on multiple skills so that resource utilization can be optimized	Jennifer Shaw	10/1/2014	7	3	2	42

Table 2.4 FMEA guideline

Parameter	Consideration	Score on a scale of 1–10	Remark
Severity	High impact on customer	High	Low score on low impact
Occurrence	High frequency of occurrence	High	Low score on low frequency of occurrence
Detection	Failure easy to detect	Low	High score if failure difficult to detect

Care should be taken to remain objective on the purpose of this analysis. The purpose is not to bring about incremental improvement, but to have at least a significant improvement. The failure modes with high RPN of the existing process should be taken into consideration while transforming the process. If FMEA for the existing process does not exist, then it may be an overkill to undertake FMEA. Rigorous FMEA should however be carried out for the transformed process to ensure that required action is taken to ensure that there is no negative impact on the customer and there is not disruption of service. In many cases the existing process is run in parallel till the new transformed process stabilizes.

2.1.3.2 Productivity Analysis

Productivity is defined as the ratio of output to input. It is a measure of performance of a particular process or organization. While at the overall level there may be metrics such as return on investment and return on equity, at the process level, productivity analysis helps in assessing the current process state. This analysis involves the following steps:

- Gap analysis of the productivity goals against the current performance.
- Analysis of the processes that is broken.
- Identification of waste in the current process.
- Gap analysis of the current productivity against expected future goals.
- Check if future goals are driven by the organization's vision.
- Analysis of barriers to productivity and ways to overcome them.
- Calculation of efficiency in terms of finding ways to minimize the inputs and maximize the outputs.

Productivity analysis concerns itself with efficiency and effectiveness. A product or service may be produced efficiently with minimum input and maximum output but may be of no use if it the output does not satisfy or exceed the requirement. In other words effectiveness of the current process also needs to be taken into consideration when creating a baseline for a process transformation.

A creative and innovative approach often leads to not only increased output with decreased input but also an increase in the actual and perceived value added to the product or service.

2.1.3.3 Customer Analysis

A process transformation, whether it focuses on the upstream or downstream processes, revolves around serving the king called "the customer." A thorough customer analysis is the key to align the process to the customer and maximize the value of the delivered product or service. It enables the process transformation team to gain an understanding of the former, current, and future customers and the market segment being catered. Besides this, the demographic features of the customers such as gender, age, and spending capacity are an additional input in devising innovative process offerings.

The information on the customers can be gathered through customer satisfaction surveys, focus groups, internal studies, etc. These are examples of direct sources of information. Indirect sources of information on customers could come from external sources such as consultancies offering reports against a payment. Very often such reports offer information on comparable businesses and outlook of their customers as well.

2.1.3.4 Functional Analysis

Functional analysis has its roots in system engineering and is useful in gaining functional understanding of the current process. The functions are identified along with their interfaces and associated resources. The function verb rule is followed wherein all the functions are verbs (action).

The flow of functions, along with data and information, is depicted with a control flow. This implies that data and information items are covered along with activation, control points, and termination of the flow. At a very basic level function comprises an input, control, enablers, activities, and output as shown in Fig. 2.3.

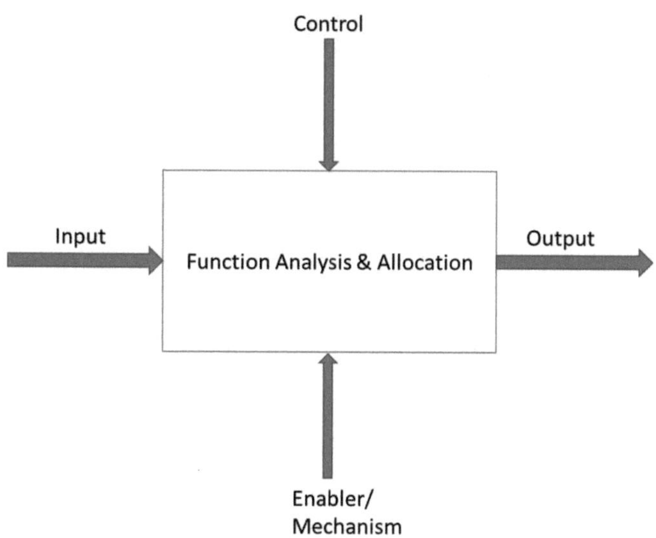

Fig. 2.3 Function analysis and allocation

The result of requirement analysis is the input for the function. Enablers are teams and tools such as function flow diagrams, IDEF, requirement allocation sheet, timelines, etc. Enablers are also called mechanisms. Controls are the constraints and organizational procedure. As an example, it could be a constraint to develop a solution using COTS product or to develop in-house solution.

Activities include system states and modes, system functions, external interfaces, allocation of functional requirements to functions, performance analysis, time and resource analysis, integration of functions, fault detection, failure mode analysis, failover, and recovery. Output is the functional architecture and supporting detail. Functional architecture is a description of requirements, but it is not the solution.

Let us consider the example in Fig. 2.4 to understand how functions are decomposed to sub-functions and how allocation of performance requirement can be done. At the system function level, an event is to be planned and executed. Within the event one function is transportation of employees. Transportation of employees has two sub-functions: transportation and distribution of refreshment. Both the sub-functions have performance requirements. Distribution of refreshment can be done in parallel to transportation. At the lowest level it is indicated how the performance requirement of covering 10 km and reaching in 30 min is allocated to the sub-functions.

The functions should be discrete and finite and are decomposed to two or more levels. A high-level function is usually decomposed to two or more levels. The input and output of the levels remain the same; however, the level of detail increases at lower levels. Sometimes processing instructions are made available which provide information on how input gets converted into output.

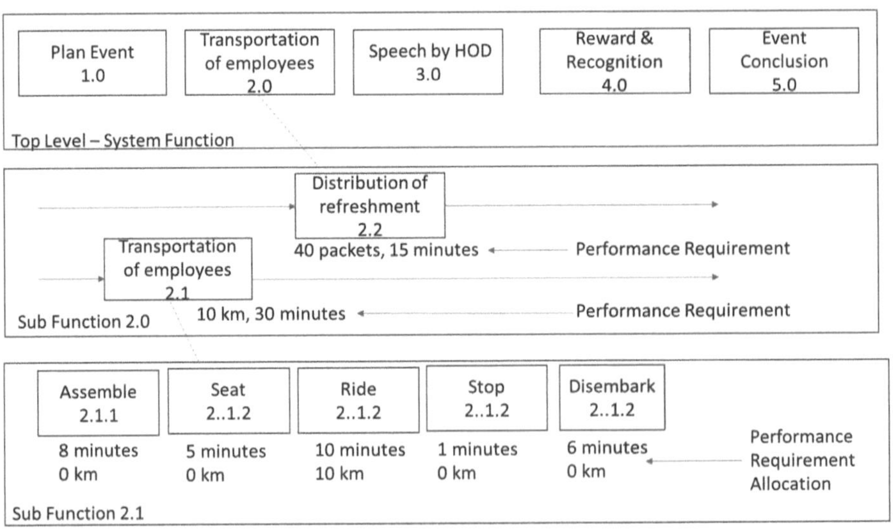

Fig. 2.4 Decomposition of functions

Functional analysis can be useful in cases where the process transformation is expected to work in tandem with automation. It is a means to transform functional, performance, and interface requirements along with constraints to come to a description of system functions.

2.1.3.5 Business Process Modeling

Business process modeling (BPM) enables in understanding of the process in a way that a complete view is presented. A complex process can be represented by way of process modeling in such a way that the participants can have a look at it in its completeness. Besides this, different roles may require different perspectives to view the process which becomes possible. The purpose of the model defines the way it will eventually look.

Process modeling is done using modeling tools, following a naming convention using a modeling language. A separate chapter is devoted to discuss business process modeling in detail.

2.1.3.6 Value Stream Mapping

Value stream mapping has its roots in "lean." Though typically associated with process improvement rather than transformation, it can be used for quickly charting a transformation plan. Value is defined from the perspective of the customer. It is something that a customer is willing to pay for! Value stream mapping begins with looking at all the items that comprise the flow.

Contrary to popular belief, value stream mapping is not restricted to the manufacturing industry. While for a manufacturer of bicycles the frame is an item, for a software provider, the technical specification is an item. Both the supplier and the customer are a part of the value stream. The material and information flows are taken into consideration as well to arrive at an end-to-end picture that can provide optimum value to the customer.

Value stream mapping differs from process analysis in terms of the level of detail and works at a higher level. Value stream mapping demands a clear vision for it to yield an effective result. A clear picture of what the customer wants in terms of price, quality, and time is required and translates into elimination of waste. The focus is on a high-level identification of the process taking the material and information flows along with the time taken in these steps. The time taken includes lead time and process time.

It is a simple paper-and-pencil tool which does not have to be perfect but functional. It enables in creating a blueprint of what should be done to create a flow that generates value. It is essential to involve the actual users of the flow to create a value stream map.

Some of the symbols used in value stream mapping are summarized in Fig. 2.5.

For the identified process, the following input may be considered (Sproull 2009):

- *Value-Added Time*: The value-added time taken to transform the product into value, excluding waiting time.

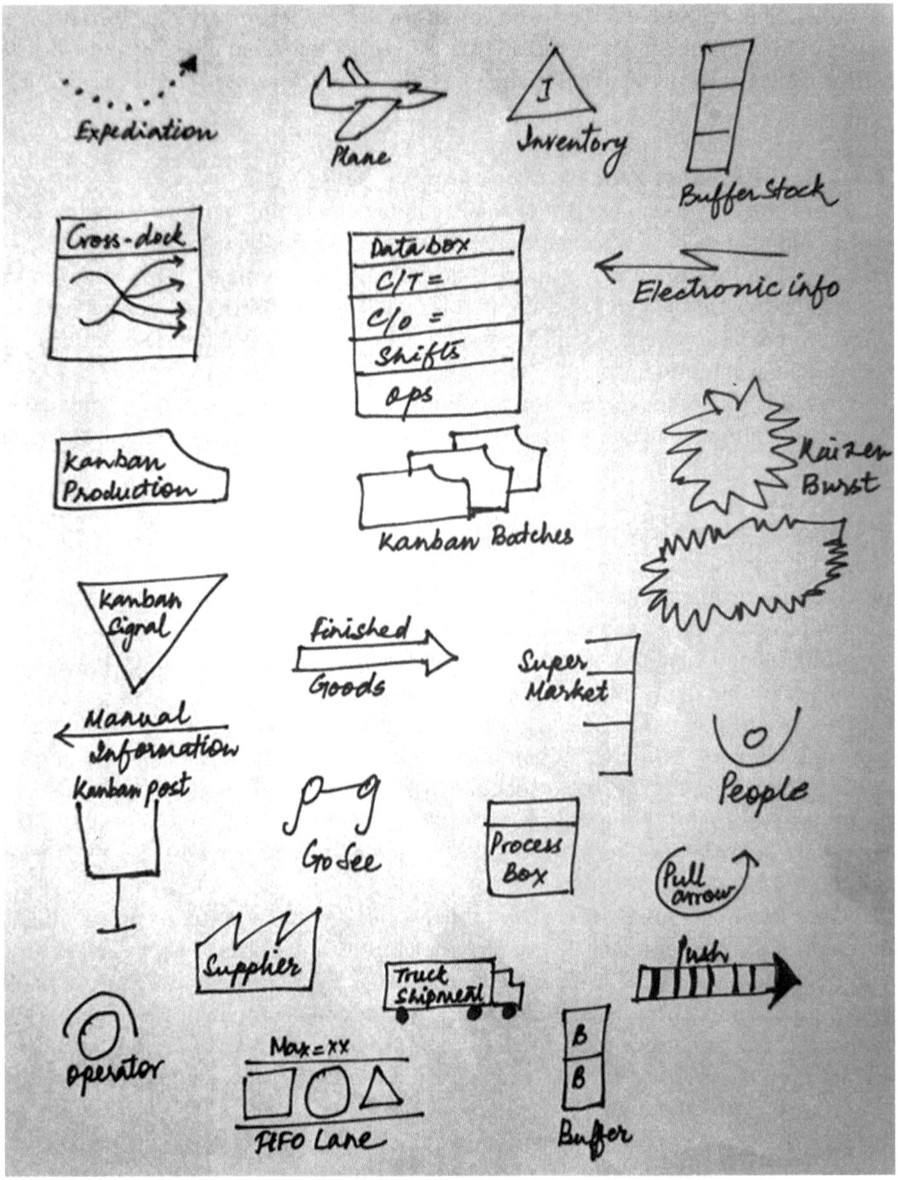

Fig. 2.5 Value stream mapping symbols

- *Wait Time*: The average time that a part waits before it can move to the next process step, for example, for inspection.
- *P/T (Process Time)*: The average time taken for a single part to be completed by a single step. Process time should be equal to the sum of value-added time and waiting time.
- *Cycle Time*: The average time taken from release of raw material into the process to the completion of finished goods ready to ship.

- *Lead Time*: This is the time elapsed between the receipt of order from the customer and the delivery of order to the customer.
- *Inventory*: The number of parts waiting to be processed in each step.
- *Actual Capacity*: The average number of parts that a process step is able to produce at a given time.
- *Actual Demonstrated Capacity*: The average total pieces or parts produced/time minus total average scrapped during the same time.
- *Percent Repaired*: Average number repaired compared to the average total produced for any unit of time.
- Customer demand or order rate.
- Actual production rate as compared to the order rate.
- Percentage on time completion.

These inputs help in identifying where the first constraints lie. These inputs give the information on internal constraints, though there could be outside constraints as well, for example, with the customer or the supplier. Once the first constraint has been identified, it is advisable to look for the second constraint as well so as to have a comprehensive picture of the constraints.

Once the process steps have been identified and quantitative data has been analyzed, the steps are categorized into the three categories of value adding (VA), business value adding (BVA), and non-value adding (NVA) (Dumas et al. 2013). The perspective remains that of the customer. To establish if the step is value adding or not, the requisite question is to establish the willingness of the customer to pay for the same. There may be some steps which may be required for reasons such as regulations; thus, even if the customer may not be willing to pay for it, they are required for running the business. Such steps are termed as business value-adding steps. The steps besides the value adding and business value adding are categorized as non-value adding.

Once the steps are categorized, a critical look is required on minimizing or eliminating non-value-added steps and business value-adding steps. The value-adding steps should be examined for better alternatives.

Very often there are possibilities of improvement not in the process steps themselves but in the lead times. The common approaches followed are from "lean" and "kanban". While lean focuses on the process steps, kanban focuses on the waiting time. The pragmatic approach sometimes requires adding additional steps in the beginning to fix the problems at a later stage.

If we take the case of LionSoft discussed earlier, the delivered orders do not get converted to cash. Here additional step of checking the current credit situation before taking the order would be required from the sales team, and additional step of providing credit information to the sales team would be required from the accounts team.

Value stream analysis is not only useful in the analysis of the current state but provides opportunity to come up with transformation plan which are called the future state and the ideal state. Once the desired state is reached, then value stream mapping acts as a deterrent for the process to digress back to the original state.

2.1.3.7 Best Practice Analysis

Best practice analysis is also called benchmarking. This involves looking at best performing comparable functions within the organization, best performing comparable functions outside the organization, and looking across industries and sectors even for noncomparable functions. For example, a nonperforming supply chain process may look at the successful HR process of the same organization, it may look at the supply chain processes of other organizations, and it may also look at finance process of another organization to look for best practices.

There are advantages in all the methods. Looking inside the organization has the advantage that the overall vision of the organization is the same and the best practices are easy to port since the overall environment, vision, variables, etc. are the same. A classic example of this is that once a shared service succeeds for the finance process, HR process may follow the same example and set up shared services.

Looking outside the organization has the advantage of expanding horizons and learning from others. It prevents reinventing the wheel and energy can be focused on taking on from where others have reached. The critique to this approach is, however, that this has a limiting impact on innovation and does not facilitate out-of-the-box thinking.

Considering another sector or industry which is not comparable, requires a lot of clarity of purpose and openness to embrace ideas irrespective of their source. A product development company, for example, may look out to Tibetan monks to transform its product innovation process. It may reach out to their way of peer-to-peer learning, commitment, and self-organizing groups to fuse talent with learning and passion in teams and deliver innovative best-in-class products.

Best practices are sometimes available in the form of frameworks, and the organizations may choose to take that path towards transformation. These frameworks are mostly crystallization of best practices. As an example CMMI (http://www.sei.cmu.edu/reports/10tr033.pdf) for Development offers benchmarking the capability of an organization as well as a path to further development. While it may be a useful path for organizations at a lower level of capability, for organizations that are at a higher level, it is not something that can be a differentiator.

There are many consultancies, databases, etc. that can facilitate the search for appropriate best practices. It depends on the goals and the starting point that the method should be chosen. Best practices are a rich source for filtering out and adopting the relevant while designing the transformed process. The focus in benchmarking is on learning from best practices that lead to superior performance.

2.1.3.8 Competitive Analysis

This is a systematic approach to look out for competitors. It not only involves looking for the existing competitors in the addressable market but also to look out if there is competition from elsewhere. While what the competitor is doing should not overshadow the organization's process transformation endeavor, it is relevant to consider their strategic moves and to recognize who the new competitors are and what could be the new technologies and intents they bring in.

Competitive analysis is different from benchmarking as here the focus is on performance parameters, differentiating capabilities, market information, and perception, while benchmarking is more on how the best in the lot achieve something.

This is relevant while identifying the end-to-end process for transformation as well as for subsequent positioning in the market for process excellence as it provides a perspective on both strengths and weaknesses. Parameters that satisfy the need of the customer should also be taken into consideration while undertaking a competitor analysis. Many organizations conduct or receive (from research agencies) such analysis on regular basis so it may actually be readily available.

2.1.3.9 Market Trends

Market trends can have a profound effect on process transformation. Consider a traditional insurance company which has always relied on a large network of insurance agents for generating and retaining business. The market trend of virtualization of value chain through technology would considerably lower the barriers to entry. Unless the company transforms its business processes, it could lose out on business or may not remain in business.

Another example could be the impact on data centers with the advent of cloud computing. Their processes would need to undergo significant transformation to offer more and more IT services instead of data hosting capabilities to compete with public cloud computing.[2] The IT departments of organizations face severe threat and would need to leverage the cloud to their benefit by looking into options such as hybrid IT[3] and internal or hybrid clouds.

These two examples indicate that the organizations cannot be oblivious to the market trends while undertaking process transformation; rather they should take advantage of the market trends to provide a better fit between the transformed process and the customer requirement.

2.1.3.10 Lesson Learned Logs

Very often process transformation efforts are not taking place for the first time in an organization. While some efforts would have been successful, some do not fly. All these efforts, irrespective of their outcome, are a rich source of information for subsequent programs. Typically organizations maintain lesson learned logs, though many a time they are updated at the end, rather than through the life of the program. These provide information with respect to improvement opportunities, challenges, corrective actions, resolutions, and strategies in the context of the organization. This helps in ensuring that the wheel is not reinvented and mistakes are not repeated.

---

[2] Cloud computing is the practice of using network of remote servers hosted on the internet to store, manage, and process data.

[3] Hybrid IT relates to the setup where IT organizations act as intermediaries to provide services which are hosted partly internally and partly externally. Internal cloud relates to a setup where the IT department creates its own cloud offering IT as a service. Hybrid cloud relates to a connection between internal cloud and external cloud allowing for easy augmentation for data.

In case the lessons learned are not properly maintained, it is interesting to interact with people who led similar projects to understand the learnings from the past.

2.1.3.11 Life-Cycle Analysis

Process transformation is not a one-time activity, and a holistic approach is required while planning the implementation. The level at which a service operates is an important input in planning the entire life cycle of transformation. While cost and time have an impact on the phasing, they need to be logically planned, implemented, and sustained to a particular level before the subsequent phase can be started. As an example it would not be realistic for a service provider to plan for customer delight when basics of incident, change, and problem management are not in place. In such a situation, perhaps, incident and change management could be the part of first phase, problem management a part of second phase, and customer delight the third phase.

In the example discussed earlier, it could be envisioned that as the process evolves, supplier support would be seamlessly integrated and automated. Besides this, the service desk would go beyond complaint resolution and advise the customer on maximizing productivity and innovation. While the evolution of process subsequent to the transformation should be thought of and documented taking the life cycle into consideration, its implementation may be out of scope. This, however, helps in providing a road map for the processes as they mature.

2.1.3.12 Organization Analysis

Process transformations involve not just revisiting the processes across the selected value chain; it brings with it structural changes that frequently involve reorganization. This requires an understanding of organizational behavior, relationships, and measures of organizational performance (Hausser 1980).

There are many models available that can be utilized for understanding and comparison with other organizations. These differ on the basis of the level of analysis. Individual analysis models focus on the individual's relationship and effectiveness with reference to the organization, while group analysis models focus on group interactions and effective systems of management. Organization analysis models study the differentiation and integration in terms of interface with the environment and central role of organization structure, while integrative models integrate the levels of analysis and synthesize domain of organizational behavior. Irrespective of the model adopted, the important aspect is to scope this analysis to the selected value chain.

Understanding of context and function helps in gaining an insight into the degree of specialization, standardization, and formalization of the functional activities in the organization. Organizations function in the context of the environment in which they operate such as size, technology, dependence, and location. Organizational structure can be broken in terms of structure, concentration of authority, line control of workflow, and relative size of the supportive component (Hickson et al. 1969).

The degree of autonomy, span of control, application of controls, and the support staff are impacted by the context of the organization. The organization structure has an impact on how groups within the organization interact with each other as well as their performance which in turn impacts the success of a transformed process.

Information for organizational analysis can be found in organizational goals and objectives, mission statements, strategic plans, annual reports, audit reports, and reward systems. Other sources could be short- and long-term staffing needs, skill level of existing staff, and impending reorganization. Interplay of context, structure, and overhead can be used to facilitate process transformation.

Organization analysis differs from organization structure covered under the culture "tan" in terms of perspective. The focus of organization analysis is to study the current state, whereas organization structure covered under the culture "tan" looks at how the structure can be changed.

2.1.3.13 Performance Metrics

Performance metrics are relevant not only as a source of information while undertaking a process transformation; they are very important to keep the process transformation on track. They are moreover required to ensure that the transformed processes do not regress back to the old state.

Performance metrics cover the critical work processes and their relation to customer requirement. They indicate how the results are measured, what are the agreed goals and standards with the customer, and most importantly how the performance has been over a given period.

These, however, need to be studied with a pinch of salt as it is not always the case that what is being measured is what should be measured. There are often a plethora of metrics that are defined, and considerable effort goes into populating them especially in cases where they are not completely automated. As with many other functions in an organization, metrics have an imprint of legacy, and it is not uncommon that something gets measured because it was done by the predecessor.

Typically performance metrics are designed around elements such as alignment with organization's mission, process performance, cost reduction/avoidance, product quality, reduction in cycle time, on-time delivery, and customer satisfaction. The process team should not get overwhelmed with existing performance metrics but at the same time sift out the objectives, criteria, and measurements.

While designing new performance metrics for the transformed process, it should be ensured that the metrics are SMART (specific, measurable, attainable, realistic, and timely). In other words, the way the metrics are defined should ensure that they can be easily interpreted and quantified. They should enable statistical analysis and comparison with itself in terms of time and possibly with others in the industry and should be realistic in terms of expectation and achievable in the expected time period. For every metric, the possible methods of measurement, benchmarks, assumptions, possible targets, ownership, frequency of measurement, and responsibility should be defined.

Besides this, it should be ensured that the focus is on outputs which include the end product as well as the significant intermediate products. The customer's perspective should be taken into consideration while designing the metrics. Customer may be internal or external and have expectations with respect to the delivered product, and the metrics should be able to capture the same. Metrics should not be designed around the ease of data capture; rather first the objective should be defined which should lead to defining of the metric, and then the important aspect of measurement should come into picture. If the starting point is how the data would be captured, the process teams can get bogged down and miss out on the important metrics.

Mostly performance metrics are a combination of "what has already happened" as well as "what is in the offing." While the former leads to root cause analysis or celebration, the latter is required to keep things under control. These are often termed as lagging and leading indicators. If, for example, a Service Level Agreement (SLA) calls for average resolution time of 2 days on a calendar month, one perspective could be the average resolution time for the preceding months, giving a trend of performance, and the other perspective could be to look at weekly average which would help to ensure that the monthly average remains within the agreed-upon SLA and timely corrective action is taken.

For new processes and setup, initially a yes/no (quantitative) performance can be measured before the qualitative aspect can be taken into consideration. For example, if a service desk setup has to be taken into consideration, initially, a measure of performance is to be able to ensure that all calls get logged into the system and that they are not getting resolved through other mechanisms. Subsequently the SLA targets can be met.

Organizations differentiate between its own key performance indicators (KPIs) which are monitored for strategic, tactic, and operational reasons and service level agreements which are agreements to deliver a particular level of service. Different levels of service may apply for different customers. In an effort to promote performance, it is a common practice to define levels of achievement.

There are many ways of grouping performance metrics. One way is to look at it from the customer's point of view, often called the voice of the customer (VoC). Critical to quality (CTQ), critical to delivery (CTD), and critical to cost (CTC) are classifications based on the understanding of critical customer requirements. Another way is to group them in terms of operational, tactic, and strategic level KPIs.

Metrics are not static; therefore, as the organization changes, they should be objectively assessed for any requirements to change. Mostly, organizations review the metrics on a yearly basis. Each organization is unique, and the objective of credible metrics is to link them to the organizational goals. At operational level, the objective is to ensure that an accurate picture of process performance is available for analysis and trends and if required to undertake corrective action.

2.1.3.14 Financial Metrics

Financial metrics provide a picture of both the top line and the bottom line. They tell what is pulling the organization down and where are the gains. If required, the process transformation team can take the help of the finance team to gain a greater understanding of the story that the numbers tell. These metrics are also useful while trying to link the benefits of process transformation with its financial implication.

Although there are vast number of specialized metrics and can be adopted as per requirement, the common metrics that are useful at the time of process transformation are listed below.

Gross Profit Margin

Gross profit margin is an indicator of profitability and can be used to make a comparison against industry benchmarks. It is calculated by dividing the gross profit by sales. Gross profit is calculated by subtracting the cost of goods sold from the revenue. It is also called gross margin.

$$\text{Gross Margin} = (\text{Revenue} - \text{Cost of Goods Sold}) / \text{Revenue} \tag{2.1}$$

$$\begin{aligned}\text{Cost of Goods Sold} = {} & \text{Beginning Inventory} + \text{Purchased Inventory} \\ & \text{for a particular period} - \text{Ending Inventory}\end{aligned} \tag{2.2}$$

Usually, the gross profit margin should be stable. Besides comparing with the industry standards, the transformation team should look out for fluctuations which can indicate substantial changes in industry affecting pricing and cost of goods sold. If organizations have many components or products that contribute to the profitability, gross margin may be drilled down to lower level to enable analysis depending upon the accounting practice in the organization.

Gross margin is affected by increase or decrease in revenue and cost of goods sold, so both the aspects should be given thought while designing new processes.

Inventory Turnover Ratio

This is defined as the ratio of the cost of goods sold to the average inventory level. This is a measure of operational efficiency and can give insights in terms of focus on operational efficiencies.

$$\text{Inventory Turnover Ratio} = \text{Cost of Goods Sold} / \text{Average Inventory} \tag{2.3}$$

$$\text{Average Inventory} = (\text{Beginning Inventory} + \text{Ending Inventory}) / 2 \tag{2.4}$$

Although it depends on the industry, higher inventory turnover level is preferred over lower ones as low levels indicate that stocks are tied up for a long time meaning ineffective inventory management or poor sales. A ratio that is too high may indicate insufficient inventory levels, losses due to shortages, and poor customer service. This ratio may be useful to analyze while transforming sales or supply chain processes.

The days inventory outstanding (DIO) is a measure of the average time taken to convert inventory purchases into sales.

$$\text{Days Inventory Outstanding} = 365 / \text{Inventory turnover ratio} \tag{2.5}$$

Receivable Turnover Ratio

This is a measure of how quickly an organization collects its outstanding cash balances from its customers and thus provides insight into any troubles on the collection of sales made on credit. Usually, a high receivable ratio is good, though the benchmark varies from industry to industry.

$$\text{Receivables turnover ratio} = \text{Net receivable sales} / \text{Average accounts receivables} \tag{2.6}$$

Using the receivable turnover ratio, the days sales outstanding (DSO) can be calculated, which is the average number of days (average collection period) that a company takes to collect its accounts receivable.

$$\text{Average collection period}\left(\text{Days sales outstanding}\right) = 365 / \text{Receivables Turnover Ratio} \tag{2.7}$$

Account Payable Turnover Ratio

Account payable turnover ratio is a measure of short-term liquidity of a business as it shows how many times an amount equal to average accounts payable is paid to the suppliers. A higher ratio indicates that the business was able to pay the suppliers quickly which makes it interesting for suppliers; on the other hand, the longer the organization takes to pay, the better it is for its working capital.

The longer they take to pay their creditors, the more money the company has on hand, which is good for working capital and free cash flow.

$$\text{Average Payable turnover ratio} = \text{Cost of Goods Sold} / \text{Average Payables} \tag{2.8}$$

The days payable outstanding (DPO) can be calculated using the account payable turnover ratio and shows how long it takes a company to pay its invoices from trade creditors, such as suppliers. Typically the DPO is 30 days, though it may vary as per industry standard.

$$\text{Days Payable Outstanding}\left(\text{DPO}\right) = 365 / \text{Average Payable Turnover Ratio} \tag{2.9}$$

Combined together, inventory turnover, accounts receivable, and accounts payable are referred to as cash conversion cycle or operating cycle. It is the length of time between the firm's purchase of inventory and receipt of cash from accounts receivable. In other words it indicates the number of days the cash of a business remains tied up.

Operating cycle or cash conversion cycle (CCC) can be calculated as

$$\text{CCC} = \text{DIO} + \text{DSO} - \text{DPO} \tag{2.10}$$

Short cash conversion cycles are considered better and often process transformations may have a goal to shorten the cash conversion cycle. When compared with competitors and previous year's performance, it may also help in establishing a broken process and subsequent target setting.

Return on Equity

Process transformation should result in increase in value, though it may not necessarily translate into higher return on equity which is defined as the net profit expressed as a percentage to the shareholder equity.

$$\text{Return on Equity} = \text{Net Income after tax} / \text{Average Shareholder Equity} \quad (2.11)$$

$$\text{Shareholder Equity} = \text{Assets} - \text{Liabilities} \quad (2.12)$$

In order to calculate the average, the average of shareholder equity at the beginning and end period can be taken.

2.1.3.15 Investment Analysis

Like any other program, process transformation requires funding, and to justify the same, a sound investment analysis is essential. Before the start of the process transformation as a program, a high-level business case is made, which is subsequently refined and updated. Investment analysis covers costs and benefits, a clear picture of whether the returns justify and outweigh the costs, return on investment, and time value of money to establish a go-ahead for the program.

For each of the options in consideration, investment analysis should be worked out and presented for the sponsor's approval. Once approved, it sets the boundary for the program and any deviation requires change management process to be followed. The following techniques are commonly followed while undertaking investment analysis for a process transformation proposal.

Cost-Benefit Analysis

There are three basic steps in this technique. The first step is to identify the cost and benefits, the second is to evaluate the costs and benefits and associated benefits, and the third is to select the best option on the basis of costs and benefits. Tangible, intangible, fixed, variable, direct, and indirect costs and benefits are all taken into consideration while evaluating the costs and benefits. Selection of the best option is dependent on many factors. In a very simplistic way, the option with the least cost and most benefits would be the one that should be selected, although many times the maximum benefits may have the maximum costs. The decision on selection is a combination of financial prudence and the overall objectives of the transformation project.

To understand this, consider the case of an IT organization which wants to move from simple commoditized packaged solutions to large complex and business critical custom or packaged solutions (Raichura and Rao 2009) (http://www.infosys.com/cloud/resource-center/documents/achieve-business-agility.pdf, accessed 20 Oct 2014). Business expects a shorter time to market new products and services, adherence to service and operational level agreements along with agile and flexible business functions.

Among the options being considered for IT services is to either set up a shared service center (SSC) or to outsource for customized application-related services. While the SSC can be utilized by other departments and have organization-wide benefits from a long-term perspective, a setup for the IT department may have higher costs in comparison to outsourcing. The infrastructure costs would be substantially reduced by leveraging the service provider's pricing models such as pay per use, pay for capacity, etc. On the other hand, for an IT organization which would have wanted to enter the market of service providers, setting up an internal shared service center could be the first step.

Typically, three options are considered for making a choice. In the above scenario, the three options would be improvisation of existing processes in as is situation, transformation of processes by utilizing shared service center, and transformation of processes by utilizing outsourcing.

The important components of cost in the case of the in-house model would be process design, building of shared service operation, and subsequently transition and operation of service. In the outsource model, on the other hand, the build and design work would be done by the service provider, and the client organization would be focused on the development of the retained functions to ensure successful implementation.

The costs are bifurcated into one-off costs and recurring costs. The one-off costs involved could be the costs of designing of requirement, staffing, funding, service continuity, transition, disaster recovery, and contingency. In the case of outsourcing, there would be additional costs of supplier selection, designing of retained organization, downsizing if applicable, agreement on transition, and transformation approach.

In terms of benefits, both the approaches would have their benefits. Outsourcing of noncore operations would result in cost avoidance by eliminating big upfront investment. There would be benefits in terms of access to updated technology, skilled staff, and operational efficiencies.

The one-off costs would be higher in the case of insourcing model as compared to the outsourcing model, while recurring costs may be higher in the case of outsourcing.

Once the costs and the benefits for the various options have been quantified, they are tabulated. A simplistic example is shown in Tables 2.5 and 2.6 for comparison of the two options under consideration, viz., to create in-house capability using shared service center or to utilize the services of an outsourcing agency. Depreciation based on agreed-upon method can be calculated on the total one-time cost. In the example shown, the straight line method has been used to depreciate the cost over 5 years.

Based on this, calculations can be done on a number of investment criteria such as net present value, benefit-cost ratio, internal rate of return, and payback period. The first three measures take into account the time value of money, while payback period ignores the same.

Table 2.5 Cost-benefit analysis of SSC

Shared service center model (values in $)	Year 0	Year 1	Year 2	Year 3	Year 4	Year 5	Total
Total one-time cost	1,316,574	200,000	300,000	0	0	0	1,816,574
Total recurring cost	1,056,667	1,359,167	1,863,817	1,974,746	2,092,330	2,217,870	10,564,596
Total annual benefit	350,086	2,046,811	2,663,735	3,357,967	3,369,427	4,048,242	15,836,269
Less tax at 33.66 %	(239,097)	180,874	324,662	1,265,228	0	0	1,531,667
Net incremental after-tax cash flow	(1,784,057)	306,770	175,256	117,993	1,277,097	1,830,372	29,749,106
Cumulative cash flow	(1,784,057)	(1,477,287)	(1,302,031)	(1,184,038)	93,059	1,923,431	

Table 2.6 Cost-benefit analysis of outsourcing model

Outsourcing model (values in $)	Year 0	Year 1	Year 2	Year 3	Year 4	Year 5	Total
Total one-time cost	1,711,389	50,000	50,000	0	0	0	1,811,389
Total recurring cost	673,836	975,686	1,302,876	1,681,723	1,712,209	1,744,924	8,091,253
Total annual benefit	1,569,583	1,646,667	2,126,867	2,086,145	2,797,981	3,512,526	13,739,769
Less tax at 33.66 %	101,025	131,959	169,998	25,406	234,552	592,596	1,255,536
Net incremental after-tax cash flow	(916,667)	489,022	603,993	379,017	851,220	1,175,006	24,897,947
Cumulative cash flow	(916,667)	(427,645)	176,348	555,364	1,406,584	2,581,591	

Net Present Value

It is the sum of present values of all cash flows irrespective of their being positive or negative expected to occur over the life of the project (Chandra 2011):

$$\text{NPV} = \sum_{t=1}^{n} C_t / (1+r)^t - \text{Initial Investment} \tag{2.13}$$

where Ct is the cash flow at the end of year t, n is the life of the project, and r is the discount rate.

As an example, the cost of capital has been taken 14 %. The net present value for the shared service model can be calculated as shown in Table 2.7.

The NPV is positive which indicates that the proposal can be accepted. In a similar way, the NPV for the outsourcing model can be calculated (Table 2.8) which is positive as well indicating that both the proposals can be accepted taking into consideration the net benefit over and above the compensation for time and risk.

Benefit-Cost Ratio

This is also called profitability index and is defined as the ratio of the present value of benefits (PVB) divided by the initial investment (I)

$$\text{Benefit Cost Ratio}(\text{BCR}) = \text{PVB} / \text{I} \tag{2.14}$$

The calculations for the shared service model and outsourcing model are shown in Table 2.9.

For both the models the BCR > 1 which indicates that the proposals can be accepted. For a value of BCR = 0, the proposal is indifferent, while for a value of BCR < 1, the proposal should be rejected.

Table 2.7 NPV shared service model

306,770/ (1.14)	+	175,256/ (1.14)^2	+	117,993/ (1.14)^3	+	1,277,097/ (1.14)^4	+	1,830,372/ (1.14)^5	–	1,784,057
269,096	+	134,854	+	79,642	+	756,144	+	950,638	–	1,784,057
								2,190,374	–	1,784,057
								NPV	=	406,317

Table 2.8 NPV outsourcing model

489,022/ (1.14)	+	603,993/ (1.14)^2	+	379,017/ (1.14)^3	+	851,220/ (1.14)^4	+	1,175,006/ (1.14)^5	–	916,667
428,967	+	464,753	+	255,826	+	503,991	+	610,261	–	916,667
								2,263,797	–	916,667
								NPV	=	1,347,130

Table 2.9 Benefit-cost ratio calculation

BCR shared service model											
306,770/ (1.14)	+	175,256/ (1.14)^2	+	117,993/ (1.14)^3	+	1,277,097/ (1.14)^4	+	1,830,372/ (1.14)^5	/	1,784,057
269,096	+	134,854	+	79,642	+	756,144	+	950,638	/	1,784,057
								2,190,374	/	1,784,057
								BCR	=	1.23
BCR outsourcing model										
489,022/ (1.14)	+	603,993/ (1.14)^2	+	379,017/ (1.14)^3	+	851,220/ (1.14)^4	+	1,175,006/ (1.14)^5	/	916,667
428,967	+	464,753	+	255,826	+	503,991	+	610,261	/	916,667
								2,263,797	/	916,667
								BCR	=	2.47

Internal Rate of Return

Internal rate of return is the calculation of the discount rate (cost of capital) which equates the present value of future cash flows with the initial investment.

$$\text{Investment} = \sum_{t=1}^{n} C_t \,/\, (1-r)^t \tag{2.15}$$

where *Ct* is the cash flow at the end of year *t*, *r* is the internal rate of return, and *n* is the life of the project.

To find out the IRR, the NPV is set to zero to find out the rate which satisfies the condition.

Let us take the shared service model as given in Table 2.10.

Similarly the internal rate of return for the outsourced model comes out to be 57 %. Both IRR and NPV can be easily calculated using a spreadsheet such as Excel.

All the measures have their share of deficiencies, yet IRR seems to be more popular than NPV because to calculate NPV, the cost of capital or discount rate should be known; on the other hand, a high IRR such as that of the outsourcing model makes it easy to rule out that the discount rate could be higher.

The general rule for IRR with conventional cash flows (first cash flow is negative) and independent projects is to accept the proposal if the IRR is greater than the cost of capital and reject if it is lower than the cost of capital.

Payback Period

This is a very simple measure of the length of time required to recover the initial cash outlay. The caveat is to give preference to the proposal with shorter payback period. Payback period is affected by whether the cash flows are even or uneven. Even cash flow is an expectation of equal cash flows per year, whereas in uneven the cash flows vary.

Table 2.10 IRR shared service model

Year	0		1		2		3		4		5		Investment	Comment
Cash flow	(1,784,057)		306,770		175,256		117,993		1,277,097		1,830,372			
	(1,784,057)	=	306,770/ (1+r)^1	+	175,256/ (1+r)^2	+	117,993/ (1+r)^3	+	1,277,097/ (1+r)^4	+	1,830,372/ (1+r)^5			
Try r=18 %			259,975	+	125,866	+	71,814	+	658,712	+	800,072	=	1,916,440	Higher than the initial investment, so try higher rate
Try r=19 %			257,790	+	123,760	+	70,019	+	636,848	+	767,016	=	1,855,433	Higher than the initial investment, so try higher rate
Try r=20 %			255,642	+	121,706	+	68,283	+	615,884	+	735,585	=	1,797,100	Very near to initial investment, try slightly higher rate
Try r=0.2 %			255,216	+	121,301	+	67,943	+	611,795	+	729,486	=	1,785,741	Very near to initial investment, try slightly higher rate to check if this is the correct rate
Try r=0.3 %			255,004	+	121,099	+	67,773	+	609,763	+	726,459		1,780,100	Lower than investment, so take rate as 20.02 %

Payback period for even cash flows:

$$\text{Payback Period} = \text{Initial Investment} / \text{Cash inflow per period} \quad (2.16)$$

Payback period for uneven cash flows:

$$\text{Payback Period} = X + |Y| / Z \quad (2.17)$$

Where

X = Last Period with Negative Cash flow

$|Y|$ = Absolute value of cumulative cash flow at the end of period X

Z = Total Cash flow during the period after Y

In the examples considered above, the cash flows are uneven payback period. The calculation of payback period for shared service model is shown below:

$$\text{Payback Period} = 3 + |1184038| / 1277097$$
$$\text{Payback Period} = 3 + .92$$
$$\text{Payback Period} = 3.92$$

The calculation of payback period for the outsourcing model is shown below:

$$\text{Payback Period} = 1 + |427645| / 603993$$
$$\text{Payback Period} = 1 + .70$$
$$\text{Payback Period} = 1.70$$

The payback period for outsourcing model is less than the payback period for shared service model so the outsource model should be preferred.

Although this method is very simple and gives a rough estimate, it does not take the time value of money into consideration. For example, if the shared service model would have substantially higher cash flows as compared to the outsourcing model in later years, that would have been ignored by the payback method.

A summary of the results of all the techniques for the two models considered is provided in Table 2.11.

Table 2.11 Summary of financial results for SSC and outsourcing

	Shared service center	Outsourcing	Criteria for acceptance
Cost of capital	14 %	14 %	
Benefit-cost ratio	1.23	2.47	If >1, accept; =0, indifferent; <1, reject
NPV	$406,317	$1,347,130	If NPV>0, accept; = 0, indifferent; NPV<0, reject
IRR	20.0 %	57 %	If IRR>cost of capital, accept; IRR=cost of capital, indifferent; IRR<cost of capital, reject
Payback period	3.9	1.7	Prefer shorter payback period

As per the capital investment analysis, all techniques indicate that the outsourcing model should be preferred, though the overall strategy of the organization may result in the shared service model being chosen.

2.1.3.16 Quality Tools

Some of the quality tools that can be helpful through the process transformation journey are listed below.

Brainstorming

Brainstorming is a tool that is primarily useful in planning and analysis. It may be used to determining possible causes or solutions to existing problems as well as looking out for opportunities (Chang and Niedzwiecki 1998). Although it is predominantly used as a tool for improvement of an existing process, the essence can be utilized while undertaking transformation.

The basic steps and rules for brainstorming are:

- Set the time limit for the session.
- Initially, quantity is the key and no idea can be criticized.
- Creativity and building on other ideas are allowed.
- Sticky notes can be distributed at the beginning of the session for everyone to write their ideas.
- The participants can either call out their ideas all at once or everyone can take a turn to offer their idea.
- The collected ideas can be subsequently grouped to bring out meaningful information.
- Since brainstorming is based on opinions, substantiating the ideas with data makes it usable.
- As a rule of thumb for a 30-min session, 25–30 ideas may be generated in a group of 7–8 participants.

Root Cause Analysis

Typically associated with the problem management of the as is process, it can be useful in not only gaining the understanding of the current problems but may provide ideas on new solutions. The level of granularity can be adjusted to push it to a higher level so that it can be useful for the purpose of transformation. For example, if an organization is faced with diminishing sales, one approach could be to focus on the sales process, and another could be to look at it from an organization's perspective.

Within root cause analysis, the following techniques are useful:

Cause-Effect Diagrams

This technique is also called fishbone diagram due to its visual appearance. Kaoru Ishikawa was a pioneer in this technique; therefore, these are also called Ishikawa diagrams (Fig. 2.6).

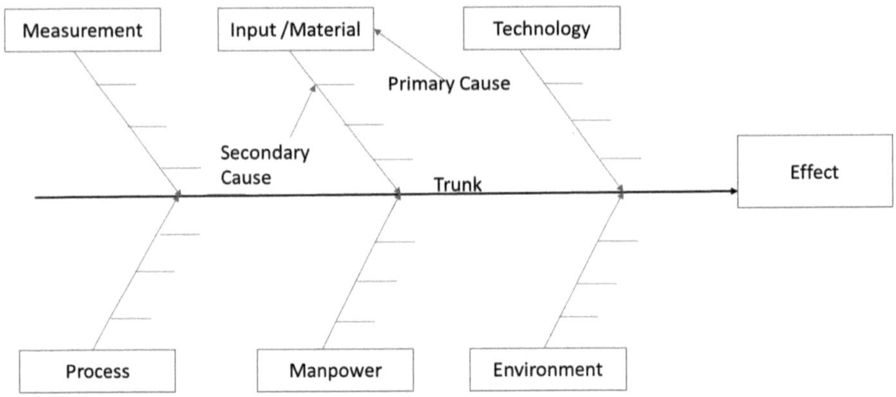

Fig. 2.6 Primary and secondary factors in Ishikawa diagram

These diagrams propose categorization and subcategorization of causes which lead to a certain effect. The main cause is referred to as the primary factor, while a cause that may be a secondary cause that leads to the primary cause is referred to as secondary factor (Dumas et al. 2013). The thick central line is referred to as the trunk. Often these factors are categorized as 6 Ms, namely, measurement, material, machine, method, man, and milieu.

Measurement concerns itself with the factors relating to measurements or calculations made during the process. Material refers to factors relating to input which could be consumables, raw material, data input, etc. Machine or technology refers to factors arising out of machinery or technology. While older machinery could be a factor so could be a server that is unable to synchronize real-time data. Method which implies the process refers to factors that arise due to process definition, its understanding, and implementation. Manpower concerns itself with factors that arise due to human activity. Example could be wrong calculation and incorrectly performed process step. Milieu or environment refers to factors arising out of the environment in which the business operates.

To understand this further, let us consider a simple scenario where payments to suppliers are getting dishonored. This can be a serious issue for the reputation and future supplies. The root cause analysis shows the following causes/factors (Fig. 2.7).

Another way of identifying the root cause would be to use the Why-Why or five Whys technique. The premise of this technique is to repeatedly ask the reason of occurrence. As the levels go deeper, the focus shifts towards the solution. If we look at the occurrence of defaulted supplier payment, it could be presented in Fig. 2.8.

In a way similar to the analysis of the factor “mistake in checking the available balance,” analysis could have been done for “delay in payment from customer.”

Once the identification of the contributing factors has been done, the priority can be established using Pareto’s analysis. This principle is commonly known as 80–20 principle which is a generalization that 80 % of the effects may be caused by 20 %

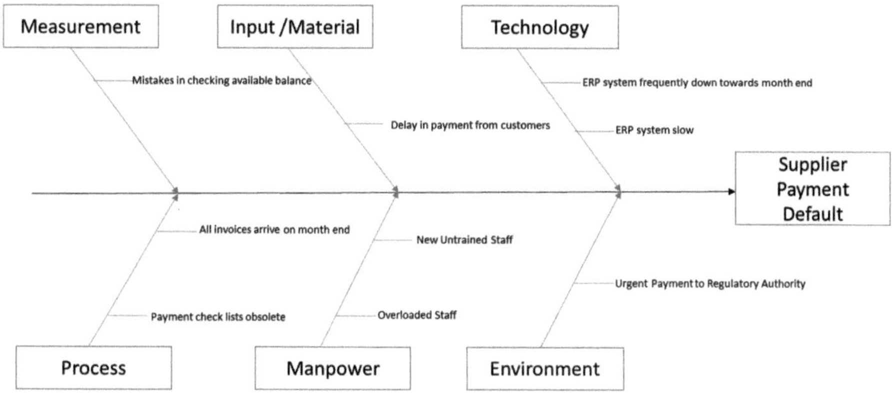

Fig. 2.7 Factors in supplier payment default

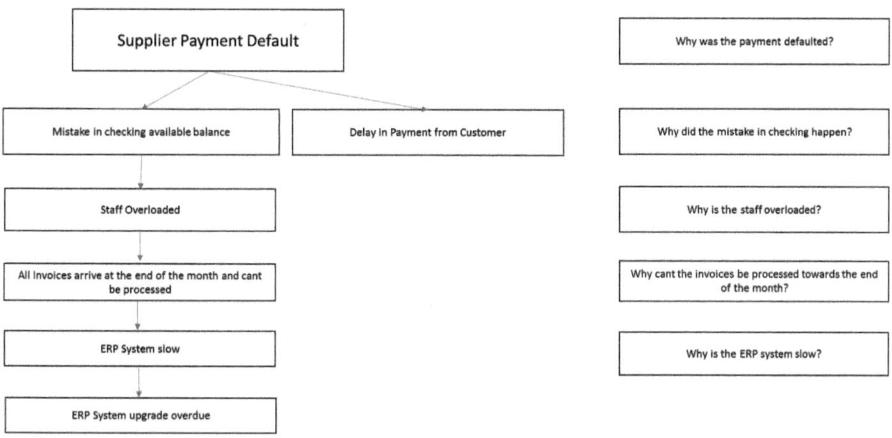

Fig. 2.8 Why-why analysis of supplier payment default

of the causes. If in the example of defaulted supplier payment, data was available, we could look at which cause was having the maximum impact. A curve is plotted for cumulative percentage impact of the issues or a simple bar chart is constructed in descending order. The cumulative values of causes are plotted along the x axis, while cumulative percentage values of effects are plotted along the y axis (Basu 2011).

As a sample the case of supplier payment default is worked out in Table 2.12 (Fig. 2.9).

It is important to realize that 80–20 rule is a generalization and it may vary as per situation. In the case of supplier payment default, 33 % of the factors are causing 86 % impact.

Table 2.12 Frequency and impact of causes in defaulted supplier payments

Defaulted supplier payments	Frequency	Impact per default ($)	% impact	Remark
ERP system slow	200	100,000	49	10 days delay in payment with $50 penalty per day
Delay in payment from customer	50	75,000	37	30 days delay in payment with $ 50 penalty per day
All invoices arrive at month end	150	22,500	11	3 days delay in payment with $50 penalty per day
Urgent payment to regulatory authority	5	2,500	1	10 days delay in payment with $50 penalty per day
Overloaded staff	20	2,000	1	2 days delay in payment with $50 penalty per day
New untrained staff	25	1,250	1	1 day delay in payment with $50 penalty per day

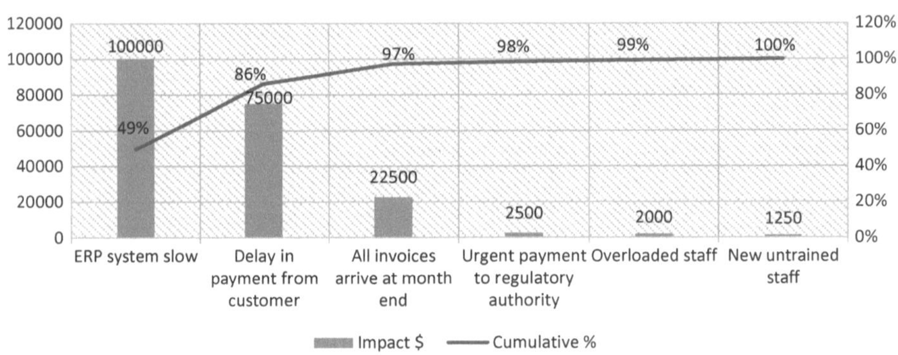

Fig. 2.9 Cumulative plotting of cause and effect

2.1.3.17 Data Analytics

Data analytics is a powerful tool that enables setting the direction of a transformation effort. It uncovers information not only from internal but also data that is external to the organization. In a simplistic manner, data analytics involves sourcing and optimizing data, its analysis, and interpretation and subsequently using this data to model and predict for future. Data analytics has moved beyond the traditional databases to encompass what is termed as big data. Examples of big data are real-time data coming from sensors, devices, transactional applications, Web, and social media. The scale of such data is very large and it is systematically analyzed to provide interpretations for future.

There are four dimensions of data analytics (Ohlhorst 2012):

Volume – Data analytics amasses terabytes and petabytes of information.

Variety – Data is not limited to one structure but comes in a variety ranging from audio video streaming to log files.

Veracity – Since massive amount of data makes it prone to errors in interpretation and analysis, purity of information is of utmost importance.

Velocity – Data is often time sensitive; therefore, maximum benefit can be derived by using real-time information.

Taking these dimensions into consideration, organizations can take advantage of current and expected scenarios making use of information sifted out of big data in an “outside-in” as well as “inside-out” manner.

2.1.3.18 Cost Analysis

Cost is defined by accountants as a resource sacrificed or foregone to achieve a specific objective (Horngren et al. 2009). It is important to have an understanding of costs as aid to decision making (Khan and Jain 2010). Through the life of process transformation program and subsequent to handover, cost concepts are helpful in income measurement, profit planning, cost control, and long- and short-term decision making.

An actual cost is historical cost and has been incurred, while a budgeted cost, which is a forecast, is incurred in future. The object for which the cost is found is called the “cost object.” The cost object could be a project, customer, department, service, or any other entity.

From the various cost objects, the transformation team can identify the relevant cost objects required for decision making, budgeting, and planning or for valuing products or services (Eldenburg and Wolcott 2005). There are various cost concepts that help in the judgment.

Direct and Indirect Costs

Costs are easily traced to a cost object because a cause and effect relationship exists. The salary of staff that works exclusively for a department can be attributed as a direct cost. Costs that are not directly attributable, such as electricity at the facility, are examples of indirect cost.

In order to facilitate the distinction, traceability of costs in terms of origin can be checked. If the costs can be traced completely to the cost object, they are direct costs, and if they are being allocated from some other cost object, they are indirect costs.

Opportunity Costs

The benefits that are foregone when an alternative is chosen over the next best alternative are called opportunity cost. While these are difficult to measure and are dependent upon takers for the other option, they aid in high-quality decision making.

Sunk Costs

Expenditures that have been made in the past and cannot be changed are called sunk costs. Sunk costs should not influence decision-making process as they are unavoidable.

Variable, Fixed, and Mixed Costs

This concept is based on cost behavior, which implies variation in costs relative to the variations in organizations' activities. Variable costs are costs that change in direct proportion to change in activity.

Fixed costs do not change with activity, for example, the rent of premise will remain the same for a particular period irrespective of the volume of products produced. Fixed costs do change over a period of time and increase in steps with increase in capacity.

Variable costs increase with an increase in volume and decrease with a decrease in volume, while fixed costs per unit decrease with an increase in volume and increase with a decrease in volume.

Mixed costs have components of both fixed and variable costs. Examples are telephone, power, etc.

Incremental/Differential Cost

Incremental costs are the costs that would be incurred if one course of action is chosen over another, while differential cost is the difference in cost between two available alternatives.

Marginal Cost

It is the incremental cost of producing a unit of product or activity in relevant range. Relevant range is a span of activity where the fixed cost remains constant and the variable cost per unit remains constant.

The total cost is a function of fixed and variable costs and is driven by inputs or activities which are termed cost drivers. It can be very relevant to identify existing and potential cost driver while undertaking a transformation. Many a time people on the floor can provide useful inputs on cost drivers.

Cost-volume-profit (CVP) analysis technique can be used with the help of accountants when input is required for examining change in sales volumes, costs, and prices. This forms input for emphasis on products or services, necessary volume of sales required to achieve target profit, revenue requirement to avoid losses, etc.

While detailed discussion of CVP is out of scope for this book, the important tenets are:

$$\text{Profit} = \text{Total Revenue} - \text{Total Cost} \tag{2.18}$$

$$\text{Profit} = \text{Total Revenue} - \text{Total variable Costs} - \text{Total Fixed costs} \tag{2.19}$$

$$\begin{aligned}\text{Profit} = {} & \text{Prices of Goods sold} * \text{Units of goods sold} - \text{Variable Cost per unit} \\ & * \text{Units of goods sold} - \text{Total Fixed Costs}\end{aligned} \tag{2.20}$$

Contribution margin ratio (CMR) is the percent by which the selling price per unit exceeds the variable cost per unit.

$$\begin{aligned}\text{CMR} = {} & (\text{Selling price per unit} - \text{Variable Cost Per Unit})/ \\ & \text{Selling Price Per Unit}\end{aligned} \tag{2.21}$$

An increase in percentage in sales mix of an item with a higher contribution margin can lead to a higher after-tax income due to reduction in variable costs.

Time-Driven Activity-Based Costing

Time-driven activity-based costing is an approach which relies on costing based on capacity cost rate and capacity usage (Kaplan and Anderson 2007).

Suppose the total cost of a department per quarter is $1,000,000 and there is a staff of 40 who are actually performing the work which includes three activities – create customer record, update customer record, and handle customer inquiries. These employees work 24 days a month, 8 h a day. They spend 60 min per day on break, training, and "all-employee meeting" (Table 2.13).

Once the capacity cost rate has been calculated, assigned cost can be derived taking the number of requests and unit time into consideration (Table 2.14).

This enables calculation of unused capacity. With the help of ERP, stepwise calculation of activities can be done at a lower level of granularity, which offers insight into possibilities of improvement. Any transformation ultimately needs to deliver and an understanding of costs will facilitate in chalking out a program for desired results.

Table 2.13 Capacity cost rate calculation

Cost of department per quarter	$1,000,000
Number of direct employees	40
Hours of work per day	8
Hour of break, all-employee meeting, training	1
Number of working days per quarter	96
Practical capacity of resources supplied	40*(8–1)*60*96
Practical capacity of resources supplied (minutes)	1,612,800
Capacity cost rate $1,000,000/1,612,800 min	$0.62 per minute

Table 2.14 Unused capacity calculation

Activity	Unit time (minutes)	Rate ($0.62 per minute)	Number of requests	Assigned cost
Create customer record	15	$9	30,000	450,000
Update customer record	5	$3	20,000	100,000
Handle customer inquiries	25	$16	10,000	250,000
Used capacity				800,000
Unused capacity				812,800

Tools and techniques are the means to achieve the goals of transformation. The next chapters will cover the tan's culture and communication which are crucial in achieving and sustaining the desired results.

References

Basu R (2011) FIT sigma a lean approach to building sustainable quality beyond six sigma. Wiley, Chichester

Chandra P (2011) Financial management, theory and practice. Tata McGraw-Hill Education, New Delhi

Chang RY, Niedzwiecki ME (1998) Continuous improvement tools: a practical guide to achieve quality results, vol 1. Wheeler Publishing, New Delhi

Dumas M, Rosa ML, Mendling J, Reijers HA (2013) Fundamentals of business process management. Springer, Berlin/Heidelberg

Eldenburg LG, Wolcott SK (2005) Cost management – measuring, monitoring and motivating performance. John Wiley, Hoboken

Hausser DL (1980) Comparison of different models for organizational analysis. In: Lawler EE III, Nadler DA, Cammann C (eds) Organizational assessment: perspectives on the measurement of organizational behavior and the quality of work life. Wiley, New York, p 133

Hickson DJ, Pugh DS, Pheysey DC (1969) Operations technology and organization structure: an empirical reappraisal. Adm Sci Q 14(3):378–397

Horngren CT et al (2009) Cost accounting – a managerial emphasis. Dorling Kindersley (India) Pvt. Ltd, New Delhi

http://newsroom.cisco.com/press-release-content?articleId=1240830. Accessed 21 Aug 2013

http://www.amazon.com/b?ie=UTF8&node=8037720011. Accessed 20 Oct 2014

http://www.cisco.com/web/learning/certifications/specialist/bus/bus_transformation.html. Accessed 21 Aug 2013

http://www.sei.cmu.edu/reports/10tr033.pdf. Accessed 28 Oct 2014

Kaplan RS, Anderson SR (2007) Time-driven activity-based costing: a simpler and more powerful path to higher profits. Harvard Business School Publishing Corporation, Boston

Khan MY, Jain PK (2010) Management accounting: text problems and cases. Tata McGraw-Hill, New Delhi

Ohlhorst FJ (2012) Big data analytics: turning big data into big money. Wiley, New York

Raichura B, Rao V (2009) White paper – Lean IT transformation – reduce total cost of ownership, guarantee quality of service and achieve business agility. http://www.infosys.com/cloud/resource-center/documents/achieve-business-agility.pdf. Accessed 20 Oct 2014

Sproull B (2009) The ultimate improvement cycle – maximizing profit through the integration of lean six sigma and theory of constraints. CRC Press Taylor and Francis Group, Boca Raton

Suggested Reading

Barfield JT, Raiborn CA, Kinney MR (2001) Cost accounting traditions and innovations. South Western, a Division of Thomson Learning, Ohio

Bogan CE, English MJ (1994) Benchmarking for best practices: winning through innovative adaptation. McGraw-Hill, New York

Boxwell RJ Jr (1994) Benchmarking for competitive advantage. McGraw-Hill, New York

Brealy RA, Myers SC, Allen F, Mohanty P (2007) Principles of corporate finance. Tata McGraw-Hill Education Private Limited, New Delhi

Burke R (2003) Project management – planning & control techniques. Wiley, Singapore
Cabinet Office (2011) Managing successful programmes. The Stationery Office, London
Cappels TM (2004) Financially focused project management. J. Ross Publishing, Boca Raton
Chang RY, Niedzwiecki ME (1998) Continuous improvement tools, vol 2. Wheeler Publishing, New Delhi
Chin CMM, Spowage AC (2012) Project management methodologies: a comparative analysis. J Adv Perform Inf Value 4(1):106–118
Cleland DI (1999) Project management – strategic design and implementation. McGraw-Hill, New York
Coulson-Thomas C (1993) Transforming the company – bridging the gap between management myth and corporate reality. Kogan Page, London
Davies C, Demb A, Espejo R (1979) Organization for program management. Wiley, New York
Dragan ZM, Martinelli RJ, Waddell JM (2007) Program management for improved business results. Wiley, Hoboken
Macdougall C (2014) Evolving programme governance models in a digital world. http://www.axelos.com/gempdf/Evolving_programme_governance_models_in_a_digital_world_White_Paper.pdf. Accessed 31 Oct 2014
Gitlow H, Gitlow S, Oppenheim A, Oppenheim R, Irwin RD (1989) Tools and method for the improvement of quality. CRC Press, Homewood Irwin
Harrington HJ (1996) The complete benchmarking implementation guide: total benchmarking management. McGraw-Hill, New York
Lawler EE III, Nadler DA, Cammann C (1980) Organizational assessment – perspectives on the measurement of organizational behavior and the quality of work life, vol 2. Wiley, New York
Project Management Institute (2013) The standard for program management. Project Management Institute, Newtown Square

3 Culture and Communication

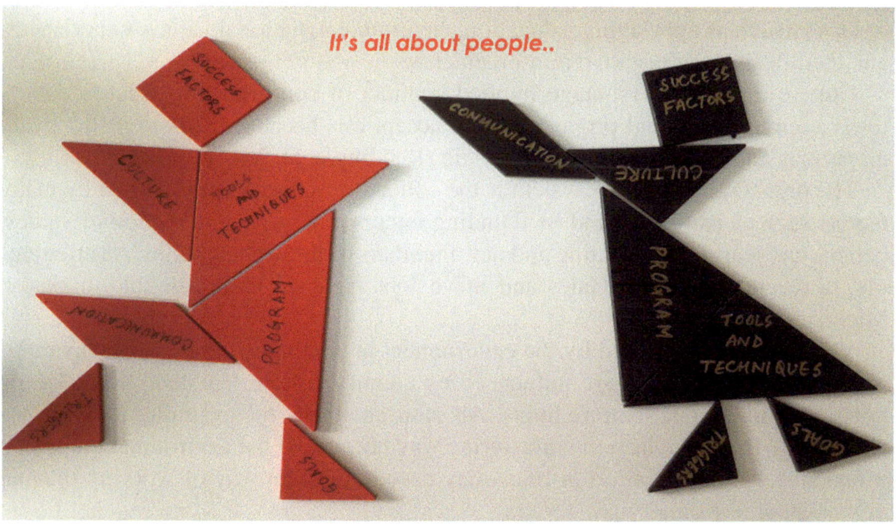

3.1 Culture

Schein (2010) defines culture as "a pattern of shared basic assumptions learned by a group as it solved its problems of external adaptation and internal integration, which has worked well enough to be considered valid and, therefore, to be taught to new members as a correct way to perceive, think and feel in relation to those problems."

Cameron and Quinn (2006) suggest that "An organization's culture is reflected by what is valued, the dominant leadership styles, the language and symbols, the procedures and routines and definitions of success that make the organization unique."

C. Sharma, *Business Process Transformation*, Management for Professionals,
DOI 10.1007/978-81-322-2349-8_3

To begin with, culture binds people and gives them a sense of identity (Weiss 2001). In the context of process transformation, the focus is to identify and consolidate the attributes of the relevant subunit cultures. The relevance should be established by identifying the target for transformation, for example, if the supply chain process is to be transformed, the finance subunits would be out of scope.

The "tan" culture is divided into value system, organization structure, motivation, change management, conflict management, and capability development.

3.1.1 Value System

Culture binds individuals to the group and takes care of their need to belong, feel stable, and undertake a meaningful endeavor. When they work in a group, this involves conformance with group norms and values. When this happens, an interplay of value systems comes into picture. Individual value systems are a net result of factors such as upbringing, education, environment, national values, experiences, and their positive or negative reinforcements.

Culture inspires a first-stage implied contract of conformity to what is collectively seen as "right and proper." People accept this because they are instinctively gregarious and dependent on membership (Redding et al. 2014).

The organization's value system is the collective values and is affected by many factors such as its history and its founding fathers and by the interaction of values, beliefs, and learning of existing and new members of the organizations. As an example, in recent times, Bill Gates and Steve Jobs have set their indelible marks on Microsoft and Apple.

Value system is affected by the environment in which the organization operates. Values of the workplace are influenced by country culture Hofstede (http://geert-hofstede.com/national-culture.html). An auto ancillary, for example, may have a tendency to think in a lean manufacturing way because of the environment in which it operates. An organization in India may have a different way of working than an organization in Korea.

When the individual and organizational value systems are aligned with each other, there is a level of comfort in the functioning of employees. Alignment reduces anxiety to change, therefore enabling employees to flow as per requirements. A complete alignment will rarely happen as none of the value systems are static. Understanding of the value system gives the transformation team the context of operation. There are various explanations and studies that provide an understanding of value system and how they can be uncovered; two of them are explained below:

3.1.1.1 Levels of Culture

The transformation team can look at various sources in the organization to dig out the three levels of culture (Schein 2010) and gain understanding of the value systems. The first level is of artifacts, which are the visible products that are available such as its language, technologies, stories, symbols. These are easily available and accessible to an outsider though may be sometimes difficult to decipher. The second level is that of espoused beliefs and values which are to be found in the philosophy and guiding principles of the organization. These set the moral tone of the organization and are the guiding factors in the time of uncertainty and difficulty. The third level is that of the basic assumptions. These assumptions hold together our understanding and coherence of the world around us. This level is the most difficult to identify and change.

3.1.1.2 Dimensions of Culture

Another perspective is to look at culture using the Organizational Culture Assessment Instrument (OCAI) proposed by Cameron and Quinn (2006). This instrument assesses organizational culture on the six dimensions, viz., dominant characteristics, organizational leadership, management of employees, organization glue, strategic emphases, and criteria of success. These are assessed for the current situation and for the preferred situation. OCAI is based on the competing values framework which classifies organizational cultures on the basis of two dimensions and results in four clusters. The first dimension differentiates effectiveness criteria that emphasize flexibility, discretion, and dynamism from criteria that emphasize stability order and control. The second dimension differentiates effectiveness criteria that emphasize an internal orientation, integration, and unity from criteria that emphasize an external orientation, differentiation, and rivalry.

On the basis of these criteria, four culture types have been identified:

The Hierarchy Culture

This organizational culture is characterized by formalized and structured place to work. Procedures govern what people do. The long-term concerns of organization are stability, predictability, and efficiency and formal rules hold the organization together. Effective leaders are good coordinators and organizers.

The Market Culture

This culture is oriented toward competitiveness and productivity. The basic assumption in a market culture is that the external environment is not benign but hostile, consumers are choosy and interested in value, the organization is in the business of increasing its competitive position, and the major task of management is to drive the organization toward productivity results and profits. Profitability, bottom-line results, strength in market niches, stretch targets, and secure customer bases are primary objectives of the organization. The core values that dominate market-type position are competitiveness and productivity. Effective leaders are tough, demanding, hard-driving producers, and competitors. Outpacing the competition and market leadership is important.

The Clan Culture

This culture has similarity to a family-type organization. Shared values and goals, cohesion, participation, individuality, and a sense of "we-ness" permeate in clan-type firms. Typical characteristics of clan-type firms are teamwork, employee involvement programs, and corporate commitment to employees. The basic assumption is that the environment can be best managed through teamwork and employee development, customers are best thought of as partners, the organization is in the business of developing a humane work environment, and the major task is to empower employees and facilitate their participation, commitment, and loyalty. Leaders are thought of as mentors and perhaps even as parent figures.

The Adhocracy Culture

This form of organization is most responsive to the hyper-turbulent, ever-accelerating conditions that typify the organizational world. These organizations are mainly in the business of developing new products and services and preparing for the future. The major task of management is to foster entrepreneurship, creativity, and activity "on the cutting edge." The root of the word adhocracy is ad hoc – implying something temporary, specialized, and dynamic. Unlike markets or hierarchies, adhocracies do not have centralized power or authority relationships. Instead, power flows from individual to individual or from one task team to another. This culture is characterized by a dynamic, entrepreneurial and creative work space. People stick out their necks and take risks. Effective leadership is visionary, innovative, and risk-oriented. The organization's long-term goal is on rapid growth and acquiring new resources. Success means producing unique and original products and services.

Cameroon and Quinn suggest that typically as the organization matures, the culture changes from adhocracy to clan to hierarchy to market. Once the organization reaches a mature state, the change patterns are less predictable and culture change needs to be managed consciously.

The "Right" Approach to Culture

As such there is no ideal culture style and an organization may or may not strongly identify with a particular culture type. In order to gain a deeper understanding, comparisons can be made on various perspectives of the type of culture. These could be, difference between the current and preferred future culture, dominating culture style, alignment of culture profile of different attributes, and alignment of culture profiles from leadership and employees. Comparison could also be made to current industry culture profiles and available trends.

Irrespective of whether the process transformation team chooses to undertake a culture assessment through artifacts, espoused beliefs and values, and basic assumptions or through OCAI, the culture assessment can be limited to 1–2 days by way of holding workshop or administering the instrument. This assessment provides the team the canvas on which the team can draw the new picture. For example, if a hierarchical organization (the solution delivery team of a bank) wants to segregate a subdivision to focus exclusively on innovative customer-focused solutions, then besides the process transformation, emphasis may also be required on initiating some culture change toward adhocracy in the subdivision.

It is important to realize that while the older members are crucial in passing on the existing culture to new entrants, new entrants have an opportunity to bring in new thoughts, values, ideas, and ways of working and contribute to the development of culture. Culture is therefore dynamic and rejuvenates itself. Factors such as changes in how processes are carried out have consequences in how people think, behave, and execute work, and the converse holds true as well. This understanding can be used while selecting the core team and super-users.

Leaders have a higher chance of influencing the culture of an organization as by virtue of their position they can push to implement their beliefs and assumptions. If these turn out to be successful, the likelihood of their becoming ingrained in the culture becomes high. The other side of the coin is that individuals who experiment and come out with successful ideas tend to be recognized as leaders.

Care should be taken to address sub-cultures which often exist, especially when a transformation is happening after a merger or acquisition. Besides this, the organizations of today are truly multicultural in terms of diversity. Attempt should be made to integrate diversity into the mainstream so that their contribution can be utilized to gain a competitive advantage to the organization. The dimensions of culture change continuously creating new synergies and forms. The attributes of culture should be channelized and/or changed to create a momentum to achieve the goal of transformation.

3.1.2 Organization Structure

Organization structure may be defined as the network of relationships that exists among various positions (Ulrich and Wieland 1976). Organization structure influences culture. A transformation more often than not requires changes in the way departments or functions are organized. Structures can be hierarchical, consisting of a vertical dimension of differentiated level of authority and responsibility. Structure can also be differentiated on the basis of specialization such as on the basis of function, location, process, or product. The organizational structures are not mutually exclusive; an organization that has a hierarchical structure may still be subdivided on the basis of function.

3.1.2.1 Span of Control

Span of control which implies the number of subordinates that can be supervised by one manager is an aspect that needs to be considered while organizing for transformation. While earlier researchers suggested that a span of control of five to eight subordinates is ideal, subsequent research has pointed to the fact that span of control is a function of many factors (Gupta 2009). These include complexity of tasks performed by subordinates, the amount of subordinate-superior interaction, and the capabilities of the manager and the subordinates. This often culminates in a combination of line and staff functions. Line implies the executives who contribute directly to the profitability, whereas staff has an advisory role and usually comprises specialists. In virtual organizations where it is not uncommon to have the manager at one location and subordinates at another, it is very difficult to establish the ideal span of control.

3.1.2.2 Centralize or Decentralize

Centralization or decentralization of decision making decides the spread of power in an organization. A transformed process may not necessarily be decentralized and some level of centralization may be still required. In a process where the execution of process is to be done by semi-skilled workers, it might be necessary to keep the decision making centralized. The skill level of the resources and the required agility in decision making are two of the key deciding factors in centralization of an organization.

Large spans of control and centralized operations generate a regimental atmosphere in comparison to a start-up agile software organization that is highly decentralized. An outsourcing service provider may structure on the basis of process such as supply chain or compensation and payroll to provide highly optimized, decentralized, and efficient process to the end customers. A government department may be structured on the hierarchical model ensuring tall centralized structure and procedural compliance.

The essence is that each form of organization has behavioral consequences on the culture which can be utilized to facilitate transformation.

3.1.3 Motivation

Transformation involves a big change and introduces certain degree of stress which they need to cope with. The coping mechanisms can be visible in a variety of ways ranging from resolve to work harder to seeking support or venting anger (Colquitt et al. 2013). Stress can also lead to methods such as strategizing, changing priorities, and avoidance being deployed. In light of this, it is a challenge to titrate the optimum mix of reward, recognition, and penalty such that stress levels improve performance and motivation.

Motivation has been defined as a set of energetic forces that originate both within and outside an employee, initiate work-related effort, and determine its direction, intensity, and persistence (Colquitt et al. 2013). Transformation requires that employees energetically engage themselves into achieving the desired results. Their internal and external forces need to be directed in such a way that the employees choose a course of action and engage in certain behaviors that lead to achievement of goals (Newstrom 2007).

Although a lot of research has been done on motivation, expectancy theory and equity theory can be particularly relevant for a transformation and are discussed below:

3.1.3.1 Expectancy Theory of Motivation

Expectancy theory of motivation proposed by Victor Vroom proposes that work effort is directed toward behaviors that people believe will lead to desired outcomes (Vroom 1964). The three factors that affect individual's effort are the following.

Effort to Performance Expectancy (E → P)

This is the individual's perception that his/her effort will result in a particular level of performance. The expectancy will lie between zero and one. There are two aspects that play a role here, the highest level of effort that the individual perceives that he or she can take and what they perceive would be their performance. These two aspects would be based on self-perception and past experiences.

Performance to Outcome Expectancy (P → O)

Performance to Outcome Expectancy is the perceived probability of a particular performance level leading to a particular outcome. A programmer may know if by writing 1,000 lines of code per day (current performance level), he would finish coding in a month. The outcome could either be that he would be able to finish (probability 1.0) or not (probability 0). It could also be that he would be able to finish half of the coding (probability 0.5) and so on.

Outcome Valences

A valence is the anticipated satisfaction or dissatisfaction that an individual feels towards an outcome, whether it is positive or negative. Outcomes that are consistent with our values and satisfy our needs are positive, whereas the ones that inhibit our values and need fulfillment are negative.

The catchphrase of Bob the Builder animation series where Bob asks "Can we fix it" and his group replies "Yes we can" offers an interesting example (http://www.bobthebuilder.com/uk/about_bob.html accessed 01/10/2014). This emphasizes the first two aspects of the expectancy theory. The group believes that their efforts will result in the performance of the work they have been assigned and when they perform the assigned work, the outcome would be completion of the project.

If we take it further to the case of transformation, it would help to increase E → P expectancies, P → O expectancies, and outcome valences. In simpler words, to increase E → P expectancies, the teams should believe that with a certain level of effort, they would be able to achieve a certain level of performance. To do so the transformation team should have people of high levels of skill and knowledge. For the process that is undergoing a transformation, there could be requirement for additional resources, time, training, coaching, etc. (McShane et al. 2011). Increase in P → O expectancy can be achieved by emphasizing the outcome of expected performance levels. As an example, if the workforce upgrades their knowledge levels and follows the newly deployed help desk process, the number of tickets that can be handled would increase. To increase the valence, it could be said that the outcome of higher number of tickets handled would increase the profitability of the organization and higher raises. This would make the valence positive.

3.1.3.2 Equity Theory of Motivation

Equity theory proposed by John Stacey (Adams 1963) dwells on employee's feeling of equity by comparing their own outcome to input ratio to the outcome to input ratio of others. Inputs include skill, effort, performance, experience, etc. Outcomes are the reward they receive in return of their inputs such as salary, recognition, bonus, important role, etc. Employees experience feeling of negative emotion when they feel that they are under-rewarded in comparison to others and equality when they feel equally rewarded. Over-reward usually does not create any feeling of equality and is less frequent.

In case of transformation, the team should ensure that the employees are treated fairly and communicate the same. Even if job cuts are required, objectivity should be maintained with clearly defined criteria. Allowing employees to voice their opinions, platforms for discussion, exemplary behavior, and explanation of why things need to be done in a particular way helps in creating a feeling of equality. Suppose there are three team leaders of which only two can remain in the same department as per the new structure while one has to be moved. In such a scenario, the three must be clearly informed on the criteria of selection and reason of choice. Feeling of inequality may change perceptions and comparisons but can also lead to demotivation.

3.1.3.3 Reward and Recognition

Rewarding employees and recognition of their effort play an important role in motivating employees. Exceptional performance should be recognized in monetary or non-monetary way. If there are multiple teams who need to deploy the new process, it may be an idea to felicitate the team that deploys it first. Recognition should be genuine; otherwise it does not achieve the desired result and creates inequality for the rest. Support to the teams who are undertaking tough tasks prevents the team from getting demotivated. It is very important to keep employees motivated to ensure that they whole heartedly become a part of transformation, strive as hard as they can, show initiative, and collectively attain the desired goals.

As such penalty is not advisable for transformation program, but it can be sometimes deployed to create an urgency to initiate action for transformation.

3.1.4 Change Management

Change management is an integral part of any transformation program and is covered as a separate chapter.

3.1.5 Conflict Management

Conflict is a necessary byproduct of any transformation exercise. In an organization, conflict is not limited to individual conflict but may be between groups. As per Pondy (1972), there are three types of conflicts: bargaining conflict amongst interest groups for scarce resources, bureaucratic conflict from superior-subordinate relationship, and systems conflict among group members in lateral working relationships.

Let us consider the case of a transformation subsequent to a merger and try to understand the kind of conflicts the employees may be experiencing. The employees of the new organization may be faced with one or more of the following scenarios:

- Redesigned task
- Change in work environment
- Disruptive interpersonal relationships
- Organization redesign
- Insufficient information leading to reliance on informal channels of communication
- Support or resentment towards newly defined goals of the organization
- Change in position in the organization

Depending on the individual capacity to cope with conflict, they will perceive it in a constructive manner. When the employee(s) are unable to handle the conflict in a constructive manner, the manager would need to jump in to adapt the conflict in a manner that the impact remains positive. On the other hand, sometimes conflict is also utilized to create way for new talent and ideas.

It is not necessary that conflict is related to negative outcomes. An employee who has to make a choice between apparently two equally good new job roles with little visibility of future prospects may still experience conflict. The reverse situation where the perception is that choice is to be made between equally bad roles is definitely a reason of conflict. Conflict may also arise in situations where the new role is a mismatch between the expectations of the new role and current capabilities. For an employee who primarily sees his future in sales and marketing, a shift to the systems department may create a conflict situation.

All individuals are different and differences in culture, education, status, ideology, values, experiences, and upbringing bring out a different perception of conflict.

To ensure smooth sailing with conflict through the transformation, the following factors can be considered:

- Communication should be clear, well planned, and continuously updated through the program.
- Differences in ideology should be respected while providing a firm direction.
- While manning the restructured organization, it is a good practice to open vacancies with detailed job descriptions, allowing people to achieve a fit between their goals, aspiration, and possibilities within the organization.
- Individual conflicts that can become group conflicts should be dealt with strongly to avoid a snowball effect on others.
- Depending on the plans of restructuring, financial support should be extended to compensate for job losses. Provide opportunities to educate/enhance skills to facilitate job search in the outside market.

Conflicts can lead to resistance which may be overcome by involving, problem solving, manipulative techniques, and persuasion. The form of persuasion should be so directed that it leads to acceptance. Negotiation requires preparation and the following tips can be helpful while negotiating:

- Focus on the issue(s).
- Stick to context.
- Exercise emotional control.
- Listen and understand the other person.
- Observe body language.
- Discuss from position of strength and not of weakness.
- Avoid personality clash.
- Give minor concessions in lieu of major benefits.
- Move towards the desired goal by reinforcing the discussion that is in sync with final goal.

As the intensity of conflict increases beyond an individual's tolerance levels, defensive mechanisms come into picture which provide a temporary relief from symptoms and if continued for a long time could develop into psychosomatic conditions (Harigopal 1995). This does not, however, imply that conflict is bad. Within acceptable levels, conflict aids in meeting challenges, looking out for alternative options, decision making, solutions, perseverance, creativity, and zeal. This level of conflict should be channelized to optimize individual and group performance. The implication is that if conflict is stimulated in work situations taking people to more effective motivational zones and is monitored so that it does not become unproductive or disruptive, it can be optimally utilized during transformation.

3.1.6 Capability Development

In order to ensure that the employees are able to live up to the expectations of the transformed process, often an upgrade of capability is required. Capability concerns itself with not only the abilities required to fulfill a particular role but also to realize the individual and organizational goals. It involves functional skills, technical skills, aptitude, and soft skills such as attitude and behavior. The process will fail to deliver if the capabilities are not built in line with the requirement and leave the employees demotivated.

The training requirements need to be carefully analyzed and undertaken as shown in Fig. 3.1

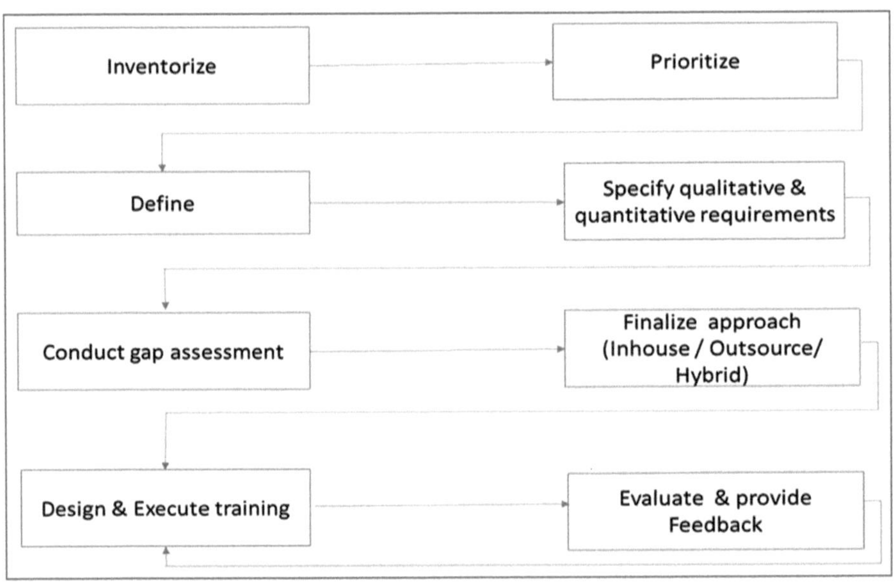

Fig. 3.1 Training design and execution

3.1.6.1 Inventorize

The first step toward a training design is to inventorize the requirements. The major input for requirements comes from the people in charge of the process as they can outline what they need, to take the process to the next level, in terms of both short term and long term. When there are multiple departments, the inventorization should be done across the departments so that common trainings across the departments can be identified.

3.1.6.2 Prioritize

Once the capability requirements have been identified, they need to be prioritized on parameters such as short term and long term, high priority, low priority. The prioritization should be on the basis of criteria such as urgency, impact if not rolled out, ball park cost of rolling it out, and the number of employees having requirement to undertake a particular training.

3.1.6.3 Define

On the basis of prioritized requirements one can define the capability development requirements that fall in scope for the transformation program. There is no hard and fast rule for selection, but it may be logical to pick up most high priority short term, some low priority short term, and some high priority long term. The requirements that were collected but not implemented should be archived.

3.1.6.4 Specify Qualitative and Quantitative Requirements

The next step after the definition of the capability requirement is the specification of quantitative and qualitative aspects. This would depend on factors such as the following: What kind of training does it need to be? Should it be a conference, a workshop, or a conventional classroom training? How many hours of training are required? Should there be a different level of detail corresponding to difference in seniority or can the training be generic? Should the training be in blocks of weeks or flexible over weekends? Does it have to be digital or face to face? Trainings should support application of skills in the workplace; otherwise the training effort does not yield any result.

3.1.6.5 Conduct Gap Assessment

Once the requirements are specified, a gap assessment can be done in terms of current capability vis-a-vis the envisaged capability. Depending on the organization, this can be done in a number of ways. One way could be to theoretically compare capability requirement of existing roles to the capability requirement of future roles; another could be to ask the delivery and/or line managers of the future process to look at employee profiles and indicate the gaps. It should be explored if change of roles of employees could create a better fit between the employees and the future roles.

3.1.6.6 Finalize Approach (In-House/Outsource/Hybrid)

Trainings do not come for free, so the next step is to finalize who can deliver the training. Should the training be in-house or should be outsourced or should be a mix of the two? The cost of the training is an important criterion in making this decision, yet cost is not the only basis to make the decision. The level of specialization required, availability of space to conduct large-scale trainings, availability of trainers, and current schedule of planned in-house trainings are some other criteria.

3.1.6.7 Design and Execute Training

Once the approach is finalized, it comes to actually designing and executing the training. This is very important as all the previous steps could be rendered useless if this step is not done carefully. The finalized training should be piloted with Subject Matter Experts (SMEs) first before it is launched for the employees.

3.1.6.8 Evaluate and Provide Feedback

The employees, the managers, and the trainers can all have feedback in various forms which should be directed to subsequent trainings so that the feedback loop ensures that the trainings remain on track.

Any process transformation impacts the people and is impacted by them. Collectively the people form the culture of any organization, and at the same time the organization influences the culture of the people. Culture transformation is beyond the scope of process transformation, but it is very important for the transformation team to be aware of and derive the most and contribute to the organizational culture.

3.2 Communication

Communication can be defined as the deliberate or accidental transfer of meaning (Gamble 2013). It is the process that occurs whenever someone observes or experiences behavior and attributes meaning to that behavior. Communication can range from interpersonal to mass and online communication, thus occurs in many forms and can be spread in space.

In order to understand communication, the essential elements of communication should be considered.

For a communication to happen, a sender, a receiver, and a message are essential. In case of intrapersonal communication, the sender and receiver can be oneself. The sender encodes and sends out the message, while the receiver decodes and receives it.

Channels are the media that are used to carry messages. The role of sender/receiver is not limited to one person, and sending and receiving occur simultaneously.

While communicating, anything that interferes with or distorts the ability to send or receive messages is termed as noise. Noise is not related to sound alone. People have their own thoughts and feelings which can block or distort communication. This blocking or distortion can be termed internal noise. Distraction due to external factors can be termed as external noise.

There is always a context to communication which affects the way one acts toward others or determines the nature of communication. There are times when the context is so natural that one may hardly notice it, and at another time, the impact of context may be so obvious that it may lead to change of posture, manner of speaking, etc.

The verbal or nonverbal cues that are perceived in reaction to our communication function are termed as feedback. Feedback can be internal, external, negative, or positive.

Lastly as people communicate, influence is exchanged in various degrees and that can be termed as effect of communication.

What is it that makes the communication at the time of a transformation so special? Why does it need to be planned and executed in a structured way? The reason is that transformation involves substantial change, and unless communication is designed to support this endeavor, it will lead to employees being frightened or angry (Ginsberg 2008). The employees need to be engaged in the transformation for them to feel a part of the transformation rather than having something imposed upon them. Engaged employees are the ones who are willing to walk that extra mile and are crucial for the success of a transformation effort.

Within the "Process Tangram," communication is divided into engagement strategy, stakeholder analysis, communication plan, identification of barriers to communication, communication package, and feedback and evaluation.

3.2.1 Engagement Strategy

Defining the engagement strategy is complex as engagement is not something tangible and is difficult to measure. Since individuals are different with their own value systems, it is a challenge to ensure that the communication reaches the employees in a way it is purported to be. We discussed earlier that noise in communication is not only external but also internal. The communication should be so strong and powerful that it cuts through the noises in a reassuring way, aligning individual objectives with the transformation goals. The way an individual receives a communication is dependent on the message, the sender, and the receiver, yet engagement drivers can be selected which then become the key drivers in framing engagement strategy.

There are various techniques that can be deployed to engage employees:

- *Employee Action Teams*: Within this technique, a group of people are selected who along with the management identify the engagement goals and create strategies to achieve them.
- *Appreciative Inquiry*: This involves collaborating with a greater number of employees to collectively come to a conclusion on what the strengths of the organization have been and how they can be applied to achieve the transformation goal. Though participation in such an exercise may result in engagement, utilizing this technique across the organization should be done only during the initial days. At a later stage, this form of engagement may prove to be counterproductive and confusing for employees.
- *Message Maps*: This technique provides a clear picture of the objectives of transformation, depending on the category of audience relating to them to explain the

past, present, and the future. Message maps help in visualizing the core business message in a simple yet crisp manner.
- *Storytelling*: This technique involves utilizing the power of narrative to propagate the crux of the transformation program in a manner that the people can relate to it and make it their own.

Communication is a support mechanism to the overall strategy envisioned for the process transformation program and is inextricably linked to culture (Riel 2012). For the engagement strategy to be effective, an alignment with stakeholders is essential. An understanding of their beliefs and viewpoints enables the organization to identify the ones that would support and the ones who would oppose. This can help the transformation team to decide on their engagement strategy. The input from culture analysis and value system provides an inside perspective, while specific surveys, stakeholder issues, and specific industry level information could be sources for the outside perspective.

A mixture of both negotiation and confrontation strategies is often required. Most managers lean towards negotiation when trying to align colleagues with new strategic ideas. The need for communication support increases exponentially if a confrontational approach strategy is adopted.

The important aspect to consider while chalking out the engagement strategy is to ensure that core message is developed and validated in a manner that it becomes compelling. Employees need to understand why things around them are being transformed and how the transformation affects them. There are times when it is possible to gauge the reaction to the message being communicated to a subset of the organization and then reframe to get optimal results. On the other hand, when teams are spread across the world, such opportunities may be limited. What works very often is a way that communicates the universal idea but is communicated with a local flavor to increase its acceptance.

3.2.2 Stakeholder Analysis

Once the engagement strategy has been finalized, a clear picture of stakeholders is required. All stakeholders should be identified, and for each stakeholder, the following aspects should be considered:

- What is the impact of the transformation on them?
- What is their role in the organization?
- How influential are these stakeholders in terms of the power they yield and leadership they display?
- What is their representation in the organization?
- What is their knowledge of the processes that will undergo transformation?
- What is their position with respect to support of transformation? Are they neutral or in support or in opposition of transformation?
- Are they associated with an association/union etc.?
- What could be their issues or concerns?

- How can the identified issues/concerns be addressed?
- What are the themes and messages that can be used to address their concern?

Stakeholders can be internal as well as external. Stakeholders are usually identified as a category rather than as an individual, for example, if the process affects the engineering department, then one of the influential stakeholders could be the head of engineering and not Mr. John Miller who is the person holding the position. Once the categories have been identified, people can be mapped against the categories.

3.2.3 Communication Plan

Once the engagement strategy has been decided and the stakeholders identified, it comes down to chalking down the details of actual implementation activities which form the communication plan. Communication plan is a live document and helps in creating a context and simplifying complex ideas. This is required to ensure that the stakeholders can see a connection between the transformation and their own self.

The communication plan documents themes and messages that will be communicated and the reason behind undertaking the effort. It answers the question of "who" will be responsible for taking up the tasks, for example, whether it will be someone called Jonathan Brown or Lisa Donner? A special communication team/role may be assigned for carrying out communication-related activities. Often the communication department of organization supports the endeavor by nominating someone from their department who not only fulfills the role but also acts as a conduit between the transformation team and the communication department. The tasks are associated with a timeline, for example, what are the dates on which Lisa needs to participate in the cascade meetings? The stakeholders should get information on an ongoing basis and should be repeated as far as possible so that it can be internalized. The communication plan is linked to the overall project plan. A part of the communication plan may also be coaching the leadership on effective storytelling such that the transformation hits a chord with the stakeholders.

3.2.4 Identification of Barriers to Communication

To deal with barriers to communication, first they need to be identified so that they can be dealt with. Communication barriers are detrimental to effective communication as they create difficulties in proper understanding of the conveyed message. From the perspective of transformation, the barriers can be categorized into four categories as shown in Fig. 3.2.

3.2.4.1 Sender

Communication is more of a push mechanism which makes the role of the sender (originator of the communication) very important. Despite the fact that the same information package may be used, it often delivers a different result with different speakers. The reason is that the person, style, method, communication skills,

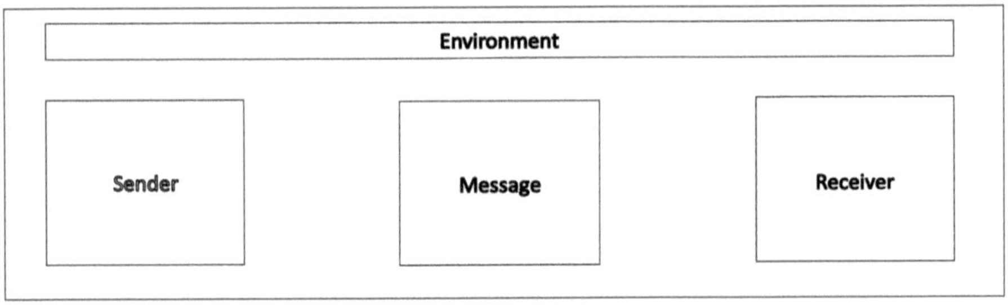

Fig. 3.2 Barriers to communication

attitude, and knowledge distinguish the message sent by different senders. This is particularly important in case of methods such as face-to-face meetings and webcasts. In case of written communication, the style, who the sender is, his/her position in hierarchy and influence in the organization, etc. take over. A common strategy to win over the affected stakeholders is to get the people who may seem to be apparent opponents to endorse the changes that encompass transformation. Not all senders may be at ease with communicating; therefore, some coaching may be required.

3.2.4.2 Message

Consider the messages:

> "I expect you to do everything you can to achieve this goal of transformation. Let's transform ourselves into a stronger and more efficient team" as compared with "If we are not able to transform ourselves in line with the transformation program, we may not exist, heads will start rolling."

Both the messages show urgency to transform. The focus of the first message is to motivate people to participate and be a part of the process, whereas the focus of the second message is on the consequences of not transforming. Depending on the culture, the message may be interpreted differently. This barrier that relates to different understanding and interpretation of the words used to communicate is called semantic barrier. If the company is known to follow a hire and fire policy, some would interpret the second message as a lot of firings are going to follow soon. If the company has been employee-friendly, it may be interpreted as a transformation for survival and so on.

These two messages are from face-to-face all-employee meetings, but if the same message was to be sent as a mailer, it might have been worded differently, although it might have worked well for a webcast. This makes the choice of communication channel important for the transmission of the message. Feedback is quick in case of face-to-face type format and slow in case of written messages. As far as transformation is concerned, all channels are important and should be made use of while transmitting the message to the stakeholders. The message should be clear and designed to meet the objectives of communication. The message should be politically correct and should be designed keeping the context of the culture in mind. Context defines the impact of verbal and non-verbal cues with respect to the content of the communication.

3.2.4.3 Environment

Consider the case of Eagle Star which is a global organization with offices in all major cities around the world. This makes transformation very complex, and communication is affected by the sheer distance between the offices. It is impossible to hold face-to-face kickoff meetings at all the offices, so it has been decided to make five hubs where the face-to-face communication will happen and representatives from various locations may join. The onus is subsequently on the representatives to cascade this information to the members of their respective locations. Within 48 h, written communication and links to webcast in various languages will be sent to all the offices. In this case, the endeavor is to ensure that the environmental variables such as of physical distance, language, space, and time do not create a barrier to communication.

3.2.4.4 Receiver

The message sent is not good enough unless the receiver understands it the way it is intended. This is not as simple as we may want it to be. Individual and group factors come into play when it comes to reception of a message making understanding and interpretation complex. If the receiver does not trust the sender due to past experiences, the chances are high that the message will be filtered selectively to construe a meaning that may be different from the intended message. The background, interest, knowledge level, and attitude all make a difference to the interpretation of the message.

There can be certain topics that can evoke emotions, for example, for a team who implemented the existing process, a transformation of the same process could evoke an emotional reaction as they could perceive it as belittling of their past efforts. Even ego can come into picture in cases especially where the proponent of the transformation happens to an ideological opponent. Gender differences can also attribute to barriers to communication.

Another practical problem in the current times is that of information overload. People get so much information to process that it exceeds their capacity to imbibe and understand. In such a scenario, the feeling of "yet another transformation" coupled with overload on processing capacity creates a significant barrier. People need time to adjust to the changes and to make it their own; when it seems that the time is not available, they may create barriers to communication.

The question arises that when so many barriers exist, how does one ensure that these barriers are minimized and the message reaches the receiver in the intended manner?

The following may be done to achieve the same:

- Design the message carefully taking best practices into consideration. Cascade is a practice wherein the message is communicated down to the lowest hierarchy level wherein each leader apprises their direct reports and takes their feedback. This can be utilized in the transformation program.
- Have leaders who are respected and influential as an integral part of the communication plan.
- Make use of existing channels of communication along with new channels designed specifically for the transformation without introducing too much redundancy. Since transformation communication needs to be repeated till people understand the message, some redundancy is acceptable.

- Create themes and messages that create a visualization of the end result and remove anxiety and fear from the minds of people.
- Message may be aggressive but should not be offensive.
- Validate the message with a select group of people before full rollout and continuously update the message based on feedback.
- Ensure that the communication plan is a living document to incorporate the feedback and subsequent action.

3.2.5 Communication Package

The communication package is the actual artifacts, supporting material, training, and instructions of their deployment. In other words communication package constitutes the resources. Guidelines on how the communication should be done are also a part of the package. A communication package may contain the following components: email templates, information packages, links to Internet and intranet pages highlighting the transformation, audiovisual materials, informal communications, external media information, posters, FAQs, and visual maps.

3.2.6 Feedback Mechanism and Evaluation

Feedback and evaluation are activities that measure the outcomes of success and run through the life of the transformation program. It is necessary to do so to ensure that the overall communication objectives are met, and if required, corrective action can be taken. The approach to the feedback and evaluation should be pragmatic to ensure the money spent in the evaluation exercise is commensurate to the expected result.

Feedback is a response from the receiver of communication which can be gathered in multiple ways. It could be informal by way of face-to-face interviews with stakeholders or people who actually deliver communication through workshops or all employee sessions. Feedback can also be gathered through queries, comments, etc. posted on dedicated pages on the intranet. It could be done in more structured ways like conducting online surveys. These could include questions on what they recalled of the communication, what they understand and how they feel about it, and whether they have received enough communication so far. The target for such activities could be a selected group of people or the complete target audience. Web metrics can also be deployed to see if the people are accessing communication items.

Evaluation implies an assessment of the performance of the planned communication activity. While feedback is an important input, there can be other quantitative criteria such as the number of times the communication was sent, whether it was sent out on the planned date, how many people turned for a communication session, whether the activity was completed within budget, and so on. While interpreting and analyzing the data, consideration should be given if some external factors influenced the data, for example, if the communication activity coincided with another important meeting resulting in low turnout.

Feedback and evaluation should not be a one-time activity as the result enables improvement while the communication exercise is still on. Once the transformation program is over, final evaluation can be done and archived to serve as learning for subsequent transformation programs.

Culture and communication deal with the heart and soul of the organization. Once that is dealt with, the only "tan" left to make a transformation program successful is the "success factors" which will be covered in the next chapter.

References

Adams JS (1963) Towards an understanding of inequality. J Abnorm Norm Soc Psychol 67:422–436

Cameron KS, Quinn RE (2006) Diagnosing and changing organizational culture – based on competing values framework. Wiley, San Francisco

Colquitt JA, Lepine JA, Wesson MJ (2013) Organizational behavior improving performance & commitment in the workplace. McGraw-Hill Irwin, New York

Gamble TK, Gamble M (2013) Communication works. McGraw-Hill, New York

Ginsberg G (2008) Melcrum's top international communication case studies: an anthology of best selling research to tackle key communication issues. Melcrum Publishing, London

Gupta M (2009) Principles of management. PHI Learning Pvt. Ltd, New Delhi

Harigopal K (1995) Conflict management – managing interpersonal conflict. Oxford and IBH Publishing, New Delhi

Hofstede G http://geert-hofstede.com/national-culture.html. Accessed 30 Oct 2014

http://www.bobthebuilder.com/uk/about_bob.html. Accessed 1 Oct 2014

McShane SL, Glinow MAV, Sharma RR (2011) Organizational behavior emerging knowledge and practice for the real world. Tata McGraw-Hill, Boston

Newstrom JW (2007) Organizational behavior human behavior at work. McGraw-Hill, New York

Pondy LR (1972) Organizational conflict: concepts and models. In: Thomas JM, Bennis WG (eds) Management of change & conflict. Penguin, Harmondsworth, pp 360–366

Redding G, Bond MH, Witt MA (2014) Culture and the business systems of Asia. In: Witt MA, Redding G (eds) The Oxford handbook of Asian business systems. Oxford University Press, Oxford, pp 358–382

Riel CBMV (2012) The alignment factor: leveraging the power of total stakeholder support. Routledge, London

Schein EH (2010) Organizational culture and leadership. Wiley, San Francisco

Ulrich RA, Wieland GF (1976) Organization theory and design. Richard D Irwin Inc, Homewood

Vroom VH (1964) Work and motivation. Wiley, New York

Weiss JW (2001) Organizational behavior and change, managing diversity, cross-cultural dynamics, and ethics. South Western College Publishing, Cincinnati

Suggested Reading

Bamrough J, Reeves M (2003) The HR management manual, training your staff, evaluation of training. Penguin Books, New Delhi

Cameron KS, Duton JE, Quinn RE (eds) (2003) Positive organizational scholarship – foundations of a new discipline. Berret-Koehler Publishers Inc., San Francisco

Coghlan D, Rashford NS (2007) Organization change and strategy. Routledge Taylor and Francis Group, Cornwall, UK

Colquitt JA, Lepine JA, Wesson MJ (2013) Organizational behavior improving performance & commitment in the workplace. McGraw-Hill Irwin, New York
Ginsberg G (2008) Melcrum's top international communication case studies: an anthology of best-selling research to tackle key communication issues. Melcrum Publishing, London
Giri AK (1999) Values ethics and business challenges for education and management. Rawat Publications, Jaipur
Guirdham M (2005) Communication across cultures at work. Palgrave Macmillan, Houndmills
Harvard Business Review on The Innovative Enterprise (2003) Harvard Business School Publishing Corporation, Boston
Harvard Business Review on Turnarounds (2001) Harvard Business School Press, Boston
Holliday A, Hyde M, Kullman J (2004) Intercultural communication an advanced resource book. Routledge Taylor and Francis Group, London/New York
Ingham J (2007) Strategic human capital management creating value through people. An Elsevier Imprint, Butterworth-Heinmann, Malden
Jardins JD (2006) An introduction to business ethics. McGraw-Hill International Edition, Boston
Jones P (2008) Communicating strategy. Gower Publishing Limited, Aldershot
Kenton B, Penn S (2009) Change conflict and community – challenging thought and action. Elsevier Limited, Butterworth-Heinemann, Amsterdam
Kirton G, Greene AM (2010) The dynamics of managing diversity, a critical approach. Elsevier Imprint, Amsterdam
Liu S, Volcic Z, Gallois C (2011) Introducing intercultural communication. Sage, London
Luthans F (2005) Organization behavior. McGraw-Hill International Edition, Boston
Martin J (2002) Organizational culture mapping the terrain. Sage, Thousand Oaks
Neuliep JW (2011) Intercultural communication – a contextual approach. Sage, Thousand Oaks
Newstrom JW (2007b) Organizational behavior, human behavior at work. McGraw-Hill, New York
Ott JS (1989) The organizational culture perspective. Brooks Cole Publishing Company, Pacific Grove
Parker M (2000) Organizational culture and identity. Sage, London
Phegan B (1996) Developing your company culture – the joy of leadership. Business Publications Inc., Mumbai
Pheysey DC (1993) Organizational cultures – types and transformations. Routledge, London
Phillips JJ, Friedman W (2008) Communication and implementation – sustaining the practice. Wiley, San Francisco
Riel CBMV (2012b) The alignment factor: leveraging the power of total stakeholder support. Routledge, London
Ritti RR (1998) The ropes to skip and the ropes to know fifth edition, Studies in organizational behavior. Wiley, New York
Samovar LA, Porter RE, McDaniel ER (2007) Communication between cultures. Thomson Wadsworth, Belmont
Schein E (2009) Corporate culture survival guide. Jossey-Bass, a Wiley company, San Francisco
Sharma RR (2012) Change Management and organizational transformation. Tata McGraw-Hill Education Private Limited, New Delhi
Stanford N (2011) Organization culture getting it right. The Economist in association with Profile Books Limited, London
Thomas CC (1992) Transforming the company – bridging the gap between management myth and corporate reality. Kogan Page, London
Thomas CC (2004) Transforming the company – manage change, compete win. Kogan Page, London
Varkkey B, Brahma G, Ghoshal S (2004) Building business capability, perform or perish. Business Pub Inc/Bpi India Pvt Ltd, New Delhi
Ybema S, Yanow D, Sabelis I (eds) (2011) Organizational culture, volume II. An Elgar research collection, Cheltenham

Success Factors 4

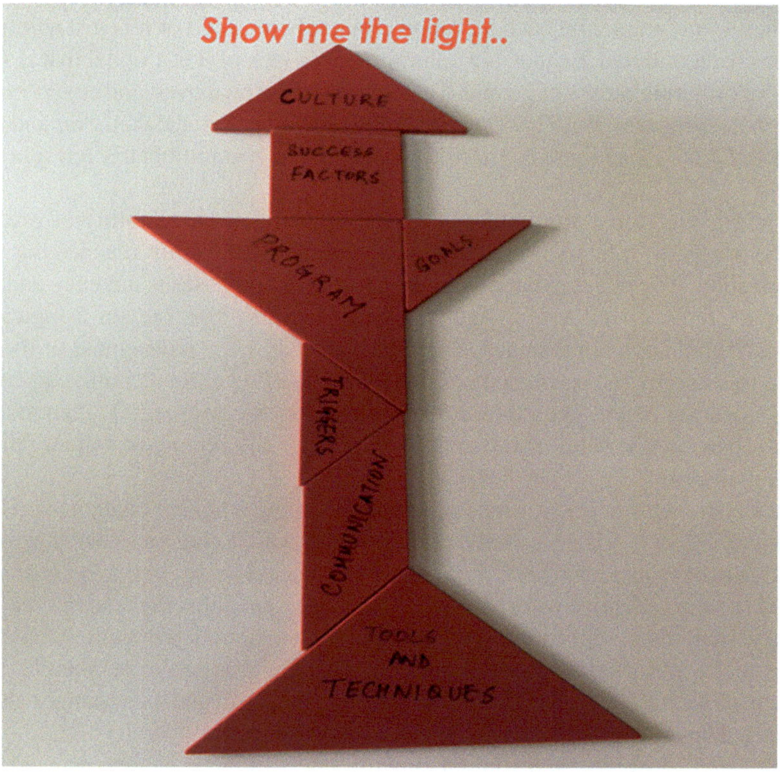

C. Sharma, *Business Process Transformation*, Management for Professionals,
DOI 10.1007/978-81-322-2349-8_4

4.1 Success Factors

The success factors are discussed below:

4.1.1 Leadership Commitment

Leadership is accepting responsibility to create conditions that enable others to achieve shared purpose in the face of uncertainty. Leaders accept responsibility not only for their individual "part" of the work but also for the collective whole (Ganz 2010). The transformation team and the rest of the organization who impact and are impacted by the change look up to the leadership and take cues for themselves through an assessment of the leadership commitment to the program.

The organization seeks out the leadership to inspire and guide them and to feel their support. A transformation is a change that affects people. Since it affects people, they want to assess if such a change is actually required or it is just another fad that has been initiated. Leadership commitment or lack of it is a signal that is sought in the information radars of people. This impacts their own overt and covert involvement in the program. With backgrounds of people more diverse than ever and crossing boundaries of nations, the impact of leadership commitment is felt more than ever.

While leadership commitment is visible by sufficient availability of resources for the program, it is also reflected in the way the leadership reaches out to the organization. The change that a transformation encompasses is not easy and at the minimum requires unlearning and relearning. People look out for a logical reasoning behind such big changes. They are affected by the willingness of the leadership to stand by the cause and empathy with its effects. Leadership can connect to organization better when they know what makes the people tick, then make the link to their own feeling, and can empathize with the feeling of others (Halpern and Lubar 2003).

Leadership commitment supports people in facing adaptive challenges (Heifetz and Laurie 1998). Adaptive challenges are those which challenge our deeply held beliefs, the ones that have been responsible for success so far. In this sense transformation requires adaptive work. A committed leadership helps in the identification of the key challenge, supporting the program from external pressures, challenging norms and conflict resolution, and empowering the program to achieve its objectives. It strikes a balance between the running business and the changes that the program demands.

Very often, however, in the initial kick off, many of the program sponsors representing the leadership are present, but as time passes by, their interest is no longer visible. Leadership involvement through feedback, regular evaluation of the program at review moments, and time-to-time communication is what the organization sees and perceives as visible signs of leadership commitment.

A leader who is committed should also be able to show its commitment. Besides one to one interaction, the other means to reach out the organization is through communication. An articulate leader is able to inform, influence, instruct, and engage as per the requirement (Barret 2014). This could include information on why transformation is required, what are the plans to achieve that, what it means to the leadership, what it means to the transformation team, what are the benefits, what would be the pain points and challenges, how and why the things that have worked in the past are no longer applicable, progress of the program, and so on. While detailed communication plans are drawn out as a part of transformation program, it is important that the leadership takes out time to be a part of the communication plan so that they can show they stand behind the changes that come along.

There are times when the leadership even when committed is faced with many initiatives that run in parallel. Besides this, they need to attend to the constant requirements of actually running the business. They also deal with disruptive changes which are spread all over. Such changes can sometimes even challenge the very existence of the organization. The business environment is complex with interplay of large number of variables that are required to be managed. In such times leadership is hard pressed with time resulting in limited follow-up and involvement. This makes their commitment and support to the program less visible.

The question arises, what can be done to structurally ensure management's commitment to the program. Although there is no substitute for involvement, one way could be to delegate their role to "active sponsor." An active sponsor is someone who can devote more time and can have a high degree of involvement. Active sponsor has the mandate of the sponsor and represents the sponsor to ensure that the pace of the program is not compromised. It is necessary that this person should be empowered enough to take decisions based on available inputs. It does not mean, however, that the active sponsor should not consult the leadership as and when required.

Another way could be to embed the transformation goals in the incentive and performance systems. The target group is not only the members of the transformation team, but this group cuts across the organization to the employees who are touched upon by the transformed business processes.

Similarly, measures can be built in the team performance goals, initially to make use of the changed process and subsequently to show the overall benefits. An objective assessment should be done to establish if the process adherence is being done for name only, while the benefits are coming in from elsewhere or they are not coming at all. In case the transformed process is being followed and results are not being achieved, it should be taken as feedback to establish if the business scenarios have changed, or the process needs to be fine-tuned.

Committed leadership helps in establishing a sense of urgency (Kotter 1996), which gets people interested and helps in gaining the necessary cooperation to achieve the desired objectives. It also invigorates people to gather the courage to tackle the most difficult challenges and therefore is a factor necessary for a successful transformation.

4.1.2 Clear Strategy and Vision

Vision refers to a visualization of future, provides direction, motivates people to take action in the right direction, and helps in coordinating actions of different people (Kotter 1996). Strategy lays down the path to be taken to achieve the goals set out in the vision.

What does this mean for the transformation program? The program-level vision cannot be totally unrelated to overall vision of the organization, yet it should be something that people can understand in the context of change. It is very difficult to get a buy-in from people if the goals are absurdly ambitious and seem too far-fetched. It is not necessary that a transformation program is undertaken only in case of dire circumstances where the need for a transformation is self-evident for survival. In such cases as well in the case of good times, the vision paints a picture that provides a direction to the people to get out of comfort zones and become a part of transformation.

It is the vision that helps people remain motivated as it is something they can visualize and connect to. The associated benefits guide to a better future, even if in the long run sacrifices are required. The vision should be clear so that it can provide direction. The overall end objective could be picked up from the goals mentioned in the "goals" tan of the Process Tangram, yet a certain level of quantification would be required to make it real for the organization.

The "do-ability" of the vision is established through the strategy. For a transformation program, various strategies can be adopted. Consider the following example of three hospitals given in Table 4.1.

Hospital A reaches out to the customers by offering them the best quality and service without exorbitant costs. Hospital B specializes in offering a luxurious experience to the end customers. Hospital C is known for its super specialists and high success rate.

The change vision gives the transformation team direction on the objectives of the transformation, yet it is not at the level of detail of a transformation plan. Hospital A can use the benchmark of the current market leader in value segment as its reference point. Similarly Hospital B can look at the market leaders offering the maximum luxury, and Hospital C can look towards the hospitals that are the best performing in selective surgery. The three hospitals could try to reach or surpass the reference points by achieving new levels of service.

The strategies of the three hospitals dwell on the details of how the change vision can be realized. These are still not at the level of a transformation plan, yet it provides information on how the change vision can be achieved. Transformation strategy could also include a guideline on the rollout of transformation program, such projects in parallel or sequence, phased rollout, or a big bang approach.

A clear transformation vision and strategy serve as the guiding principles in how the transformation should be carried out and is very important for a successful transformation.

Table 4.1 Comparison of hospital transformation

	Hospital A (HA)	Hospital B (HB)	Hospital C (HC)
Value proposition	Maximum value	Luxury healthcare	Super specialty
Transformation vision	Become market leader in corporate segment by offering value for money	Offer the most luxurious customer experience to high-end customers	Offer the best elective surgery in the state
Transformation strategy	Value maximization through cost reduction, comfort, and service level enhancement. Transformation of patient treatment and care delivery process as well as marketing process to highlight quality care at reasonable prices to target corporate customers	Transform "intake to discharge process" for high-end customers. Online intake, relationship managers for intake, at home sample collection, panel of specialists for selection, and post-discharge home visits will be the salient features. This will lead to greater number of high-end customers reaching to HB without a pressure on bed capacity, thereby maximizing revenue	Transform the elective surgery process to reduce the surgery and recovery time along with a higher success rate. This will lead to the accommodation of a greater number of patients and potential for higher surgery billing rates. Happy customers will pave the way for maximizing revenue

4.1.3 Value Focus

Every transformation must have a value focus. When this happens, the business objectives are always a priority. It ensures that the big picture is always on the mind irrespective of the activity being undertaken. Value focus enables in aligning processes with business strategy.

Every organization has a value proposition, the offering that it has for its customers, that differentiates its products and services from competitors. It is something that enables a customer in assigning value to the products or services received. Whatever may be the goals of transformation, value enhancement and creation are central themes that a transformation should be concerned with.

Let us reconsider the three hospitals that we discussed earlier:

Hospital A The value proposition is to maximize value, which is guided by a balance in quality cost and service. When the transformation starts as per the strategy of value maximization through cost reduction, comfort, and service level enhancement, there will be choices that would have to be made.

For example, the hospital can go for the best treatment possibility but that may be too steep in terms of cost. There may be choices of lowering the service levels to reduce the costs. The quality should be such that the patient is cured of the disease although there may be no music and aroma of fresh flowers in the waiting rooms.

The focus would be on no frills yet good service and reasonable cost, which would be roughly 95 % of what is covered by standard insurance packages. This value focus provides the parameters that should be kept in mind to be able to sustain the benefits of transformation, once the program is over. To make the customers aware of the offered value, the marketing process would have to be revamped to counter popular notion that quality service is not available at a reasonable price.

Hospital B The value proposition is to provide luxury healthcare. The target customers are the high-end customers who do not want to get out of comfort zones even when they are unwell. At every interface, they want to have a superior customer experience.

This will require transformation of "intake to discharge process" for high-end customers. While doing so, it may face dilemmas, and value focus can be very useful in establishing the right way. Suppose hospital B wants to decide if it should transform the intake to operation theater subprocess on lines of 7 star hotels. This subprocess, which might be very efficient and valuable to the customer, would have very high associated costs, therefore, the cost versus feature discussion is bound to come up. In such a scenario, cost considerations would be overlooked in line with the value focus of providing luxury.

Hospital C The value proposition of the super-specialty hospital C is the ability to provide surgery. While transforming its chosen elective surgery process, a value focus can again help in making wise choices. Providing the best elective surgery implies getting the best surgeons, the best training, the best equipment, the shortest procedure, new techniques, the fastest recovery, greater collaboration with international surgeons when required, and so on. This comes at a high price; however, the value focus will help in establishing that, while cost should not be ignored, there should be no compromise on the super-specialty proposition. No matter who the surgeon is, the success rate should be every competitor's envy. Ultimately, the success rate will create goodwill to eventually maximize revenue.

A value focus ensures that the transformation program remains connected to the business and eventually contributes to the achievement of the value proposition.

4.1.4 Quality

Quality is an aspect that should be ingrained not only in the transformation team but also in the people who ultimately run the transformed process. For only then can the end objectives be achieved, free of deficiencies and satisfying the acceptance criteria.

Deming WE (1993) defined quality in terms of its characteristics as "A product or service possesses quality if it helps somebody and enjoys a good and sustainable market. Trade depends on quality."

The American Society for Quality (ASQ) (http://asq.org/glossary/q.html) defines quality as: a subjective term for which each person or sector has its own definition. In technical usage, quality can have two meanings: (1) the characteristics of a product or service that bear on its ability to satisfy stated or implied needs and (2) a product or service free of deficiencies. According to Joseph Juran, quality means "fitness for use"; according to Philip Crosby, it means "conformance to requirements."

Garvin (1984) identified five major approaches to quality: transcendent, product based, user based, manufacturing based, and value based. The transcendent approach quality related to innate excellence is universally recognizable. In the product-based review, the preciseness and measurement aspect is highlighted. In the user-based approach, quality is based on customer's perspective. In the manufacturing approach, quality relates to meeting the specification. The value-based approach measures quality in terms of acceptable performance and cost.

All these and many more available definitions clearly indicate that there is no "one" correct definition of quality, with each one offering a different perspective. The question arises that how do these definitions link to a transformation program and why it is a success factor. When quality is established as a key criterion inherent in the work that is delivered as a part of the transformation, the results are visible in many ways. Not only does it result in producing the expected results as per specifications, it also results in reducing the unnecessary costs that are incurred due to poor quality.

Campanella (1999) identified three types of quality costs: prevention costs, appraisal costs, and internal and external failure costs. Prevention costs relate to prevention of poor quality. These are activities that are designed to prevent poor quality and services such as quality planning and process review. Appraisal costs relate to costs associated with measurement and evaluation that quality conforms to expected standards. These are activities such as measurement and auditing of product or services. The last category failure costs are divided into external and internal failure costs. These occur when the product does not conform to the specification. Internal failure costs occur before the product is passed on to the customer. This results in activities such as rework and scrap. External failure costs are the ones that reach the customer and can have the most serious repercussion in terms of warranty costs, loss of sale, and goodwill.

While an increase in these costs can be a trigger for transformation, they need to be kept in control through the life of transformation. Quality should be embraced as an attitude that enhances the value of the program to the organization.

4.1.5 Innovation

With its roots, the Latin word "innovare" implies "making something new." Innovation can be extended to include renewal, improvisation, (re)deployment, (re) positioning, or adoption of a product, service, process, or idea in a manner not done in the past to achieve desired objectives.

Organizations cannot afford to forever bask in the glory of one-time innovation. A systematic mechanism is required to ensure their innovation program is not just a fancy facade but a pot brimming with ideas that can rejuvenate current offerings and set the direction of future.

It is not necessary that the innovation comes only from one's own stable. It can well be based upon someone else's innovation yet deployed in a manner that allows a reinvention to be responsive to the changes in the market.

There are different views with respect to innovation; the traditional western view has been of a structured approach to innovation with substantial budgets to support the same. On another tangent, "Jugaad" (Radjou et al. 2012) has been suggested as an approach that can complement the structured approach to innovation. This form of innovation supports the simple, ingenious, flexible, and frugal approach to innovation. "Jugaad" innovators seek opportunity in adversity, pursue the customers who are on the margins, and follow their heart. Intuition, empathy, and passion are as important as analytical thinking.

There are other approaches to innovation as well. Hargadon and Sutton (2000) propose that innovators continuously use old ideas as raw materials for new ideas through the strategy of knowledge brokering. The knowledge brokering cycle consists of four steps:

- Knowledge brokers are constantly on a lookout for new ideas, sometimes in a generalized way and sometimes in a specific way. Not all collected ideas lead to innovation.
- Since organization memories are difficult to maintain, the best way to keep the ideas alive is by discussing them and using them.
- The ideas that have been kept alive can be put to use by applying them directly on other situations or benefitting from analogies thereof.
- The last step is to test the applied ideas to establish benefits for the organization.

The idea is essentially to bring out the fact that organizations cannot keep on waiting for a "eureka" moment of geniuses but need to approach innovation in a structured way.

Irrespective of the chosen approach, creativity plays an important role. Creativity, innovation, and competitiveness are linked to each other and operate at individual, organizational, and national level, respectively (Carayannis and Gonzalez 2003). Creativity is about perceiving and envisioning relationships and possibilities in an imaginative manner that is unlike the normal constructs.

One approach closely linked to creativity is lateral thinking (Bono 2009). It is a way of thinking that enables in generation of new ideas. Lateral thinking works along with the traditional way of thinking called vertical thinking. While vertical thinking follows logical sequence of steps, lateral thinking experiments and one can take a wrong step before reaching a conclusion. In lateral thinking, one breaks away from rigid patterns of the mind and opens oneself to restructuring of patterns. This facilitates generating ideas that may not necessarily be right yet provide a different way of looking at things. Once abundant ideas have been generated, vertical thinking can be exploited to select and strengthen the ideas. As an example, if one wanted to reach from point A to point B, vertical thinking may lead to thoughts pertaining to using the latest model of car and so on, while lateral thinking may focus on thoughts pertaining to bringing point B nearer to point A.

Creativity becomes the input for adoption of these ideas into an economically viable proposition for an organization and thereby becomes sustainable innovation. The collective outcome of innovation contributes to bringing efficiency and sophistication thus contributes to the competitiveness of the nation. The global competitiveness index has three pillars on which it assesses countries on competitiveness (http://www.gaportal.org/global-indicators/global-competitiveness-index). One of the three is the pillar of "innovation and sophistication factors" which highlights their impact on the competitiveness of a nation.

Although the stage of development of a country influence the competitiveness of country, at the level of organization creative individuals need to work together to come up to solutions that enable the organization to bring in new offerings of any kind. When creative individuals work at a personal level, they tend to be flexible, find out new ways of using existing things, and change the rule to produce great results. At the organizational level, a balance is required between individual space for thought and collective solutions. Organizations should provide an environment that fosters experimentation, enhances conceptual skills, leverages on employee attributes, and stimulates creative behavior (Gundry et al. 1994).

Innovation is like any other activity in the organization in the sense that it requires resources. For an optimal result and selection of ideals, scoping is required. Suppose a transformation program is running on the theme of bringing in efficiency in time to market, then this theme can be central in selection of ideas that could be developed.

Innovation is no longer confined to the boundaries of an organization and has moved from closed innovation to open innovation (Chesbrough 2006). There is a higher level of collaboration with opportunities for generating and commercializing innovation. While commercializing, some innovative companies may market ideas, while others may take the best ideas from all available sources and offer them competitively.

Transformation involves playing with the variables and going beyond conventional boundaries while having respect for the efficiency of systems that work. Innovation is a factor that increases the chances of success of a transformation and therefore should be an integral part of the transformation program.

4.1.6 Speed

Speed is a very important component of a successful transformation. Consider the following scenarios:

Scenario 1 A consumer is regularly facing a connectivity issue while using her laptop at her residence. She calls the customer service desk. The service agent picks up the phone, asks questions as per the standard operating procedure, and at a particular point decides that someone else should help. He transfers the call to a colleague who starts again with the same standard operating procedure. When the next agent is almost on the verge of resolving the problem, the call gets disconnected because of the connectivity issue that the customer is facing. The consumer can call all over again.

Scenario 2 A sales agent sells customized solutions. Before he can give a quote, he first understands the customer requirement and then sends the list of individual components to the centralized sales department. The central sales department adds solution design cost and overhead to the cost of individual components to come to a quote. The sales agent calls the prospect the next day but he has already ordered elsewhere.

Scenario 3 A patient goes to a hospital, in extreme pain he waits, and a nurse arrives, greets, and asks the patient to follow to a patient intake area. She asks the patient for reports, asks standard questions as per laid-down practice, makes some notes, and then leaves. The patient waits in the intake area; after a while the doctor arrives, and he starts asking questions. He starts from the same questions that the nurse had already asked, while the patient answers, not so patiently.

Scenario 4 A high-end customer takes a standard route, and every day her conference calls get disconnected while she is on her way to office. She decides she should lodge a complaint.

Now consider these scenarios with slight changes:

Scenario 1 The conversation was transcribed, and the second agent started from the point where his colleague had left. When the call got disconnected, the consumer got a call back and the problem is resolved in a short time.

Scenario 2 The sales agent feeds in the data into the CRM system and chooses components and predesigned solutions that come up on his smartphone. He discusses the solution options, finalizes the most suitable solution, and through the CRM generates an instant quote and closes the order.

Scenario 3 The nurse makes notes and updates the doctor on initial analysis. When the doctor arrives, he has already gone through the notes and asks only additional questions and provides a quick diagnosis and treatment.

Scenario 4 Based on network data logs, a network monitoring system picks up the connectivity issue. The customer is informed that the operator has picked up the issue through logs and would be resolved. Very soon the customer is informed that the issue is resolved.

In the initial scenarios, all the participants were operating as per the laid-down procedure; however, the element of speed was missing. Organizations should be able to anticipate and react at a speed like never before. This is not an easy task as anticipation alone cannot always handle disruptive changes. Organizations need to continuously reconfigure themselves to adapt to such changes.

The "to be" processes should be so designed that although they offer the efficiencies of standardized processes, they are nimble enough to offer customized solutions when required. Independently, processes may be correct to the T, but in correlation with each other, certain level of tweaking may be required.

Transcription or summarizing of information exchanged in the system and the provision for callback to the consumer would have ensured a satisfied customer and saved agents time.

A small change in the doctor's standard operating procedure to ensure a small discussion with nurse or going through the nurse's notes would have ensured that the patient's patience was not tested.

Empowering the sales agent to finalize the solution with the client would have helped him clinch the order.

Anticipating the problem with the network would have ensured that the customer did not move out to another service provider. This does not imply that exception handling has to be the norm; what it means is that the processes should be agile enough to deal with competitors, should be in a position to incorporate the best of technology, and so on.

The more an organization wants to anticipate, the greater is its reliance on historical data. When there are changes which could not have been anticipated, it is the skills, training, and empowerment of employees who are on the front that makes the difference in providing service with speed. Empowered employees can make swift decisions as all decisions do not have to go to the superior in the hierarchy whose availability can become a single point of failure.

How does this augur for transformation? The transformation team should realize that although the complete program takes long to conclude, they need to start reaping the benefits as soon as possible. This is required not only for catching the low-hanging fruit but also to satisfy the insatiable requirement of the organization to be able to respond with speed.

The team has to understand that if the "to be" processes are to be rolled out globally, there has to be a provision for local variations while keeping the global reporting mechanisms intact. Local rules and regulations could also impose additional restrictions or requirements on the process. The maturity of the operating markets also impacts the process. An "only Web" process that may be appropriate in The Netherlands may not fly at all in a remote village in Africa. The same process may perhaps require a Web interface and a service center setup in India.

Many a times speed is a part of the specification in forms such as service and operational level agreements, but as seen in the initial scenarios above despite meeting the SLA requirements, the processes were not able to provide the service with speed. Speed may actually have a component of perceived speed. When people know how long it takes to fix a certain issue and it is in their acceptable limits, they are likely to find the speed acceptable as compared to the situation when they do not know when the fix would be available or when it is beyond their acceptable limits.

The transformation team should take a holistic view of the process to look at the nuances to ensure that the processes are delivered and are perceived to be delivered with speed.

4.1.7 Process Orientation

Hammer and Champy (1993) have defined process orientation as the development of a customer-focussed, strategic business process-based organization enabled by rethinking the assumptions in a process-oriented way and utilizing information technology as a key enabler.

In his analysis of business process literature, McCormack (1999) (www.drkresearch.org/research/kmpaper.doc) suggests that process orientation seems to be centered on process culture along with systems and structures. This covers integration of suppliers and customers which fall outside the formal organizational structure. In this integration, customer occupies a central role.

When an organization is process oriented (Škrinjar et al. 2007) (http://proceedings.informingscience.org/InSITE2007/InSITE07p171-185Skri357.pdf), it leads to better nonfinancial performance and may indirectly lead to better financial performance. Nonfinancial performance refers to a better interaction between employees who work efficiently as there are no functional silos. There is greater interaction among them, and they work more effectively and efficiently. This in turn leads to improved relationship with suppliers and customers, thereby bringing in repeat orders.

A process-oriented organization may have a process-oriented organization structure. Process-oriented organization structure is different from functional organization which has the objective of achieving better coordination between similar activities and is mostly aligned with organization structure. In a process-oriented organization, the process framework of the "to be" model guides the organization structure (Kugelar and Vieting 2003).

While process orientation is a wider concept, not limited by process-oriented organization structure, the number of interfaces for a process is reduced in a process-oriented organization. Fewer interfaces counter the "throwing it over the fence" attitude. This leads to greater responsibility and accountability, successful execution of process, and streamlined reporting being vested in the organization. The process-oriented structure should not be created at the cost of resource efficiency, and an appropriate balance should be created.

In the current era of e-commerce and Web interfaces, McCormack and Johnson (2001) suggest that in the times of e-forces when organizations need to minimize non-value adding, horizontal or business process orientation is required to propel the organizations to perform at greater levels. In their model of process orientation, they propose that an organization passes through various levels of maturity before it becomes process oriented. In the initial ad hoc stage, processes are ill defined and organization structures are function based. In the defined stage, process documentation and change management exist. There is a higher degree of coordination between traditional functions. The linked stage involves process management with strategic intent and results. Besides traditional functions, broad process jobs and structures are put in place. At the highest level is the integrated stage where the organization cooperates with its vendors and suppliers. Traditional functions equal or subordinate to process in the organization structure. Process measurement and management systems are deeply embedded in the organization.

Similarly, Davenport (2013) suggests that a business view of organization is the view of processes and not that of functions, divisions, or products. Process view facilitates cross-functional solution implementation and willingness to search for process innovation.

In the context of transformation, it is not necessary to be at an integrated stage to reap benefits, but it seems only logical to have a process orientation to achieve the most out of process transformation in terms of efficiency, effectiveness, and innovation.

4.1.8 Portfolio Management Approach

A portfolio management approach to transformation implies the ability to have a holistic view so that functional silos do not jeopardize the benefits of transformation. In other words, it implies focusing on end-to-end process instead of departmental subsets. This approach has many benefits. It helps in ensuring that all the participants of the process come on the same page. It also helps in providing end-to-end visibility.

Some of the end-to-end processes that come under consideration are planning and budgeting, purchase to pay, order to cash, new product or service development, and lead to order. Let us take the metaphor of human body to understand this. Suppose someone has a problem in the vocal cord leading to speech impairment. A new medical intervention promises to restore the speech completely. One approach would be to go for the intervention, and another could be to first consider the impact on nose and ear. If there is no impact, then perhaps it is the best course of action. On the other hand, if the intervention has serious side effects on the ear, a careful consideration would be required before going in for the intervention. Here the point is not whether side effects are there or not, the point is that an overall consideration of the action and their consequences on the complete ENT system should be done before a decision is taken.

Consider another example of an automobile manufacturer who has the objective of offering world-class after-sales service to its customers. This manufacturer has earned lot of loyal customers in the past due to its superior service, which obviously came at a cost. The auto manufacturer is facing stiff competition and has no choice but to reduce fund allocation for after-sales service between 30 and 40 %. It, however, does not want to compromise on the after-sales service. There could be many possibilities on how this situation could be tackled. Few are mentioned below:

- Develop franchisees who can offer the same service at a lower cost owing to their agility
- Streamline and increase automation in its own service
- Outsource work to subcontractors who deliver services at existing location

Let us assume it goes in for the first option of developing franchisees. The franchisees are selected on the basis of merit, developed, trained, and start delivering service, yet the auto manufacturer is unable to bank the benefits. A lot of searching gives the insight that the centralized intake (the registration point for service request) was never geared up for the franchisees, resulting in deterioration of service. There was another problem with the reporting mechanism to the central finance department. Each franchisee was reporting financial data in its own way, resulting in delays and rework in consolidation of financial data. The franchises were developed with the single focus of servicing the vehicle in the best possible way. Although the actual service was done as expected, the customer's perceived benefit of services was degraded due to bad experience at the time of intake, and finance had a problem in effectively bringing the benefits to the books.

These examples highlight that an end-to-end approach many a times referred to as the portfolio management approach to transformation broadens the horizon and brings in universal benefits. It opens up possibilities of analytics and benchmarking that can drive overall performance. In cases where the organization has a process-based design instead of a function-based design, this may be simpler as the end-to-end process may reside in the same department.

4.1.9 Adequate Funding

Though this factor sounds like common sense, many transformation programs cannot reach their completion or achieve their complete objectives for lack of adequate funding.

There are many reasons for occurrence of such a situation. The foremost is inaccurate estimation of costs. Inaccurate cost estimation cannot only make the business case look rosier, but it also sets unrealistic expectations of benefits. If required, the program manager should take assistance of people with higher financial acumen to bring in as realistic estimates as possible.

In other cases, the transformation program is started with an initial corpus of funds with the promise of additional funding; however, sufficient provisions to fully fund the program are not made. When additional funds are sought, they are not available. The program is then asked to build in efficiencies to fund the projects.

While it is necessary that the program delivers the expected benefits, it can be counterproductive to shift focus on funding of the program rather than the program itself.

Sometimes there are competing programs that are started, and halfway the impact on overall business costs is realized. This might result in consolidation of competing programs or splitting of available funds.

In case of outsourcing scenario, where the transformation involves a sending and receiving organization, costs increase due to lack of desired skill set and knowledge of tools, leading to expensive substitution from the market. Factors such as staff attrition also lead to hiring of expensive consultants. All this might make the funding insufficient for the overall transformation program.

In all cases of cost overrun, there exists the possibility of additional funding through change requests which should be duly approved by the sponsors. If the transformation program is fund starved, it can prove to be difficult to achieve the objective.

There could be cases where the costs are distributed over a central fund and the underlying departments or practices. While the central funds may be available, the departments/practices may be reluctant to share costs. This unwillingness to fund may also stem from the impact on their profitability and poor visibility of perceived benefits.

It is also not infrequent that the sponsors are unable to see the benefits in line with the expectation. In such scenarios it may be better to stop the program and list down the lessons learned instead of reducing the funding and waiting for a turnaround.

Inadequate funding could result in temporary decrease in variable costs but the fixed costs continue to incur. Eventually the program may have overrun not only in costs but also in time and quality. In light of the above, the following aspects should be covered carefully to ensure adequate funding:

- Rope in people with financial acumen to make as correct estimation as possible of required funds.
- Take firm commitment for release of funds through the life of the program.
- Ensure acceptable overlay over central and departmental funds.
- Look around for opportunities of consolidation before initiating new transformation programs.
- Keep control on costs right from the beginning and ensure mechanisms are in place to make the benefits visible.

4.1.10 Cross-Functional Teams

A team can be defined as a group of people who collaborate with each other in a virtual or physical setting and are bound together by a purpose. A team may or may not have a common manager. The ability of the team members and their interaction with each other, along with the authority vested in them, influence the power and influence they can exert in the organization.

Schaffer (2010) defines cross-functional teams as "A cross-disciplinary or multidisciplinary team is comprised of two or more individuals from different disciplines interacting to solve, complex, ill structured problems." Cross-disciplinary team learns through their own knowledge, recognition of knowledge of others, appreciation of others' knowledge, and understanding of others' knowledge. New knowledge emerges as the level of understanding increases (Schaffer 2010).

In the context of transformation, cross-functional teams comprise of key members nominated from teams across the organization. Cross-functional teams offer an opportunity to take advantage of the diverse views and perspectives of its team members. When members of such teams interact, they bring in their knowledge for the benefit of the transformation program. Although it is not easy to achieve consensus in such teams, the benefits overweigh the extra effort, especially in case of rapid change (Bettenhausen 1991) that accompanies a transformation.

Collectively a diverse group can more easily bring in ideas as different perspectives push the boundaries of thinking beyond the sets of vertical thinking. This results in forced lateral thinking while trying to reconcile with difference in thoughts arising out of cross-functional setup. Cross-functional teams are in a better position to respond to the challenges faced through the transformation program.

In a transformation, the endeavor is to find novel solutions, which is facilitated by diverse points of view. These are not limited to the knowledge in a particular area but also the life experiences of the team members. The access to diverse thinking offers multiple possibilities and makes the transformation team aware that multiple solutions exist to achieve the same objective (Ganz 2010).

Weingart et al. (2005) suggest that by understanding the dynamics of driving apart and pulling back of teams through team integration and effective conflict management, organizations can increase the chances of being able to capitalize on the innovative potential of cross-functional teams.

Quite often all the members of the transformation team are not collocated which adds the dimension of virtual teams to cross-functional teams. In this scenario, interaction styles profoundly influence team performance and process outcomes (Godar and Ferris 2004). Active and encouraging style of communication and collaboration styles are associated with high-performance teams. Tools for virtualization cannot substitute collocated team which can have face-to-face interactions but can bring in significant improvements in the quality of interaction by connecting a face to the voice and mail.

4.1.11 Flexible IT Architecture

Flexibility is defined as the ability of the entity to proactively, reactively, or inherently embrace change in the timely manner through its components and its relationships with environment (Conboy and Fitzgerald 2004). A flexible IT structure thus enables in dealing with changes and is able to accommodate for changes that accompany a business process transformation.

Regev et al. (2006) (http://ceur-ws.org/Vol-236/paper2.pdf) have defined the taxonomy of flexibility in business process changes around three orthogonal

Video Branch: This convenient and secure service is offered exclusively to all you IndusInd Bank customers to connect with your Branch Manager, Relationship Manager or with our centralized Video Branch Executive. Enjoy all the banking services which are offered on the IndusInd Bank Phone Banking and additionally, perform transactions like opening a Fixed Deposit or Recurring Deposit, transferring funds through NEFT, RTGS anywhere in the world. This service is made available for all Android (2.3 and higher) and Apple mobile devices (iOS 6, 7 and higher).

http://www.indusind.com/content/home/about-us/responsive-innovation.html , 28/09/2014

Fig. 4.1 Video branch IndusInd Bank

dimensions: the abstraction level of the change, the subject of change, and the properties of the change, which include extent, duration, swiftness, and anticipation.

Let us understand the taxonomy and the role of flexible IT by taking an example of IndusInd Bank which opened a video branch http://www.indusind.com/content/home/about-us/responsive-innovation.html , 28/09/2014 to provide anytime anywhere reach to its customers. The description of this innovation in banking reads as given in Fig. 4.1.

Abstraction level of change concerns itself with the changes that usually accompany change in process type and instance. In process type change, the process changes, whereas in the instance change, an exception is handled without compromising on necessary controls. The video branch is an example of a process "type change."

The subjects of change are covered through different perspectives:

In the functional perspective, the objective of the business process changes – In the case of video branch, the functional perspective did not change as the end objective of providing standardized services remained the same as for a customer who would walk into a branch.

In the behavioral perspective, the preconditions change – In case of the video branch, the prerequisite was the availability of installed application.

In the organizational perspective, the participants and roles change – New team with different competencies was required for the video branch.

In the operational perspective, the activities are changed – The activities were changed as additional activities were added to let the process run smoothly.

In the informational perspective, the information exchanged is changed – Additional control of photograph verification through digital access was required for the video branch.

The author would like to add one more perspective, that is, the perspective of "access." It relates to how a business process is accessed by a participant. In the case under consideration, the way of accessing the bank services is changed and could now be done through mobile application or Web interface, besides the conventional access by walking into the branch.

The properties of change are extent of change, duration of change, swiftness of change, and anticipation of change.

The extent of change distinguishes between incremental (small) and revolutionary (totally new process) change. The video branch could be categorized as a revolutionary change.

Duration of change deals with whether the "to be" implemented change is permanent or temporary in nature. The video branch is a permanent change.

The swiftness of change is about whether the change is immediate (on all instances, existing and new) or deferred (on new instances). The change is immediate and applicable to all existing and new customers.

The last property is if that of anticipation of change establishes whether change is planned or ad hoc. Ad hoc changes are created with exceptional situations where an immediate fix is required. Video branch is a planned change.

In order to roll out such a business change, the flexibility of IT architecture can make a lot of difference. Suppose the IT architecture of the bank is based on service-oriented architecture, then it would be relatively easy to accommodate the envisaged change as compared to a situation where such an architecture is not in place. It would also reduce the time to market of the service while being economically efficient.

In other cases, flexible IT can facilitate running of business processes across continents, increasing collaboration and flexible business models. Information technology and business processes have fused to the extent that it is difficult to imagine business process transformation without IT. Technology changes can be utilized to the benefit of the organization. IT enables configuring of many processes which can be very helpful for experimentation without having to incur heavy expenditure on IT. Automation that is possible through IT can help in making the process IT intensive with lesser need of manual intervention.

When organizations merge or work is outsourced, flexible IT infrastructure becomes very important to enable a smooth transition possibly subsequent transformation.

Many business processes have a need of a lot of logging data for compliance reasons. When business processes change, these need to be configured as well; the fact that it is mostly possible to do so is based on the flexibility of IT infrastructure. Organizations that have Enterprise Resource Planning (ERP) software as their base are based on best practices and have a lot of in-built flexibility. Workflow structures available through them facilitate in the controlling and coordinating of tasks and activities. Flexible IT infrastructure enables both pull and push of information which makes coordination, assignment, and decision making of tasks and activities easier.

IT infrastructures facilitate information exchange and thereby enable in decision making. The metadata available through the IT systems is also useful in validating the efficacy of a business process.

Not every process transformation is linked to information technology. Business process (re)design should lead and IT should support, yet in many cases flexible architecture can play a significant role in the success of a business process transformation through offering opportunities of data analysis, data manipulation, control of process, and harnessing the most of new technologies.

4.1.12 MIS and Knowledge Assets

Knowledge is an intellectual asset that enables value creation. Lack of knowledge and inability to capitalize on the existing knowledge takes an organization into a downward spiral. In the times when knowledge is “the” product that provides the edge, people may not be always willing to share knowledge for the fear of losing power. On the other hand, if an organization has the culture of nurturing and sharing of knowledge, it can attract professionals who want to learn and grow while they share.

Knowledge assets like any other asset need management, and unless they are managed, they lose their value. A knowledge asset should have a clear idea of the objective of the asset and the audience. A difficult to understand intellectual document may not be very useful if the staff comprises undergraduates. What is knowledge for one can then easily become information overload for another.

There are conditions that play an important role in creating collaboration between knowledge professionals (Tissen et al. 2000): having a knowledge strategy that provides direction and a shared understanding of goals and opportunities to facilitate conversion of knowledge into value for the organization, providing an environment that is conducive to knowledge management and professional’s motivation and creativity, and visibility of the value addition achieved through knowledge creation and reflecting their value to the company in a transparent manner.

Knowledge assets can be identified in many forms and is not necessarily a document available on the repository. These include but are not limited to patents, manual procedures, frameworks, and implicit knowledge that resides in the minds of the people that make the organization what it is. Knowledge assets are also not limited to the boundaries of the organization and are to be found in forums and alliances as well.

Nonaka and Takeuchi (1995) have explained the process of knowledge creation through SECI model, a combination of four modes: socialization, externalization, internalization, and combination. The knowledge spiral starts with the conversion of tacit knowledge into explicit knowledge. Once the knowledge has been made explicit, it is internalized by a larger number of people and thereafter becomes the basis for new knowledge generation. Explicit knowledge can be combined to create new sets of systematic knowledge. Knowledge creation is a continuous activity so a snapshot of today differs from a snapshot of the future. Emergence of knowledge is a culmination of meaningful interaction of shared perspectives and contexts in physical or virtual space. This gives rise to the “and” perspective instead of “either/or” perspective. These contexts can be multilayered spanning beyond the boundaries of an organization.

Explicit knowledge is not necessarily created in the organization; it could be brought in from outside through hiring new people, participating in forums, outsourcing, contract research, joint ventures, acquisitions, and so on. Besides this, explicit knowledge can be developed through trainings, spreading the winning team across the organization.

Knowledge assets have their own life cycle. Many of the formalized artifacts that are relevant today may not be relevant tomorrow. A continuous effort is required to manage these assets, otherwise employees can get lost in the information and data maze.

It is important that the knowledge assets are relevant and accurate. Knowledge requirements should be identified and duplication should be removed. Avenues of development and creation of missing knowledge should be identified. At times it is possible that the available knowledge assets are not unified in their approach and meaning, thereby facilitating thought process and appreciation of conflicting views and frameworks (Liebowitz and Beckman 1998).

Information generates consequences which it cannot foresee, and information reservoir has no saturation point (Targowski 2002). Knowledge assets can therefore be leveraged in ways that they can provide significant advantage to an organization undertaking business process transformation. Artifacts that represent prior experiences provide important inputs that aid in the prevention of repeatable mistakes and utilization of best practices. Knowledge that is not yet externalized is also as useful when looking out for new paradigms.

Customer interactions generate the kind of knowledge that may not be available in many formal documents. This knowledge can provide insights in opportunities for removing bottlenecks, creating needs, and enhancing existing products and services in way that new landscapes unravel themselves.

The accessibility and availability of knowledge assets is affected by the information systems supporting it. These systems enable the utilization of knowledge in a number of ways. They provide support in decision making and can provide real-time information on performance. They facilitate in the simplification and collaboration of work (Majchrzak 2008).

Before a transformation is carried out, a lot of research is required to establish the wisdom of choosing and rolling out a particular product, solution, service, etc. This requires knowledge of the organization, the hard data for which too comes out of information systems. The analysis of data can provide insights into new possibilities and enable scenario comparison from the market.

Management information systems help in keeping a check on the impact of the activities of a transformation program while it is being carried out and subsequently ensuring the benefits and ways of working become a way of working in the organization.

The skill levels of the organization are also indirectly reflected in the formalized assets, whereby it can be used as an indicator of the receptivity of the organization in terms of understanding a proposed solution. Knowledge assets and information systems are of prime importance through the transformation program, and their benefits should be optimally utilized to achieve success.

Collectively the twelve elements of the success factors "tan" can really change the shape of a transformation program. An organization which is conscious of utilizing them for its benefits is likely to deliver processes that transform the way they do their business.

References

Barret DJ (2014) Leadership communication. McGraw-Hill Education, New York

Bettenhausen KL (1991) Five years of group research: what we have learned and what needs to be addressed. J Manag 17:345–381

Bono ED (2009) Lateral thinking. Be more creative and productive. Penguin, London

Campanella J (1999) Principles of quality costs: principles, implementation, and use. ASQ Quality Press, Milwaukee

Carayannis EG, Gonzalez E (2003) Creativity and innovation = competitiveness? When, how and why. In: Shavinina LV (ed) The international handbook on innovation. Pergamon, Amsterdam, pp 587–606

Chesbrough HW (2006) Era of open innovation. In: Mayle D (ed) Managing innovation and change. Sage, London, pp 127–138

Conboy K, Fitzgerald B (2004) Innovative systemic perspectives: toward a conceptual framework of agile methods: a study of agility in different disciplines. In: Proceedings of the 2004 ACM workshop on Interdisciplinary software engineering research. ACM, New York, pp 37–44

Davenport TH (2013) Process innovation: reengineering work through information technology. Harvard Business Press, Boston

Deming WE (1993) Foundation of management of quality in the Western world. In: The new economics for industry, government, education, Centre for advanced engineering study. MIT, Cambridge, MA

Ganz M (2010) Leading change leadership, organization, and social movements In: Nohria N, Khurana R (eds) Handbook of leadership theory and practice. Harvard Business School Publication, Boston, pp 509–550

Garvin DA (1984) What does product quality really mean? Sloan Manage Rev 26(1):25–43

Godar SH, Ferris SP (2004) Virtual and collaborative teams, process technologies and practice. Idea Group Inc., London

Gundry LK, Prather CW, Kickul JR (1994) Building the creative organization. Org Dyn, Spring, 22(4):22–37

Halpern BL, Lubar K (2003) Dramatic techniques to reach out, motivate and inspire leadership presence. Gotham Books, New York

Hammer M, Champy J (1993) Reengineering the corporation: a Manifesto for business revolution. Harper Business, New York

Hargadon A, Sutton RI (2000) Building an innovation factory. Harv Bus Rev, (May–June), pp 157–166

Heifetz RA, Laurie DL (1998) The work of leadership, Harvard business review on leadership. Harvard Business School, Boston

http://www.gaportal.org/global-indicators/global-competitiveness-index. Accessed 1 Oct 2014

http://www.indusind.com/content/home/about-us/responsive-innovation.html. Accessed 28 Sept 2014

Kotter JP (1996) Leading change. Harvard Business School Press, Boston

Kugelar M, Vieting M (2003) Design of a process oriented structure. In: Jörg B, Kugeler M, Rosemann M (eds) Process management: a guide for the design of business processes. Springer, Berlin/Heidelberg, pp 166–167

Liebowitz J, Beckman T (1998) Knowledge organizations, what every manager should know. CRC Press LLC, Boca Raton

Majchrzak A (2008) Breaking the functional mind-set, the role of information technology. In: Grower V, Markus ML (eds) Business process transformation, vol 9, Advance in management information systems. M.E. Sharpe, Armonk, pp 125–140

McCormack K (1999) The development of a measure of business process orientation and its link to the interdepartmental dynamics construct of market orientation. www.drkresearch.org/research/kmpaper.doc. Accessed 1 Oct 2014

McCormack KP, Johnson WC (2001) Business process orientation: gaining the e-Business competitive advantage. CRC Press LLC, Boca Raton

Nonaka I, Takeuchi H (1995) The knowledge creating company: how Japanese companies create the dynamics of innovation. Oxford University Press, New York

Quality glossary, ASQ. http://asq.org/glossary/q.html. Accessed 1 Oct 2014

Radjou N, Prabhu J, Ahuja S (2012) Jugaad innovation, a frugal and flexible approach to innovation for the 21st century. Random House India, Jossy-Bass, Wiley, San Francisco

Regev G, Soffer P, Schmidt R (2006) Taxonomy of flexibility in business processes, business process modeling, development, and support. http://ceur-ws.org/Vol-236/paper2.pdf. Accessed 1 Oct 2014

Schaffer SP (2010) Cross-disciplinary team learning. In: Watkins R, Leigh D (eds) Handbook of improving performance in the workplace. Selecting and implementing performance interventions, volume 2. International Society of Performance Improvement, Pfeiffer, San Francisco

Škrinjar RR, Štemberger MI, Hernaus T (2007) The impact of business process orientation on organizational performance. In: Proceedings of the 2007, Informing science and IT education joint conference. http://proceedings.informingscience.org/InSITE2007/InSITE07p171-185Skri357.pdf. Accessed 1 Oct 2014

Targowski AS (2002) Knowledge mapping and management. In: White D (ed). IRM Press, Hershey

Tissen R, Andriessen D, Deprez FL (2000) The knowledge dividend, creating high performance companies through value-based knowledge management. Pearson Education Limited, Harlow

Weingart AR, Cronin MA, Houser CJS, Kagan J, Vogel C (2005) Functional diversity and conflict in cross functional product development teams- considering representational gaps and task characteristics. In: Neider LL, Schriesheim CA (eds) Understanding teams. Information Age Publishing Inc., Greenwich, pp 89–110

Process Modeling

5

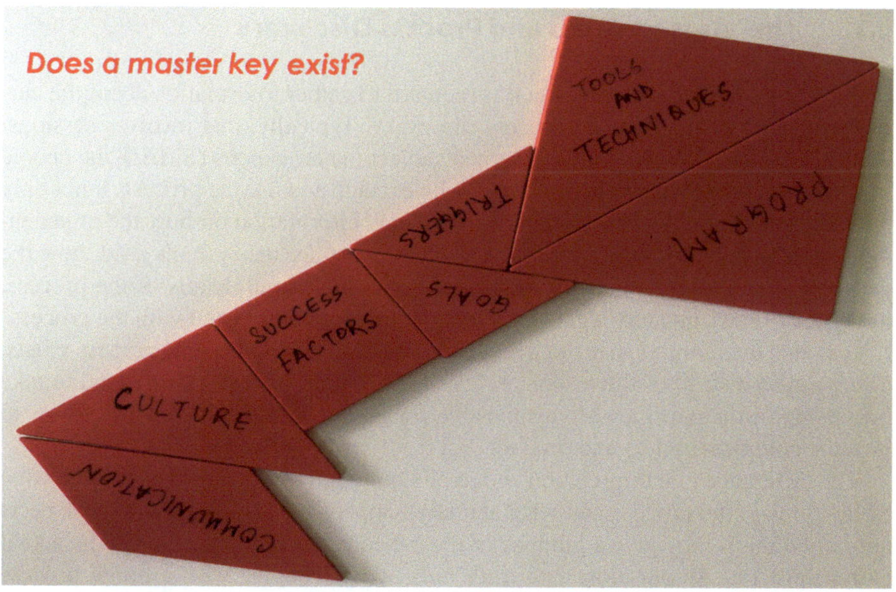

Process modeling as a technique enables comprehending and conceptualizing complex processes around us which in turn become the basis for discussion, analysis, design, optimization, and documentation. Process modeling provides a mechanism to decompose large processes into smaller chunks called sub-processes that are complete in themselves, yet are related to the main process. This hierarchy of processes helps in understanding processes as per the scope requirement. A CEO may want to look at process landscape, while a team leader may want to look at the sub-process that falls in the scope of his team.

C. Sharma, *Business Process Transformation*, Management for Professionals,
DOI 10.1007/978-81-322-2349-8_5

One can only model once one knows what is to be modeled. In cases where a totally new process has to be developed from scratch, one undertakes what is called "to be" modeling. In cases where a current process exists, before moving to the "to be" model, the "as is" model is often taken into consideration. The time spent on gathering information on "as is" model and its modeling depends on the overall plan of process modeling.

There are many modeling notations such as event-driven procedure chain (EPC) and business process modeling notation (BPMN). While EPC has been popular for many years, BPMN is gaining popularity as one can model interaction and communication between organizations. This chapter attempts to explain process modeling through examples based on BPMN 2.0 (http://www.bpmn.org). The objective is to provide an overview of how process modeling can be done, but does not substitute for books on advanced process modeling.

5.1 The "As Is" Process and Process Discovery

In order to assess the current state, it is required to gather information about the current processes. This is called process discovery. Typically, this involves sessions/workshops/interviews with the concerned subject matter experts (SMEs), the people who own the process as well as the ones who execute and use the process. It not only provides insight on the process but also provides information on how the organization is structured with reference to the process, what are the systems used, how the data is stored, etc. It provides knowledge on the functional details of the process, turnaround times, and any legal/contractual obligations associated with the process.

It is not uncommon that the no clear ownership of the current process exists. Many times, instead of the responsibility of the whole process, people tend to take ownership of the part they are responsible for. As a consequence, no one seems to own the complete end-to-end process.

The difference in interpretation and implementation may also exist between what SMEs think is the process and what actually happens on the floor. Both the aspects are important as they give a glimpse of the expected current process and the actual current process. To get closest to truth, this activity begins with a rough process model based on initial insights which can be fine-tuned with the progression of process discovery. The process analyst who is engaged in process discovery should be able to make up for lack of process modeling knowledge in the organization.

It is very easy to get swayed away and substitute feelings for facts, but the important point is to focus on facts and practice. This requires the process analyst to be systematic and friendly in approach. Once the analyst receives information from the relevant corners of the organization, she should tie all the ends together to create the bigger complete picture. This picture can be subsequently validated.

Another approach that stems from lean is "going to the Gemba" Flinchbaugh (http://www.industryweek.com/companies-amp-executives/going-gemba). In this approach, the analyst goes to the Gemba which implies "going to the real place." It involves direct observation of how work is performed by triggering the process and following what happens at each step. This allows a keen observer to figure out what is really going on at the shop floor. The analyst can use known business patterns, frameworks, etc. as a reference point while making observations. Like any other method of discovery, this also needs to be validated for correctness and exception handling.

Systems and their functional documentation can also be a source of information as far as the current process is concerned. On the data side, analysis of data that is captured through mechanisms such as system and transaction logs, offers another method called automatic process discovery. Tools can reconstruct the process on the basis of instances of process and particular activities at a specified time. Although it is applicable in places where enterprise systems are working, it can facilitate in process discovery. Automatic process discovery helps in the identification of bottlenecks, non-compliance, and repetitions based on data available through systems such as workflows. Automatic process discovery is sometimes referred to as process intelligence. It helps in process discovery as well as subsequent monitoring of the process. Automatic business discovery has its limitations as well. Besides being relatively complex to understand and interpret, it is also dependent on the quality of data.

In cases where process documentation already exists, it is convenient to use it as a starting point for discussion. Other documentations such as organization brochures can also be utilized for providing insight into the organizational processes. Before utilizing the existing documentation, a quick check is required to ascertain the validity of the documentation. Very often an external agency is hired to create the process repository and the process documents are rarely updated thereafter. This leads to dated documentation which may no longer be valid and accurate.

Process discovery costs time and effort. Discovery effort cannot be put into each and every process. The processes to be covered should be identified and prioritized as per the scope. In case of transformation, a balance should be struck between the time required to gather this information and the result it can deliver. Various discovery methods are not mutually exclusive; therefore, they can be used in combination with each other.

As such the idea is to gain an understanding of the current processes so that mistakes are not repeated and the current issues are highlighted. These issues can often help in creating a case for transformation. Process discovery has the limitation that it induces a certain level of bias which can become a deterrent to out-of-the-box thinking required for innovative process redesign.

5.2 "To Be" Process Modeling

Before one can go into detailed modeling of the "to be" process, an overview of the high-level end-to-end process is required. This enables the creation of a process-oriented organization. A process-oriented organization is efficient as the interfaces and handovers are minimized. The focus lies on the value chain and overall end-to-end process efficiency takes priority over individual process optimization (Kugelar and Vieting 2003).

In case of transformation, there could be reference models such as proprietary to the organization or to a service provider to whom processes have been outsourced. Best practices and frameworks such as Information Technology Infrastructure Library (ITIL) (http://www.itil.org/en/vomkennen/itil/index.php) and process classification framework from APQC (http://www.apqc.org/process-classification-framework) can also act as reference points. Even when the transformation is to be based on an alignment to a reference framework, it does not automatically mean that the "to be modeling" is simple. It requires effort and maneuvering to bring in the alignment.

Suppose there is a sourcing framework that suggests that "there should be a list of selected vendors with pre-negotiated yearly rates of line items." These vendors should be assessed every year on their performance before retaining them on the vendor list.

For a large company, it may be absolutely logical to have a performance-based assessment of vendors. This assessment on clearly defined parameters could become the basis of renewals. This would provide a structured way to select the best vendors who can provide the most competitive products, on time and in good condition.

For a smaller company, the same framework could translate into "buy from market leaders; compare on price, quality, and specification; and order."

For the maintenance of these products, the large company may close a well-negotiated contract with an operations and maintenance vendor, while the small company may simply buy an annual maintenance contract after negotiating the best rate.

Both the organizations achieve the same objective, but the process is customized to meet the scale and required efficiency. Creating a vendor list and spending effort on it has to be worth the return it has to offer.

What if, despite its scale, the small organization had the aspiration to have same processes as the market leader? Would that justify to having a vendor list, annual evaluation, and line item-wise rate negotiation in terms of the effort involved? Maybe yes! In case a venture capitalist would be willing to invest in the small company if and only if its vendor sourcing process was at par with the best in the market or it is a prerequisite for participating in a government tender. The business objectives are the guiding principles for process modeling.

Now consider an onshore entity which outsources work to its offshore unit. In a drive to have competitive sourcing, the onshore entity may evaluate the quality, price competitiveness, and performance on delivery of the offshore unit and compare with some onshore vendors. Even if the quality of the onshore vendor may be higher, the purchase order may still go to the offshore unit because of a directive to promote the onshore unit in its setup phase. This would be an exception to the process of awarding contract based only on merits. The process model could enforce this by assigning a parameter and policy preference and adding it into the weighted ranking system. Another way could be to check for any policy guidelines just before awarding the purchase order and if required, bypass the result of objective assessment. This could be logged in the system and could trigger an action item for the offshore unit to improve quality.

Process modeling is more than a diagrammatic representation in a particular notation. It is sometimes what fits best to size and scale, what is most effective, what is most efficient, and at other times what one aspires to be. It is a means of communication of roles and the tasks they perform within a particular scope and their interaction with each other. They are logical and enable an organization to define the path that an organization wishes to undertake. Once defined and followed, they become the basis of measurement and thereby support in process optimization.

While modeling a process, some points should be kept in mind (Dumas et al. 2013):

- Every process has a start and an end, and these points form the boundaries of the process. These boundaries define the scope of the process. For example, a call from a customer is an event that becomes the starting point for a customer relations process, while logging of corresponding ticket can be the end point of the process.
- Processes can be decomposed into activities. At the stage of process discovery, the focus should not be the sequence of activities; rather it should be the identification of activities.
- Processes can be executed by a single resource or may involve handover. Handovers enable the identification of sub-processes, although a sub-process may also involve multiple handovers.
- Process responsible can be made explicit by using pools and lanes depending on the adopted modeling notation.
- Activities can happen in parallel or in sequence.
- A process could have decision points based on conditions, which decide the subsequent activity. Decision points indicate whether activities occur in parallel, are exclusive based on the fulfillment of conditions, or take a default path when none of the conditions are applicable.

5.3 Guidelines for Process Modeling

In the context of business process model and notation (BPMN), Bruce (Silver 2011) suggests that a good BPMN model is the one which is correct, clear, complete, and consistent. Correctness implies that the rules of BPMN should be followed. Clarity stems from unambiguous process logic, which is evident from the diagram. The process diagram should indicate the start, end state(s), and communication with external entities to be complete. Consistency implies that for the same process logic, different modelers should come up with a similar diagram.

In 7PMG, Mendeling et al. (http://wwwis.win.tue.nl/~wvdaalst/publications/p574.pdf) proposed the following guidelines for process modeling:

Guideline 1: To decrease likelihood of errors and difficulty in understanding, use as few elements as possible.

Guideline 2: A strong correlation was found between the number of modeling errors and the average or maximum degree of elements in a model, so the guideline is to minimize routing paths per element.

Guideline 3: One start and one end event should be used while modeling. This makes models easy to understand and allows analysis. The number of start and end events is positively connected with an increase in error probability.

Guideline 4: A model should be as structured as possible. Split connectors should have matching joins to reduce errors and increase understanding.

Guideline 5: The OR routing should be avoided. Compared to OR routing, AND and XOR routing are less error prone.

Guideline 6: For labels, verb-object activity labels should be used.

Guideline 7: A model should be decomposed into smaller models if it has more than 50 elements in order to minimize error probability.

With the possibilities of utilizing process modeling going way beyond software development (Becker et al. 2000) (http://udoo.uni-muenster.de/downloads/publications/1717.pdf) and information management, the people involved in modeling are no longer restricted to analysts. To achieve consistency in modeling and interpretation, process guidelines prove to be very helpful and therefore should be kept in mind.

5.4 Conceptual Frameworks of Process Modeling

Franken and Weger (1997) in their modeling framework suggest two viewpoints while conceptualizing a process (re)design:

Conceptualizing Business Processes: Before documenting a process, the process is imagined, conceived, and created in mind. This is an abstraction, wherein intricate details are left out to allow for discussion with stakeholders at appropriate level.

External and Internal Viewpoint: The external viewpoint has an outside-in view, whereas the internal viewpoint has an inside-out view. The external viewpoint is an abstraction from the internal structure and behavior of the internal process. In the external perspective, the internal business process is treated like a black box and the focus is on the services provided to the environment. A person who wants a car to be delivered on a particular day does not want to be bothered about how the car reaches the showroom from the warehouse. The focus is on the customer to business interaction and not the part of process that supports this interaction. The internal viewpoint is concerned with the "how" of the process that provides services to the environment. The focus is on the (re)design of the internal process to be able to optimally provide the services. The last example would imply the transportation process from the warehouse to the showroom.

Kaplan and Murdock (1991) suggest that in order to achieve breakthrough changes, companies need to rethink the way they do their business. In a shift from traditional approach of value chain which emphasizes sequential functional areas, they view the company as being composed of three to four core processes that cut across functional, geographical, and even company boundaries. These core processes are linked to and enable realization of strategic objectives and measure cross-functional performance. Result-oriented cross-functional view identifies and monitors the upstream activities that influence downstream activities.

Melao and Pidd (2000) have organized the multifaceted views in business process around four points of view:

1. Business Processes as Deterministic Machines: Very close to Morgan's (1997) metaphor of organizations as bureaucratic machine, this view emphasizes the structure procedure and goals. Good process design ensures that all the resources are efficiently utilized to ensure satisfaction of customer needs. This view has the limitation that it lacks attention on the sociopolitical and organizational issues which are often the biggest bottlenecks in success of business (re)design initiatives.
2. Business Processes as Complex Dynamic Systems: This view is also close to Morgan's metaphor of organism. The focus in this viewpoint is on the interaction of the process with the environment, thereby focusing on the systems approach. Each system has inputs which are transformed to outputs, systems have boundaries and can be decomposed hierarchically into subsystems, and each (sub)system has interfaces through which they communicate. This view has the limitation that it ignores the sociopolitical dimension and feedback loops.
3. Business Processes as Interacting Feedback Loops: This viewpoint is an extension of complex dynamic systems with internal controls called feedback loops. This view has the limitation that it treats human beings as instruments who control and are controlled and could encourage dehumanization of business process modeling.
4. Business Processes as Social Constructs: This viewpoint proposes that a business process can be defined as abstract and subject to perceptions, meanings, and judgments of people and thus treats processes as a soft way of thinking. This has the limitation that this way is too difficult to model.

The crux lies in having an approach that amalgamates the perspectives to suit a particular requirement.

Davenport and Short (1990) have emphasized the recursive relationship between IT capabilities and business process redesign, implying each of them is key while thinking of another. Leveraging IT awareness at the time of process design enables exploiting the possibilities. They classify processes across three dimensions: entities, objects, and activities.

Once the perspective(s) is decided, the question arises as to what is required for the process to be effective.

Ramias and Rummler (2009) in their article on evolution of effective process framework (EPF) provide a performance perspective to processes. As per EPF, process must be designed to meet output requirements. These output/results requirements should be linked to organization and customer requirement. It is the output/results requirement that determines whether the process is a success or a failure so utmost importance must be given to what comes out of the process. The process does not run in isolation, but is dependent on the underlying models. The underlying model and process should be synchronized so that correct output can be produced by the process. In order to perform a process, resources are required which includes machinery, staff, and material. The performance of the process is also dependent on the quality of the inputs and how and when the process is triggered. Jobs and roles and technology must be aligned with the process to keep the execution smooth. All these elements together allow the process to be performed effectively.

Once the basic idea is clear, the next step is to model it. There are various tools and notations that can be used to model a process. A model is a means of presenting information in a way that the users can understand it, bring about improvements, and very often take the first step to automate them. The process can be captured from a functional view, data view, behavioral view, informational view, and organizational view (Curtis et al. 1992).

5.5 Process Modeling with BPMN

In this book, business process model and Notation BPMN2.0 (http://www.omg.org/spec/BPMN/2.0/PDF/changebarred) have been utilized to explain basic modeling concepts. BPMN has been developed by the object management group (OMG) with the primary goal of providing a notation that is readily understandable by all business users, from the business analysts that create the initial drafts of the processes, to the technical developers responsible for implementing the technology that will perform those processes, and finally, to the business people who will manage and monitor those processes.

This specification represents the amalgamation of best practices within the business modeling community to define the notation and semantics of collaboration diagrams, process diagrams, and choreography diagrams. Within the scope of this chapter, the basic idea behind process diagrams and collaboration has been covered. Choreography, which is the definition of expected behavior of interacting participants between pools has not been covered.

A process in BPMN is described as a sequence or flow of activities in an organization with the objective of carrying out work. It is depicted as a graph of flow elements, which are a set of activities, events, gateways, and sequence flows that define finite execution semantics. Processes can be defined at any level from enterprise-wide processes to processes performed by a single person. Low-level processes can be grouped together to achieve a common business goal.

Private business processes are processes that are internal to a specific organization. These processes are generally called workflow or BPM and have a swimlane-like appearance.[1] Consider a very simple incident management process as shown in Fig. 5.1. A sequence of activities of service desk handles incidents based on a workflow. For each request, a ticket is created and handled through the system. A complaint is handled as an incident ticket.

The process starts whenever a complaint is received. This is denoted by a circle with thin boundaries and indicates that a new instance of the process is initiated through this start event. The start event leads to activities, denoted by rounded rectangle, and is connected by a sequence flow denoted by arrows with full arrow head. The end event is denoted by a circle with thick boundaries which denotes that the process instance is complete.

[1]All the symbols and definitions used for process modeling in this chapter are as per BPMN2.0 specification. In case of any discrepancy, the specification prevails.

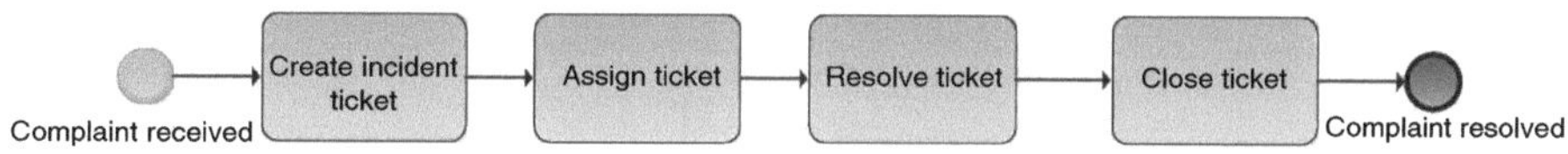

Fig. 5.1 Incident management process

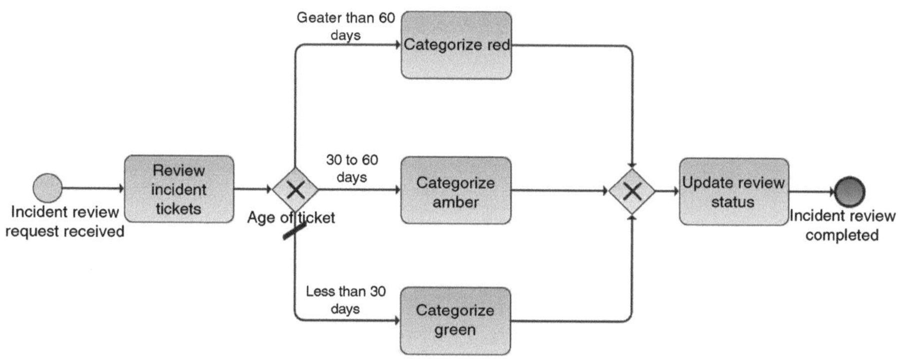

Fig. 5.2 Incident review process – (XOR) exclusive gateway

It is a good practice to use verb-adjective-noun naming convention where the adjective is optional. As an example, create incident ticket; "incident" specifies the type of ticket to be created. Care should be taken to keep labels short to enhance readability.

Since processes do not always run sequentially, activities could occur in parallel or could be mutually exclusive (only one of the activities can occur). Some situations could require a combination of parallel and exclusive activities. All the three situations are modeled using gateways which decide the path the process will take. Gateways could lead to divergence of process flow called split gateway or convergence of process flow called join gateway.

Consider the example of incident review process in Fig. 5.2 where a review of incident tickets happens on request basis. The tickets are categorized to green, amber, or red on the basis of ticket aging. The status of the incident tickets is set to "reviewed" and the process completes. At any point in time, a ticket can have only one category, and green is the default category shown by an oblique sign. This is a scenario for exclusive gateway which is also called XOR gateway, where any of the three scenarios will hold true. The exclusive gateway is denoted by a diamond sign with an X. The XOR join waits for at least one of the paths to be true before moving to the next activity "update review status."

In cases where activities are independent of each other, they can occur in parallel and therefore can be modeled using a parallel (AND) gateway. Parallel gateway is denoted by a diamond with plus sign. This is explained through a simple incident management process shown in Fig. 5.3

In this process, once the incident ticket is created, three activities diverge through the AND split gateway, namely, assign ticket, notify client, and notify stakeholders.

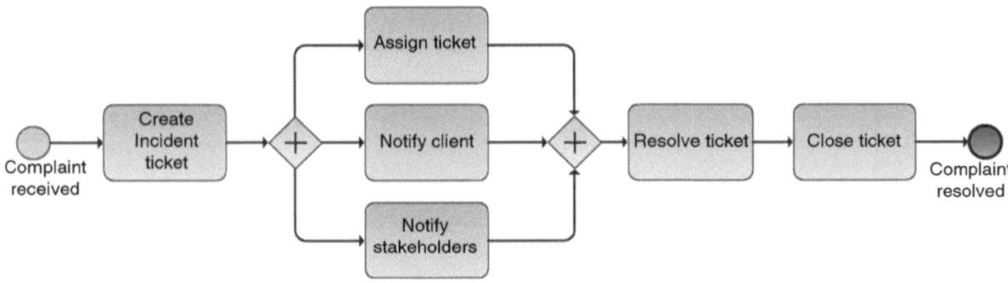

Fig. 5.3 Incident management process – parallel (AND) gateway

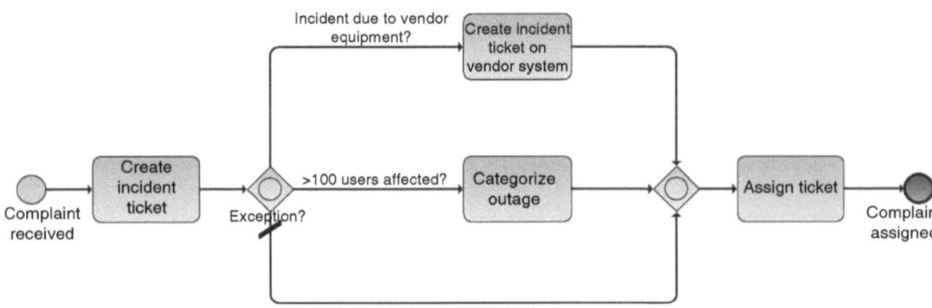

Fig. 5.4 Assign incident process – inclusive (OR) gateway

These activities can happen in parallel and are independent of each other. The AND join gateway waits for all the three activities to be completed before the resolve ticket activity starts. If the AND join gateway was not there, it would imply that resolve ticket activity should happen thrice, which is not the expectation.

A third scenario exists when a decision leads to a situation where one or more options can be taken at a time. This is called the inclusive (OR) gateway. This is different from exclusive (XOR) gateway where only one condition can be true and from parallel (AND) gateway where all conditions must be true.

To understand this, consider the example of assign incident process shown in Fig. 5.4.

The process starts when a complaint is received. After the activity create incident ticket, a decision is made based on exception, with process paths diverging through the inclusive (OR) split gateway. If >100 users are affected, incident is categorized as outage. If incident has occurred due to vendor equipment, then an incident ticket is created in vendor system.

For any other exception that occurs (both conditions being false), no action is required till the inclusive (OR) join gateway. The default path does not have any activity, but it is required to ensure there is no deadlock if any of the other conditions is not true. There can be a situation that both conditions evaluate to true; the incident could be due to vendor equipment and affect >100 users. Only one of the two conditions could be true as well implying either >100 users are affected or the incident is due to vendor system. The inclusive (OR) join gateway waits till both the conditions

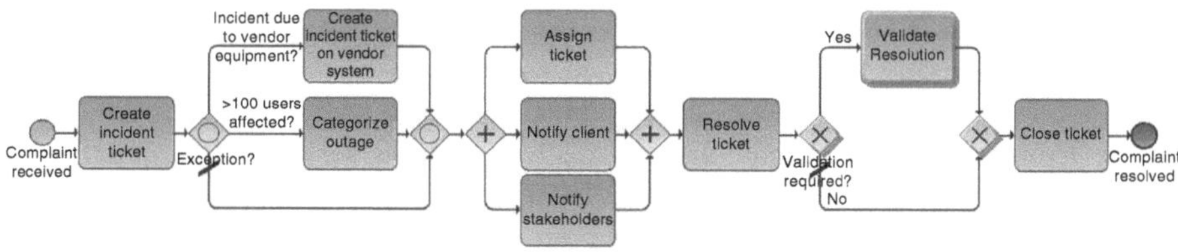

Fig. 5.5 Incident management process – combination of gateways

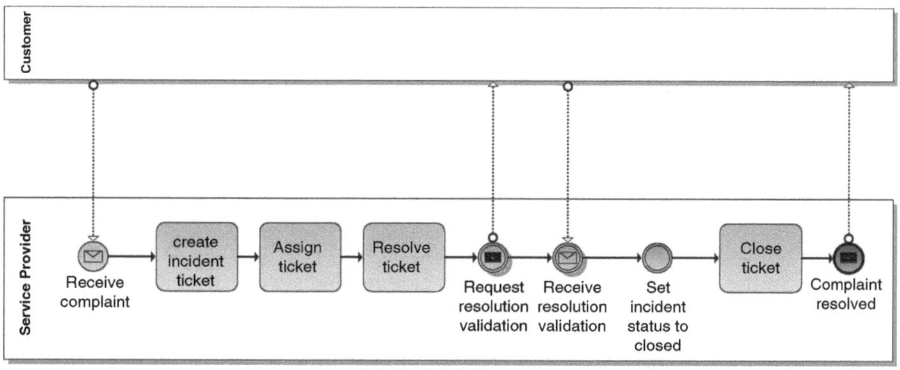

Fig. 5.6 Incident management process – participants as pools

evaluate to true or false. If both the conditions evaluate to false, the default path is taken.

All the gateways can be combined as per requirement as shown in Fig. 5.5, which combines the above flows with some variation.

The incident management process is an example of a public process. Public processes represent the interactions between a private business process and another process or participant. Only those activities that are used to communicate to the other participant(s) are included in the public process.

The discussion so far does not indicate the participants of the process. In Fig. 5.6, the participants are represented by the use of pool shape. The pool shapes for the service provider and the customer helps to create a context in the diagram. Pools are not limited to people or departments and can include systems.

The process is initiated by a message start event, represented by an unfilled envelope in the start event. A message start event can be used when the interaction is asynchronous, implying that the customer can send the complaint without someone being available at the service provider end to receive it at the same time. In the case where synchronous messaging was required, it would have been done through the use of message task, which will be explained later.

Since the focus of the process is the service provider, the customer pool is treated like a black box and its internal activities are not shown, yet the presence of a separate pool enables to show the point of interaction. The message flow is denoted by a dotted line with a circle at the starting end and an arrow head at the other. The message flows show the order of the message flows that are required for the process interaction. Message events cannot be used within a pool.

The service provider receives a complaint which is a start message event (catch event) from the customer. Once the ticket is resolved, the service provider sends an intermediate send message event (throw event) to "request resolution validation," denoted by a filled envelope in a double circle and receives back an intermediate receive message event (catch event) "receive resolution validation" denoted by an empty envelope in double circle. Upon receipt of validation, the empty intermediate event takes place. It is denoted by the double circle, indicating only a status change of the ticket. This does not delay the process, does not imply a point of synchronization, and does not have any conditions attached to it (Debevoise and Geneva 2008). Finally the customer is notified of complaint resolution through the message end event.

A segregation can be made within a pool through lanes to signify participants within the pool. Figure 5.7 shows a case of collaboration which shows two public processes communicating with each other. With a public process, the activities for the collaboration participants can be considered the "touchpoints" between the participants. In the given example, the technical team and service desk are two participants in the service provider pool. While there should be a gap between pools, there is no gap between lanes. In the other pool, the customer is not shown like a black box as in the previous example. The customer process ends with end message event.

While start message event can only receive a message (catch event), end message event can only send a message event.

Activities can be represented as tasks or sub-processes. A task represented by a rounded rectangle is the lowest level of decomposition of a process and cannot be broken down further. A sub-process on the other hand is utilized to group similar activities together to improve the readability of the main process. Depending on the

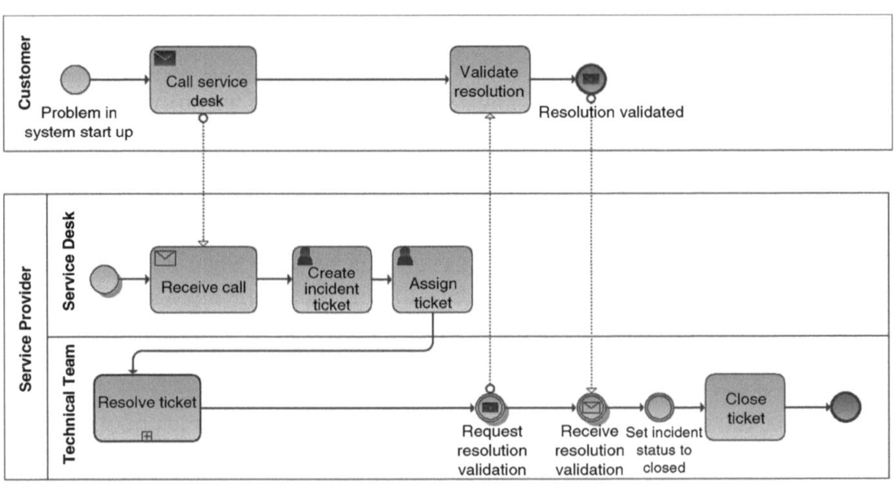

Fig. 5.7 Collaboration between public processes – pools and lanes

hierarchy, a sub-process may contain further sub-processes. A sub-process can be shown in collapsed or expanded form. As shown in Fig. 5.8, in the collapsed form, it is denoted by a rounded rectangle with a plus sign and hides the underlying activities. In the expanded form, it is denoted by a rounded rectangle with a minus sign. In the lane technical team, resolve ticket is an expanded sub-process composed of tasks and another collapsed sub-process deploy solution.

The type of tasks used in Fig. 5.8 are explained through Table 5.1.

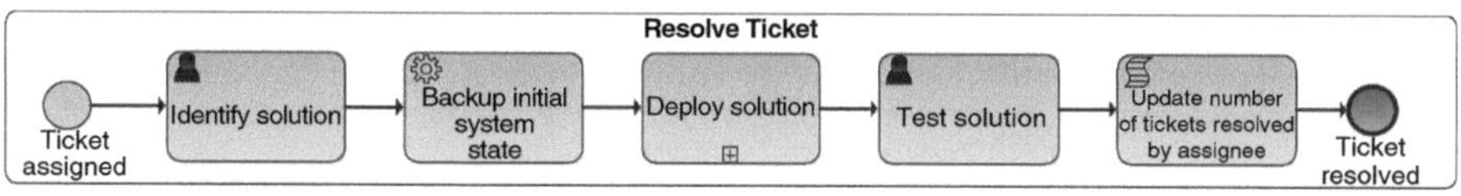

Fig. 5.8 Collapsed and expanded sub-process

Table 5.1 Types of tasks – I

Example	Task
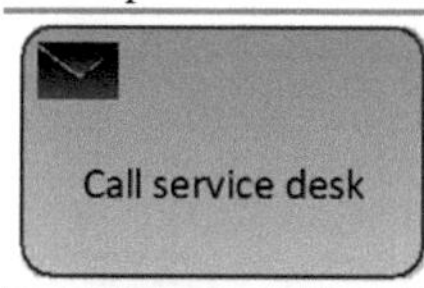	This is a send message task and involves interaction with the receive message task
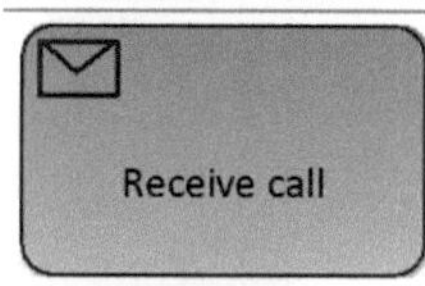	This is a receive message task and involves interaction with the send message task
	Send and receive message tasks are used for tasks that are synchronous (when both participants are required)
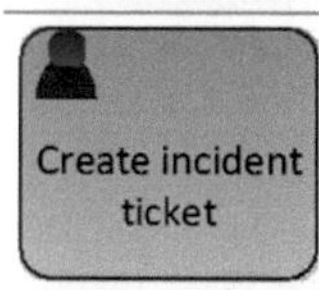	This is a human task, performed by a human within the business process management system
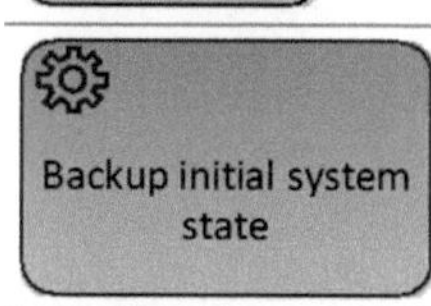	This is a service task, a task performed by a system service
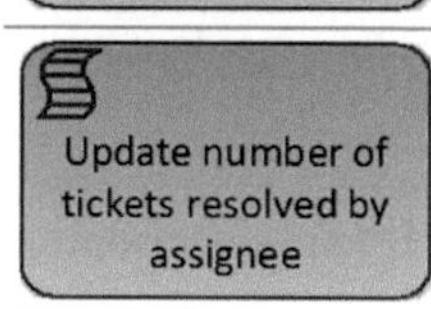	This is a script task performed by a software script automatically, usually within business process managements system

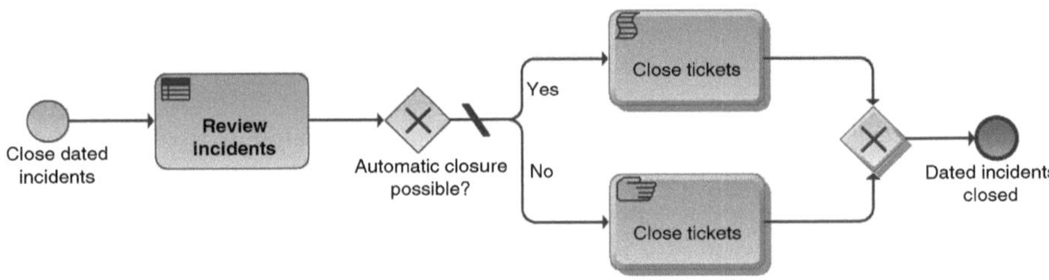

Fig. 5.9 Close-dated incident process

Table 5.2 Types of tasks – II

Example	Task
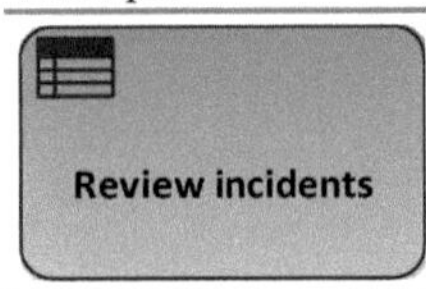	This task is performed based on a business rule. There could be many business rules, such as customer, time period, etc., that can be mapped to identify incidents that can be closed automatically
	This task represents a manual task outside the business process management system. In this case, the dated incidents that cannot be closed by system will be closed manually after confirmation from the customer

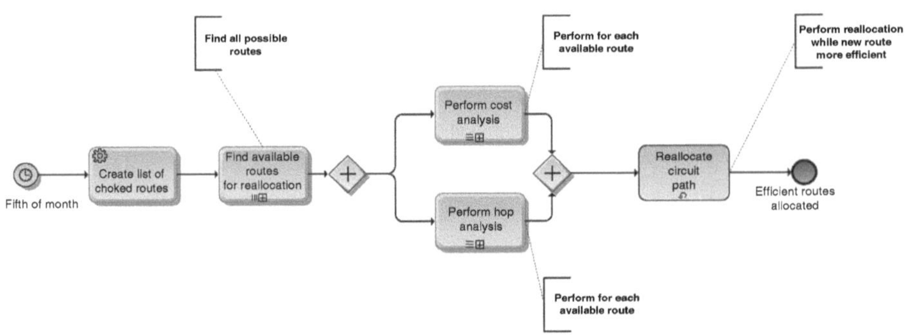

Fig. 5.10 Route allocation process – parallel and serial sub-processes

Figure 5.9 illustrates evaluation and automatic or manual closure of dated incidents in Close Dated Process through a business rule task review incident and a manual or script task close ticket tasks.

The type of tasks used in Fig. 5.9 is explained in Table 5.2.

Consider Fig. 5.10 which shows route reallocation process. It explains looping, parallel, and serial sub-processes.

The process starts with a start timer event which is denoted by a clock in a circle. It denotes that the process starts on the 5th of every month. It could also denote any other specified time such as a given day like Tuesday, at 2 am every day. In this case, therefore, the system service to create a list of choked routes is created on the 5th of every month.

Once the choked route list is created, available routes for reallocation need to be identified for the complete list. In other words, there are multiple iterations to find all possible routes available for reallocation. To make it more efficient, this activity can be done simultaneously by multiple teams for all the items of the list. This can be represented through multi-instance parallel sub-process. This is denoted by three parallel lines.

Once the available routes have been identified, for each identified route, cost and hop analysis is done to calculate its efficiency. This is an activity that is to be performed by subject matter experts who will perform cost and hop analysis for each available route. Since this multiple-instance activity will be done one at a time by subject matter experts, it can be denoted as a multi-instance serial process. A multi-instance serial process is denoted by three horizontal lines.

When both cost and hop analysis activities have been done (denoted by AND gateway), the process iterates to reallocate circuit paths wherever an available route is more efficient than the current route. This is denoted by a normal loop since this activity reallocates where the route is more efficient, hence resulting in the most efficient route allocation. This activity continues to iterate till the most efficient route is allocated and exits once the most efficient route allocation is achieved. This type of loop is dependent on a condition which is expressed through text annotation. If annotation is not used, there will be no mechanism for the loop to move to the next activity.

Consider a very simple instance of awarding a purchase order (PO) to a new vendor as shown in Fig. 5.11.

The process is initiated by a message start event "Request for New Vendor PO." The message start event is denoted by a circle with thin boundaries and empty envelope inside. For further processing, vendor registration is required; therefore, sub-process Register New Vendor, shown as collapsed sub-process, is initiated. Once this is done, the process moves to the next sub-process – Generate PO.

The Generate PO sub-process gets started with a registered vendor start event. After the registration, the company has access to the vendor's stock availability and the same is checked. Since either the stock could be available or not, XOR gateway

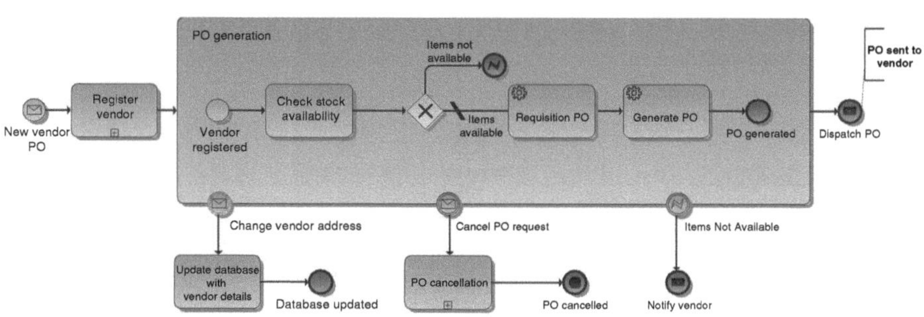

Fig. 5.11 Award PO to new vendor process

is used to denote these two options. In case the items are not available in stock, the sub-process throws end error event. The end error event is denoted by a thick circle with lightening sign inside. This results in PO generation for new vendor being stopped. The end error event is handled by an intermediate catch event "item not available" denoted by lightening sign in double circles. This catch event leads to throw message event of notification to vendor.

In case the items are available, service tasks requisition and generate POs. The generated PO is dispatched to the vendor. This is denoted by a thick circle with a filled envelope, which is a "throw" end message event. Through the sub-process, a non-interrupting message event, denoted by dotted double circles with envelope inside, can occur. A "non-interrupting event" means that it sends a message to a communication partner and afterward continues the process execution. "Change vendor address" is non-interrupting because the occurrence of this event and subsequent update of vendor details should not stop the process.

There could be interrupting message events as well. In the given example, suppose a cancel request arrives, it interrupts the sub-process PO generation as it is no longer required to continue with the same. The "Cancel PO" message event leads to PO cancellation sub-process and the process is terminated. The terminate event is denoted by a thick circle with a darkened circle inside. A terminate event triggers the immediate termination of the process instance. All steps still in execution in parallel branches are terminated.

The scenario of a customer buying a car in the car sale process is discussed through Fig. 5.12.

The process starts with the request from the customer to buy a car. It is denoted by a circle with thin boundaries called start event. Once the request is accepted, it is further processed by providing quotation. This is a send message task. Let us assume that the customer can take two actions. She can either reject offer or accept offer. These are denoted by event-driven exclusive gateway.

Event-driven gateways are denoted by a combination of a gateway diamond shape, circles, and pentagon denoting multiple events. If the event-based gateway is at the start of the process, there is a single circle around the pentagon. If the event-driven gateway is intermediate, the circles are double as shown in the example. Even though these gateways are triggered by the happening of the events, they are drawn on the left side for the sake of readability.

When the reject offer catch message event occurs, the request is cancelled, denoted by end event.

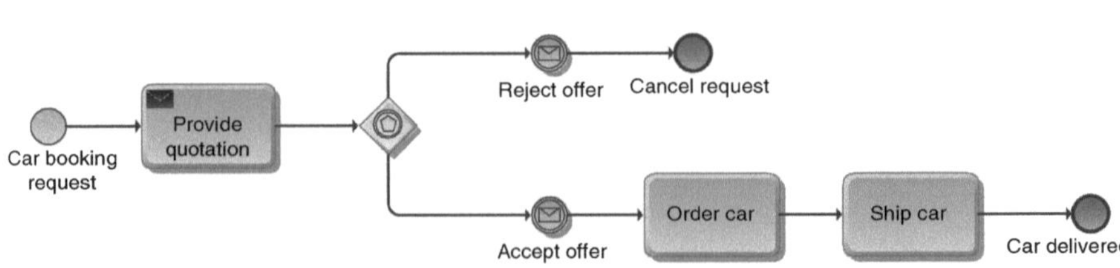

Fig. 5.12 Car sale process

When the accept offer catch message event occurs, the car is ordered, shipped, and delivered.

Events can also occur in parallel. Parallel event gateways are denoted by an "unfilled" plus sign instead of a pentagon and are also called event-based inclusive gateway. These require multiple events to be completed before the process can proceed.

Consider the car delivery process as shown in Fig. 5.13. Assume that every car booking request can be processed further only after there is confirmation of advance receipt and confirmation of specification. In such a scenario, two catch message events – advance confirmation and specification confirmation – must occur before order car activity occurs. The parallel event gateway denotes this requirement. Once both the events have occurred – order car and ship car – the car is delivered.

Let us consider Fig. 5.14 to understand the use of a signal event.

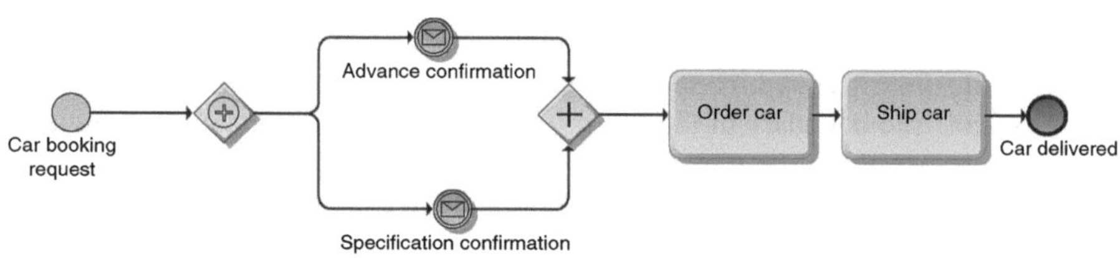

Fig. 5.13 Car delivery process – event gateway

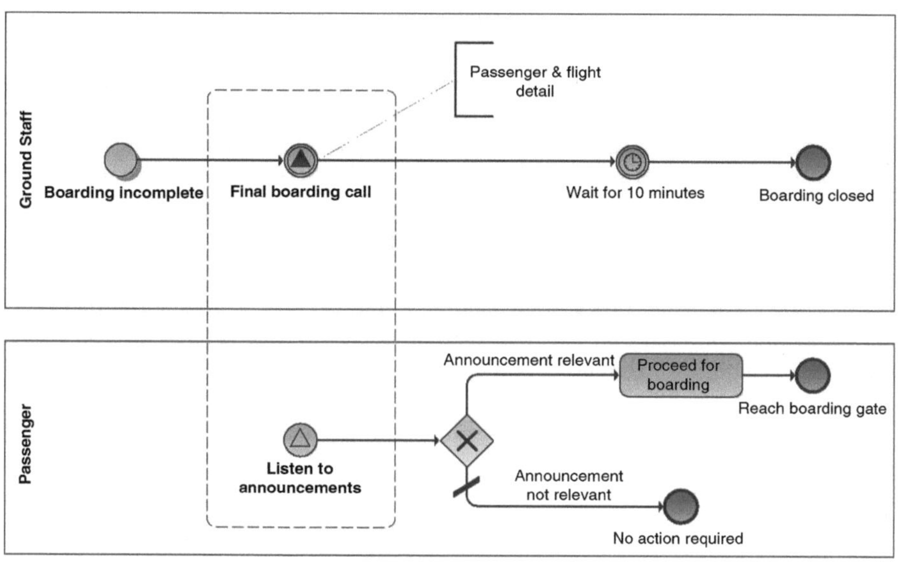

Fig. 5.14 Signal event

Signal events are denoted by a triangle in a circle. In the given example, the use of a throwing intermediate signal event and catching signal start event has been done. Signal events are used when something needs to be broadcasted, though it is not known who the recipients are. In Fig. 5.14, 10 min before closure, the boarding is incomplete. It is customary to make a final boarding call announcement for the passengers who have not reported to the boarding gate; however, it is not known where these passengers are. In such scenarios, the signal event can be used.

The intermediate throw signal event in the ground staff pool broadcasts final boarding call with passenger details. If the passengers listening to the announcement in the passenger pool find the announcement relevant to them, they proceed to the boarding gate. If the announcement is not relevant for them, they do nothing.

In the ground staff pool, since the flight should not be delayed due to no-show of passengers, after 10 min of announcement (intermediate throw signal event), the boarding is closed irrespective of reporting of the delayed passenger at the boarding gate.

The use of transaction is explained through Fig. 5.15. A transaction is a specialized type of sub-process with a special behavior that is controlled through a transaction protocol. The boundary of the sub-process is double-lined rectangle to indicate that it is a transaction. The transaction in this example is called order completion. The transaction starts once the card and address details are received.

A transaction can have three outcomes: successful completion, failed completion (cancel), and hazard. While a successful completion indicates that the sequence flow leaves the transaction normally, cancel indicates that activities inside the transaction would be subject to cancellation and could include rollback of process and compensation. If the payment is not successful, the transaction gets cancelled, and after notifying the customer, the transaction is terminated.

Compensation is concerned with undoing steps that were already successfully completed, because their results and possibly side effects are no longer desired and need to be reversed. Compensation is performed by a compensation handler. A compensation handler performs the steps necessary to reverse the effects of an activity. A compensation handler is a set of activities that are not connected to other portions of the BPMN model. The compensation handler starts with a catch compensation event. The catch compensation event either is a boundary event or, in the case of a compensation event sub-process, the handler's start event. The compensation events at the boundary of "Make payment" and "Ship book" are catch compensation events on the boundaries. Handle compensation shows the compensation event sub-process.

The compensation activity, which can be either a task or sub-process, has a marker to show that it is used for compensation only and is outside the normal flow of the process. "Recall payment" and "Return shipment" are compensation

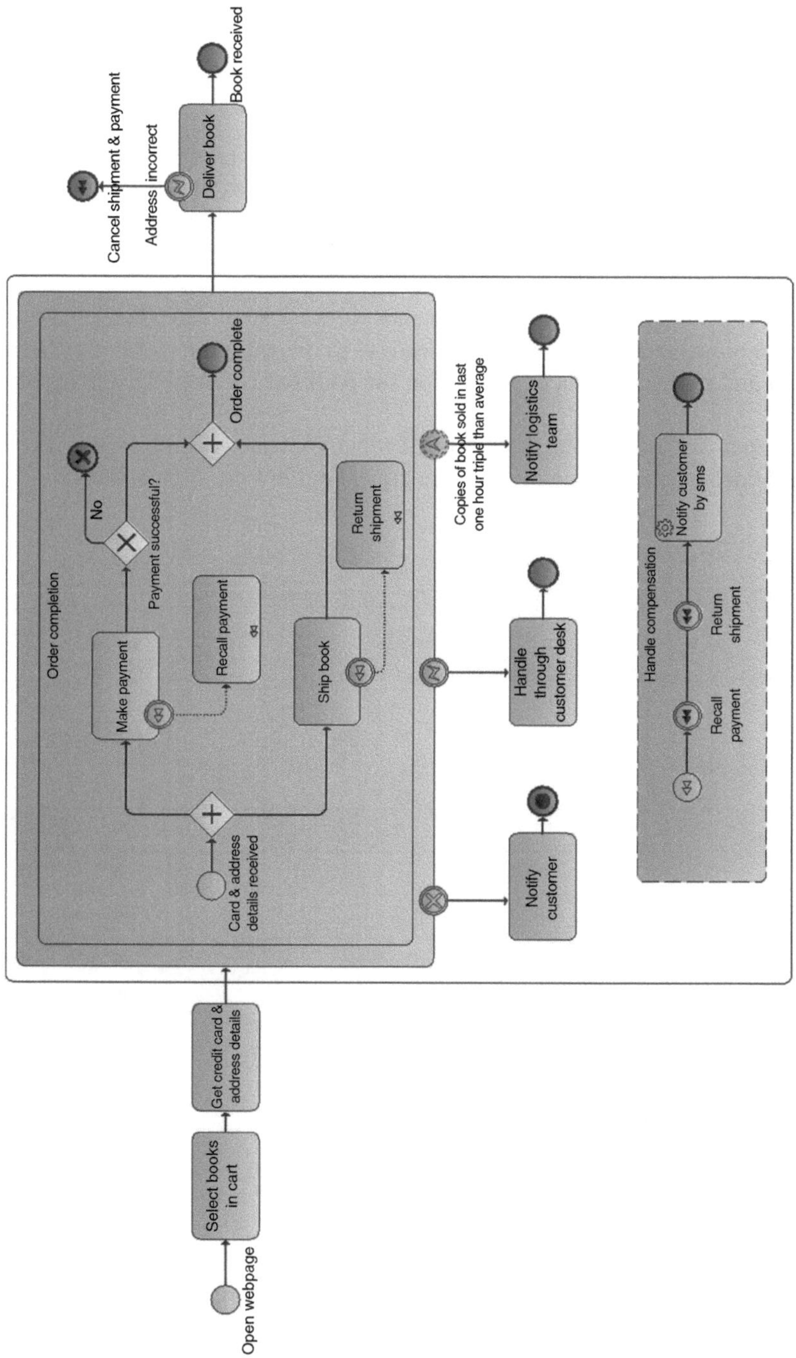

Fig. 5.15 Buy book process – transaction

activities connected through an association to catch compensation events on the boundaries of "Make payment" and "Ship book" activities.

A hazard on the other hand is a situation where normal success or cancellation is not possible. When a hazard happens, the activity is interrupted and the flow continues from the error intermediate event. In this example, the hazard is handled through customer desk.

An *escalation event* that does not interrupt the *activity* to which it is attached is called a non-interrupting escalation event. The boundary of the *event* is dashed, as is the case in Fig. 5.15. When copies are being sold at three times the average rate, it results in a non-interrupting escalation event which leads to notification to the logistics team.

Once the transaction is completed, the next process step is to deliver the books. If the error of incorrect address arises, it leads to a compensation end event of cancel shipment and payment. If there is no error, the books are delivered and the process ends.

So far many of the building blocks of BPMN have been covered to give an overview; the ones that have been covered are grayed out in Figs. 5.16 and 5.17.

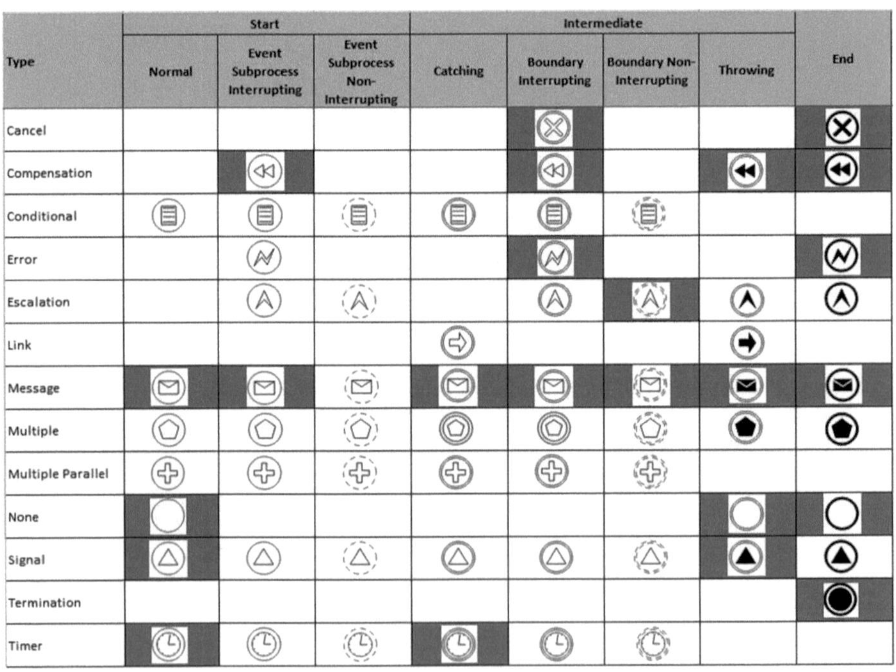

Fig. 5.16 BPMN 2.0 symbols covered – I

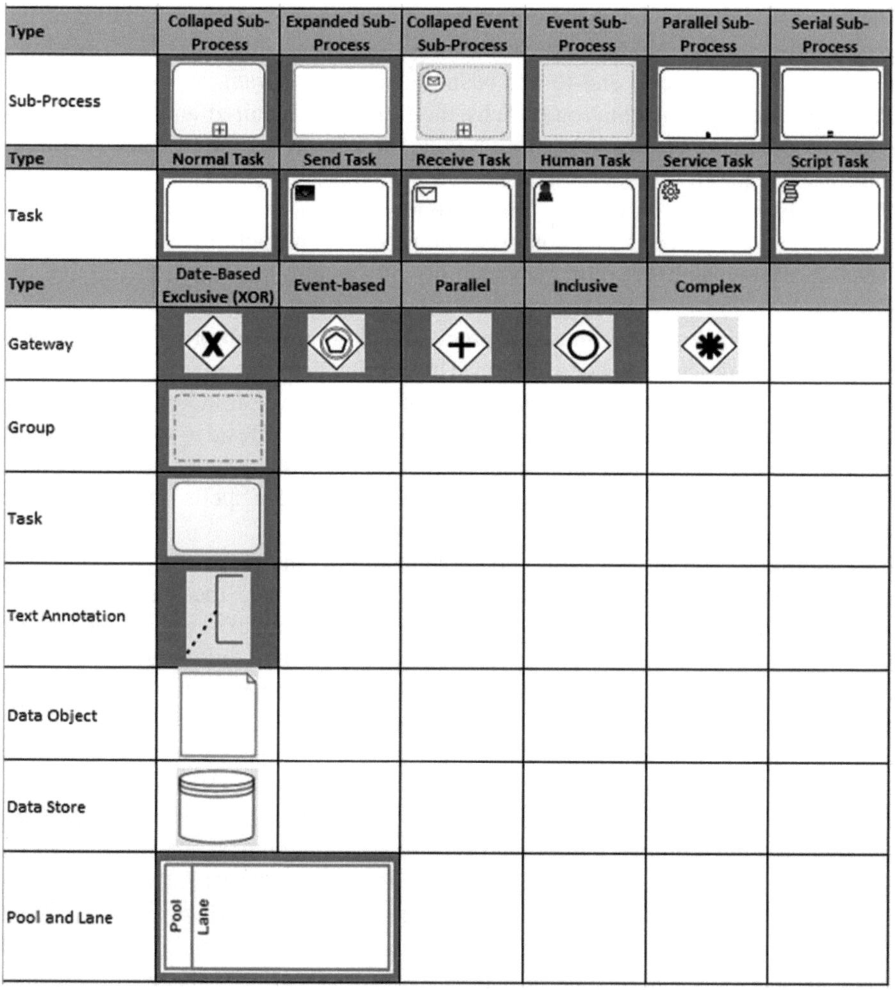

Fig. 5.17 BPMN 2.0 symbols covered – II

5.6 Business Process Documentation

Although coming to a good model requires a lot of effort, first in terms of gathering the information and then in modeling, this is not sufficient for most organizations. Organizations create their own set of process documentation guidelines. While it may be required for the purpose of understanding, it is often a legal requirement. Some of the important aspects covered in the documentation are:

Process Overview/Executive Summary This is usually at the beginning of the process documentation and helps in creating a context for the process. Sometimes this includes a high-level end-to-end business process diagram.

Purpose It covers information on why the process is required and what happens when it completes successfully. It highlights the benefits of the process as well as the consequences of non-compliance.

Process Flow This provides a visual representation of the start, sequence of activities, and end points that comprise the process. Through the use of pools and lanes, it offers insight into the responsibility of execution of activities through the process.

Process Description This includes process background, sub-processes, key process roles, and process flow description. This section provides a clear description of the activities that comprise the process. At the activity level, it includes if the activity is critical to time, quality, or success of the process. Besides this, it provides information on the role responsible for the execution of the process and, if applicable, the role responsible for any specific approvals. It also spells out any specific archiving requirements with respect to process data.

Stakeholders Internal (within the organization) and external (outside the organization) stakeholders are listed in this section. Since the stakeholders are affected by the process, depending upon their role, they should be approached as per the RASCI matrix (responsible, approve, support, consulted, informed).

Assumptions A process may have certain assumptions necessary for successful completion of the process. These are covered under assumptions.

Control Mechanism Control mechanism for a process may be internal as well as external. Control mechanisms are required to ensure that the risks associated with the process are captured to enable necessary action. Risk control matrix indicates the risks and the required control mechanisms. Documentation, system transaction information captured in system logs etc. are evidences of the presence of control mechanism. Control mechanisms should be tested for their effectiveness to avoid bureaucracy. Additionally, there may be requirements of internal and/or external audit to verify the compliance of a process. Non-compliance leads to corrective action plans. This section lists necessary audits and their frequency.

Interrelated Process: Interrelated processes should be listed to enable impact analysis of any change in those processes. On the other hand, any changes in the process under consideration could have impact on the interrelated processes.

Supporting Material Standard operating procedures, templates, training materials, etc. may be required to properly carry out a process. Such supporting material is created and uploaded on the repository.

Document Control This section contains the link to the repository where the latest approved version of the process can be found. This document is a signed-off version of the process that clearly indicates the author of the process, signing authorities, and process owner. Processes are updated from time to time, but even the previous versions should be archived and stored in a repository which handles version control of the process.

Feedback At any point in time, the process may lead or follow the practice. Keeping pace with the same feedback acts as an important mechanism to keep track of the differences and to bring about improvement. Usually a link and template are provided to give feedback on a process.
Handover When process involves multiple participants across departments and/or organizations, proper handover and acceptance are required. The acceptance and handover are signed off to formalize and approve the process. The effective date and sign-off date of the process, which may be different at times, are captured in the process document.

References

Becker J, Rosemann M, Uthmann CV (2000) In: van der Aalst W (ed) Business process management. Springer, Berlin/Heidelberg, pp 30–49

Curtis B, Kellner M, Over J (1992) Process modeling. Communications of the ACM - Special issue on analysis and modeling in software development. 35(9):75–90

Davenport TH, Short JE (1990) The new industrial engineering: information technology and business process redesign. Sloan Manage Review 31:11–27

Debevoise T, Geneva R (2008) The microguide to process modeling in BPMN2.0 How to build great process, rule and event models. Advanced Component Research, Lexington, Virginia

Dumas M, Rosa ML, Mending J, Reijers HA (2013) Fundamentals of business process management. Springer, Berlin

Flinchbaugh J http://www.bpmn.org, http://www.industryweek.com/companies-amp-executives/going-gemba. Going to the Gemba, Accessed 1 Oct 2014

Franken HM, Weger MK (1997) A modelling framework for capturing business process dynamics. Knowl Proc Manage 4:153–162

http://udoo.uni-muenster.de/downloads/publications/1717.pdf. Accessed 1 Oct 2014

http://www.apqc.org/process-classification-framework. Accessed 1 Oct 2014

http://www.itil.org/en/vomkennen/itil/index.php. Accessed 1 Oct 2014

http://www.omg.org/spec/BPMN/2.0/PDF/changebarred, formal/2011-01-04. Accessed 1 Oct 2014

Kaplan RB, Murdock L (1991) Rethinking the corporation, core process redesign. Mckinsey Q (2): 27–43

Kugelar M, Vieting M (2003) Design of a process oriented structure. In: Jörg B, Kugeler M, Rosemann M (eds) Process management: a guide for the design of business processes. Springer, Berlin/Heidelberg, pp 166–167

Melão N, Pidd M (2000) A conceptual framework for understanding business processes and business process modelling. Inf Syst J 10(2):105–129

Mendling J, Reijers HA, Aalst WMPVDA http://wwwis.win.tue.nl/~wvdaalst/publications/p574.pdf. Seven process modeling guidelines (7PMG) Humboldt University, Unter den Linden 6, 10099 Berlin, Germany, Eindhoven University of Technology, P.O. Box 513, 5600 MB Eindhoven, The Netherlands. Accessed 1 Oct 2014

Morgan G (1997) Images of organization. Sage, Thousand Oaks

Ramias AJ, Rummler R (2009) The evolution of the effective process framework: a model for redesigning business processes. Perform Improv 48(10):25–32

Silver B (2011) BPMN method and style. Cody-Cassidy Press, Aptos

6 Change Management

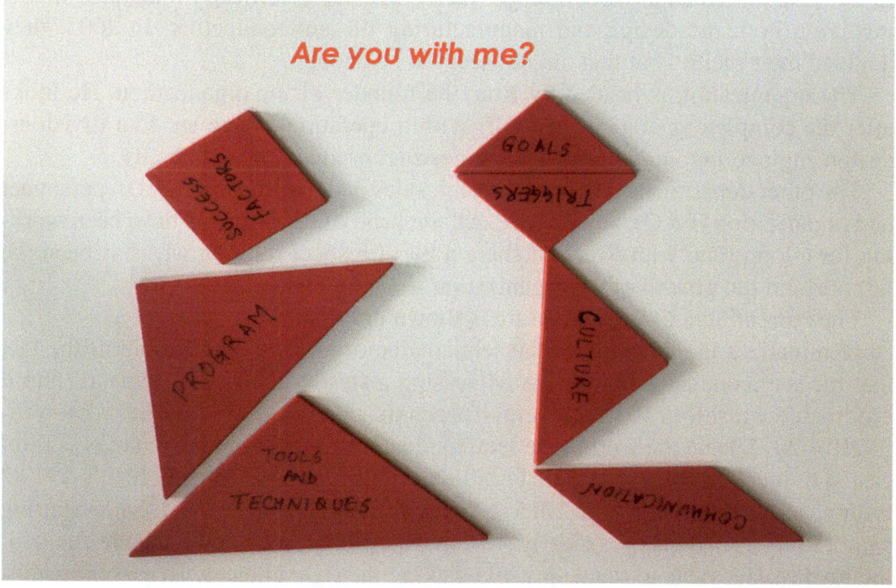

A small agile organization needs as much change management as a big hierarchical structure. Due emphasis on change management ensures a smooth transition to the desired state and its subsequent sustenance. Surprisingly, despite the abundance of recipes of success, the change management success rate remains low. The case of Semicron International, a fictitious company, illustrates how the knowledge on change management can be interpreted and incorporated during business process transformation.

C. Sharma, *Business Process Transformation*, Management for Professionals,
DOI 10.1007/978-81-322-2349-8_6

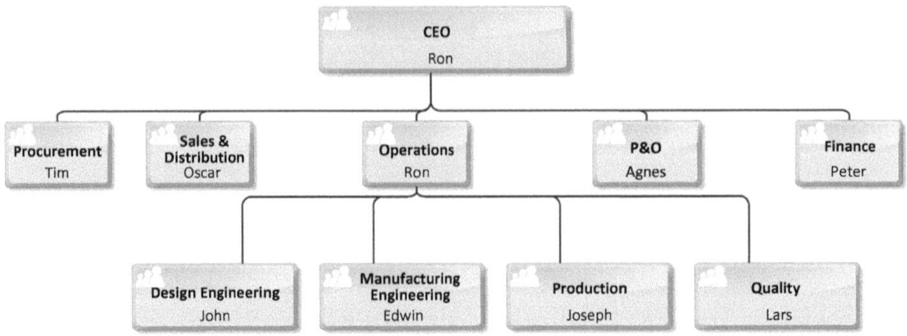

Fig. 6.1 Organization structure – Semicron

Semicron International is a company involved in manufacturing semiconductors. In 1999, it started small with a single facility. It was a vertically integrated model involving both the design and manufacturing of semiconductors. In 2005, they doubled their facility but that did not seem to be enough.

The organization is headed by Ron, the founder of the organization. He looks after the complete operations himself. Within operations, there are four divisions: design engineering, manufacturing engineering, production, and quality.

The other departments are procurement, sales and distribution (S&D), personnel and organization (P&O), and finance. All the head of departments have been working for a long time with Ron and share a lot of respect for Ron who has been the light behind the growth of the organization so far.

The current organization structure is shown in Fig. 6.1.

Ron realizes the potential of the semiconductor market. He is aware of the fact that the semiconductor industry is witnessing a steady increase in demand (http://electroiq.com/blog/2014/07/semi-forecasts-double-digit-business-growth-in-2014-2015/) and the worldwide semiconductor capital equipment market is forecasted to increase 20.8 % to $38.44 billion in 2014, compared with 2013's $31.82 billion, and another 10.8 % in 2015 to $42.6 billion (Dorsch 2014). Despite starting small, Ron has had his eyes clearly set to have a global reach and a sizable chunk of the market. He wants to scale up while making the right choices. To make the most of the possibilities, he needs to change the gear and accelerate to new heights.

Currently, his main processes are shown in Fig. 6.2.

Being in the business, Ron knows that he has many options to consider in capturing a greater market share:

Option1 – Additional integrated setup for both design and manufacturing

Option 2 – Additional capacity only for foundries (manufacturing) and cater to fabless (only design) customers

Option 3 – Additional capacity as fabless customers and outsource manufacturing work to merchant foundries

Option 4 – Joint venture with their competitors in an effort to split research and design expenditures and fab-maintenance expenses

Option 5 – Take over some competitors and save on setup cost and time

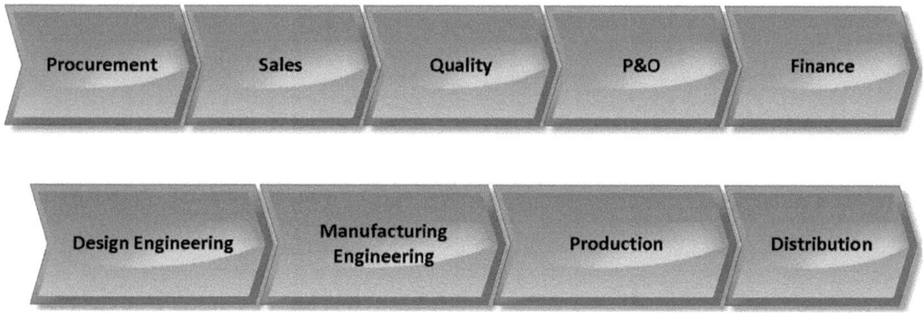

Fig. 6.2 Main processes of Semicron

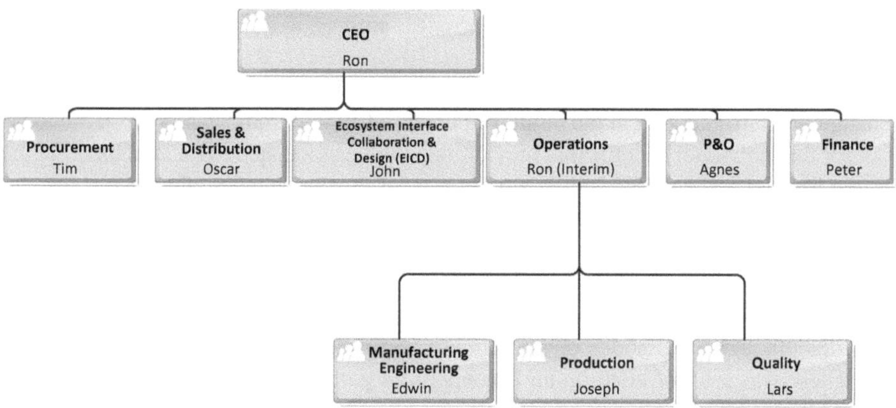

Fig. 6.3 Proposed organization structure – Semicron

After due diligence by his core management team, he is advised to go in for option 2 wherein additional capacity for manufacturing (fabless foundry) would be created to cater to fabless customers.

This would imply a change in the organization structure as well as the processes. The proposed organization structure is shown in Fig. 6.3.

His current 300+ workforce is known in the market for their loyalty to Semicron and have a feeling of belonging for their organization. They also consider Ron as their father figure. The workforce takes a lot of pride in their integrated design and manufacturing setup. Currently, the number of people in the design division is more than the manufacturing division. This would reverse in the future when manufacturing would become the core business.

This would be a transformational change. There would be a fundamental shift in what is done in Semicron and how it is done. Design engineering will primarily move out to design houses and to the customers who would be utilizing manufacturing and testing facilities at Semicron. An overview of the proposed processes is shown in Fig. 6.4.

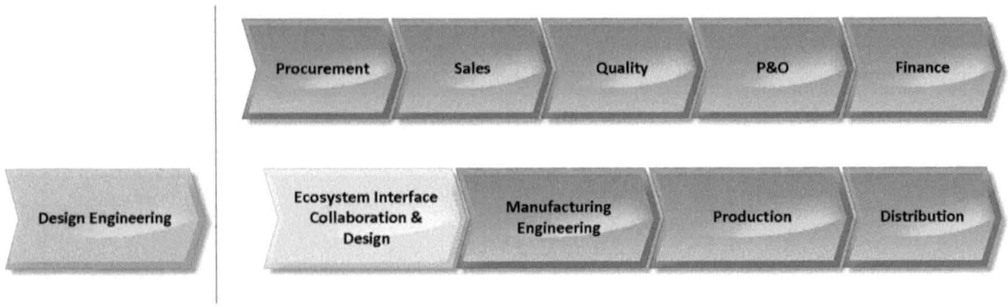

Fig. 6.4 Proposed processes Semicron

Ron is not sure if his organization is ready for a change. As such, Semicron is a profitable venture due to which there is no hunger in the mind of staff to grab more and grow more. While discussing the possible impact with the senior management team, various opinions have come up.

A senior member of management team has raised the apprehension that the news of change might trigger fear in the minds of people. They will immediately be on the lookout for the individual benefits that may or may not be associated to them, damaging the group identity and benefits. While at the moment the personnel on the design side are more, in the times to come, the balance will tilt in favor of the manufacturing team.

Another member pointed out that when a competitor had undertaken similar initiative, it turned out to be an ugly affair. They faced a lot of resistance. So many rumors were spread about the change initiative that they even reached Semicron. Besides this, nasty episodes of attempts to derail the change initiative were in the air. There was a lot of attrition and competitors gained by offering attractive offers to their best people.

If Semicron decides to undertake the envisaged change initiative, it needs to feel the pulse of the people carefully. They will have to make choices in whether it wants to force compliance through hierarchical methods or it wants to address resistance in an open manner.

Ron is not used to facing resistance or for that matter recognizing it. His organization has grown like a typical family-driven organization where the founder is respected and obeyed. He can however, not risk a fate similar to its competitor. This change, if initiated, would touch people, resources, culture, technology, processes, designs, packaging, technology, and organization. In other words, the impact of the change will be felt in every corner of Semicron.

The following things are clear to Ron:

- Semiconductor foundries have very high barriers to entry and it will take some time before the benefits would start coming in.
- If he cannot have the staff behind him, the chances of making a successful transition to the next level would be considerably low.
- The team needs to understand why the shift to a foundry setup is required and the difference it will make to their lives.

- The culture will undergo a significant change as the current staff will have to embrace new people and new thoughts. They will have to believe in the segregation of work beyond their own facilities.
- The staff engaged in the design side may feel sidelined and could lead to the formation of formal and informal groups.
- Teams would have to wipe out history and start looking afresh to the forward outlook of collaboration.
- The processes would have to be aligned/defined to fit the new scenario.
- In order to derive maximum benefit through a foundry setup, Ron will have to embrace more automation in the manufacturing process.
- Tie-ups would have to be done with fabless customers which follow design best practices, so that Semicron can cater to multiple fabless customers and optimally utilize its capacity.
- The cost of a new foundry exceeds $ 1 billion, so his current facilities should continue to work efficiently to avoid additional financial burden.
- Key performance indicators (KPIs) would need to be defined to ensure timely product readiness.
- New roles would be created for vendor management.

Ron did not want to reinvent the wheel, so a quick look at the change management approaches yielded the following result:

6.1 Kurt Lewin's Model

In his model for change, Lewin (1947) emphasizes that achievement of certain parameters cannot be the objective of a change endeavor as group performance tends to slip back to the original levels. This happens because every level is maintained by force fields.

The concept of a force field is based upon the setting of a group as a social field. The position of entities such as individuals, groups, subgroups, barriers, channels, etc., in a social group is guided by their interactions and movement within these fields. To make a change permanent, the setting of the force fields has to be brought to the next level. The force fields at the new level need to be made stronger for entities to move towards them.

A successful change involves unfreezing the current level, moving to the new level, and freezing the new level. Unfreezing and freezing are complex and often an emotional shake-up is required. Unfreezing and freezing at a group level facilitate the movement of individuals towards newly established levels. The reason for this facilitation is that individuals tend to act as group members.

6.1.1 Learning for Semicron

- Surface the driving and resisting forces.

- Visualize the desired state.
- Create dissatisfaction with current state and motivate to achieve the next state.
- Find change agents who can help in the movement to the next level.
- Create structure and reward mechanisms to facilitate remaining at the desired state.

6.2 Kotter's 8 Steps for Change

In the heart of change, Kotter (2007) has proposed 8 steps for a successful large-scale change:

- Establish a sense of urgency.
- Form a powerful guiding coalition.
- Create a vision.
- Communicate the vision.
- Empower people to act on vision.
- Plan for and create short- and long-term wins.
- Consolidate improvements and produce still more change.
- Institutionalize new approaches.

Kotter explains that though it sounds easy, half of the transformation programs fail for lack of aggressive cooperation. For establishing a sense of urgency, it is necessary for the organization to feel motivated to get out of their comfort zones. Many times, a crisis or bad performance helps in creating a sense of urgency.

From the perspective of the process Tangram, each of the triggers can be a potential source, which can be built upon to create a sense of urgency.

The person at the top alone cannot make a difference. It is the people who are actually involved with it and function together like a well-oiled machinery who are instrumental in making a transformation successful. These people are not necessarily the senior managers but could cut across the ranks but should be committed to the cause. Kotter calls such a group of people a "guiding coalition." This group of people is required to sustain the transformation effort so that it does not fizzle out before reaching its conclusion.

A sense of direction provided by the vision is required to lead a transformation effort to its end objective. A crisp and clear vision scores much above a lengthy discourse which does not provide any clarity. Besides this, the vision needs to be communicated to the point that employees can see the benefits of getting out of their comfort zones. All channels of communication should be deployed extensively to communicate the vision. A vision does not get communicated through just words but by the deeds of people who matter as well. Actions and behavior speak louder than words holds true to a great extent.

The path towards a new vision is encountered with obstacles. These obstacles could be a figment of mental blocks, previous experiences, etc., or they may be tangible and real. In all the cases, they should be dealt with firmly. There are times that people get so bogged down by the humongous changes that approach them that they get overwhelmed. In such scenarios, sometimes cutting the elephant into pieces yields results. Since all obstacles cannot be resolved, they should be prioritized and the bigger ones must be resolved to retain the credibility of the change effort.

A lot has been said and written about the low-hanging fruits; however, these do not fall on their own. These short-term wins need to be planned and achieved. These short-term wins ensure that a sense of urgency is maintained through the transformation effort. If these are not planned, the long-term goals seem too far away and the possibilities of analytical thinking and revisiting the vision are limited.

In order to ensure that the benefits of transformation are fully realized and do not regress to the original state, completion should be declared once the changes are ingrained in the culture of the organization. The success of the transformation lies in being able to anchor the change in the organization. When the organization consciously attempts to demonstrate the benefits of the change in terms of results such as improved performances, people are able to relate the efforts to the benefits. Another factor that helps is the personification of approach by the management.

6.2.1 Learning for Semicron

- Ron will have to make it clear to his organization how important it is to move over to the new semiconductor foundry setup and why this needs to be done quickly. This thought will be the base around which the weave of the change initiative will be woven.
- Ron will not be able to form a powerful guiding coalition on his own. He will have to take Semicron together in this journey. He will need to form a group of people who will relentlessly support the goal. To begin with, this number would be small but with time these numbers would grow. This would only if this group of people is committed to the cause and can work together in an effective and efficient manner.
- A link to the change initiative would need to be established with the overall vision of Semicron, to lead with excellence in the chosen field.
- Just having this vision and establishing the link of the change to the vision would not be enough, and not only the 300+ staff would need to understand the message but would require a repeated reinforcement to make it part of their own vision.
- The staff should feel every morning that they have the capability to turn the vision into reality. This will not come with empty rhetoric, but by allowing them to make changes in and around them, that could add to the "how" of achieving the change. This does not imply that people should do whatever they like but it implies a certain degree of freedom is available to innovate while keeping the process and goal in mind.
- Since change is an uphill task, Semicron would have to plan out for targets that are realistic and achievable. This will help in instilling a feeling of achievement. An example could be to have the setup of the new economic interface collaboration and design (EICD) department as one part of the target. While this is only a first step in the change initiative, yet it is substantial enough to celebrate a win.

All these will consolidate into long-term wins such as transformational foundry performance levels.

- The movement of pure design engineering out of Semicron will take a while, and the new process would not be streamlined in a day. It will take various iterations before the final shape arrives, but every iteration should add something to the previous one. The crux is to continue doing, so as to consolidate the improvement.
- It would be very difficult to institutionalize new approaches, especially for the current staff who would have to unlearn before they can reap the benefits of the new ways of working. For the new people who would be joining, it would be learning the new approaches in a way that they become their ways of working.

6.3 Beckhard and Harris Model

In their model, Beckhard and Harris (1987) provide a proposition of "when" people get motivated for undertaking a change. The premise of their model is that there is motivation for change when the impact of certain conditions is greater than the cost of change.

The first condition (A) is that there should be dissatisfaction with the current state of the organization. There should be a felt need to undertake a change. In other words, these are the triggers for change. It does not imply that things should necessarily be going wrong, but it could also be a change in strategy, market conditions, and so on.

The second condition (B) is that the future should be desirable. In other words, these are the goals for change. A positive and desirable future not only creates a feeling of optimism but also enables people to envision their role and objectives. It increases the feel-good factor by virtue of reduction in perceived insecurities.

The third condition (C) is the practicality of a path of change. A path that is practical increases the engagement of people as it makes the goals seem to be achievable. The path should be with minimum risk and disruption.

The impact of all the three conditions ABC should be greater than the costs of changing (D). The cost of changing is not limited to the associated financial costs but involves convincing people of the availability of means to achieve the same. People assess the cost of change with respect to the effort required, the level of difficulty in adapting to the changes, and the perceived and real risks.

For change to happen, $ABC > D$ should hold true, and thus the equation can be represented as

$$\text{Change} = ABC > D$$

6.3.1 Learning for Semicron

In order to create dissatisfaction with the current state of organization, Semicron can deploy many strategies such as a comparison of future cash flows in the new setup to cash flows in the current setup; another could be to see if a loss, instead of an increase, in market share would happen if they do not make transformational change. Industry trends, expert views, and Semicron's short- and long-term goals can also be deployed to strengthen the case.

To make the future state desirable, a future state business case would need to be worked out. These benefits would include both tangible and non-tangible benefits. Together they should indicate that by taking the chosen course of action, Semicron will move into a stable period, where incomes will be assured. If they continue to evolve through the change, they will be able to consolidate into a new organization which is capable, secure, and future ready.

To show that the transformation goals are achievable, it should be taken up as a program. Clear milestones should be set which become the base for short-term and long-term victories. Consolidation of effort will move Semicron to another plane of performance. It should also indicate that the current facilities would not move on to the new setup in a haphazard manner, but rather the transition would be well planned. Current outputs will only face a slight dip while moving over to the new setup. As such, there would be little disruption.

For the cost of changing, the greatest effort besides the funding would be required on convincing the design engineering team of the fact that their role is not diminishing but it is becoming more strategic. Besides this, those who are willing to move to manufacturing engineering would be provided the training to do so. The message that needs to be spread across is that though this change is not without risks, risks would be managed to ensure that Semicron will be able to achieve its goals.

All these efforts will enable the employees to assess that the three conditions of dissatisfaction with the current state, desirability of the future state, and its practicality outweigh the costs of change so the change initiative should be undertaken.

6.4 Mckinsey's 7-Step Model

Mckinsey's 7-step model (http://www.mckinsey.com/insights/strategy/enduring_ideas_the_7-s_framework) looks at organizations from the perspective of shared value and belief, strategy, system, staff, skills, style, and structure. When all these work in tandem, it creates an environment that is conducive for bringing about successful change (Fig. 6.5) (http://www.mckinsey.com/insights/strategy/enduring_ideas_the_7-s_framework).

Shared values and belief linked to transformational change provide a logical reasoning to the employees on the need for undertaking the initiative. These shared values bind people together and help them sail through the difficulties that accompany change.

Without a strategy, it is impossible to achieve the ambitious goals typically associated with a transformation. No road can lead to Rome if the capabilities are not available and a clear road map is not established to achieve the goals. It is not necessary that all the capabilities should exist within the organization itself. In many cases, the very fact that the capabilities can be distributed and alliances can be forged is the basis for transformation. A strategy is also required to counter any new or perceived threats.

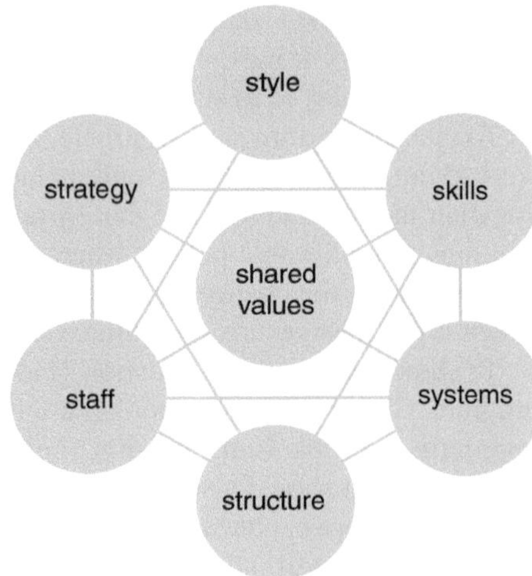

Fig. 6.5 Mckinsey's 7-step model

Systems ensure that the organization functions like a well-oiled machinery. Efficient and effective business processes supported by robust systems facilitate that the organization remains at the new state rather than digressing back to older levels.

Staff concerns itself with the needs of people that the organization is composed of. It also involves the recruitment, retention, and motivation of employees. In terms of a transformation, staffing may not involve a significant amount of new recruitment but may involve the actualization of job responsibilities, job roles, job grades, and training and development requirements.

The style of management in a transformation program type influences the management style that would be best suited. If transformation requires a movement from a family setup to a market-driven organization, the management style would definitely have to undergo a transformation. This can happen only in synchronization with a change in structure. A market-driven organization would typically require lower levels of hierarchy coupled with empowered decision making at different levels. This would be a departure from a centralized decision making in the hierarchical family culture.

The skills of the employees are a key to a successful transformation. In the perspective of a transformation, it would imply an assessment of the current fitment, gap analysis, and subsequent enhancement of skills to achieve the objectives of the goals of the organization.

6.4.1 Learning for Semicron

Mckinsey's 7-step model looks at organizations from the perspective of shared value and belief, strategy, system, staff, skills, style, and structure. When all these work in tandem, it creates an environment that is conducive in bringing about successful change.

The management team and employees would have to convince themselves on the need for transformation and how it fits in with Semicron's values. These reasons and beliefs will allow them to have a logical reasoning on the need for undertaking the initiative.

Ron will have to chalk out a clear strategy on how the ambitious goals of change would be achieved. They would have to position themselves in such a way that they are recognized as a world-class production facility. Besides the market- and production-oriented approach, their approach would have to involve knowledge management. Knowledge management would provide them an edge over other foundries (http://www.cata.ca/files/PDF/Resource_Centres/hightech/reports/indep-studies/GlobalizationTaiwaneseSemiconductor.pdf). Semicron would have to take advantage of market proximity to the design houses and huge local talent pool. It would have to grow together with the rapidly growing design houses. The new department led by John can bring in excellent results as Semicron would be uniquely placed in terms of their deep understanding of design engineering. The stock market seems to be on a bullish run, so Semicron could go public and raise funds from market to fund its expansion costs.

Semicron should develop its process-based technology platform to cater to multiple design houses who want to leverage design compatibility with multiple foundries for maximizing volumes. They should make their process design kits available to design houses so that they can design to maximize innovation in the available standards. Besides this, it should be in a position to provide test equipment for experimentation to semiconductor suppliers who may later turn out to be valuable customers. Semicron's systems should be capable of providing different levels of service to suit customer requirements. Efficient and effective business processes supported by robust systems would be required to take on the highly competitive market and to ensure that the processes do not digress back to older levels.

Staffing at Semicron will be crucial. On one hand, it has a design engineering division that will be disbanded and merged into EICD; on the other hand, they will have to recruit additional staff for their foundry expansion plans. Capable staff would have to be trained to such levels that Semicron can provide high level of flexibility along with R&D expertise as and when required by its customers.

Staffing should be optimized as understaffing would lead to loss in terms of capacity utilization and overstaffing would lead to decrease in throughput due to interference. Mechanism should be put in place to allow for quick ramp-up and ramp-down to achieve flexibility in tune into market demand. Accurate demand forecasting is very important to maximize the benefits of flexible staffing in a market which typically has variations not only in year-on-year demands but also in month-on-month demands. The fixed staff would have to be motivated to deal with the ad hoc staff, as dealing with new people every time does cost extra energy and effort. Development paths, vertical as well as lateral, should be made available to nurture Semicron's talent.

Semicron's typical family-oriented setup and style of management will have to change. With plans of expansion and greater interaction with design houses, it would have to move to a more market-oriented style of functioning. Ron realizes that he needs to give greater freehold to the management and has decided to look out for the position of operations head. He will vest more decision-making authority in his subordinates to allow them to swiftly react to market demands.

Semicron would require a change in structure as it will need to move to lower levels of hierarchy. Decision making at different levels would have to be empowered. Ron is gearing up for the same, though it will be very difficult for him to function at a strategic level and let go the hands-on operations approach that he has always had.

The skills of the employees are crucial to a successful transformation. The new establishment would require skill enhancement for the existing workers. In order to scale up and down as per market demand, tie-ups will have to be made with staffing agencies to provide skilled resources on a requirement basis.

6.5 Nadler Tushman Congruence Model

Nadler and Tushman (1982) proposed the congruence model for change. They identified four components for organizational performance, viz., people, task, and formal and informal organization. The key to organizational performance is the alignment of these components.

From a transformation perspective, the components can be interpreted as below:

The interaction of people in the organization depends on who they are: what are their personalities, their backgrounds, their skills, their motivations, etc. This aspect is captured in the people component. This captures the essence of the individual in the organization.

Congruence also depends on the "tasks" people are expected to perform, the level of interaction with other roles, how well the tasks are defined, meaningfulness of the task, and the comfort zone of the person in the tasks he or she is expected to perform.

The way people perform assigned tasks is subject to their interaction both in formal and informal organizations. A formal organization refers to the structure, processes, tools, rewards, recognition, etc., that hold the functioning of the organization together while an informal organization refers to culture, politics, power centers, and aspects that are usually unwritten.

The interaction of these four components is more than the individual components added together. These can work both ways for an organization.

If formal and informal organizations are harmonized, a common scenario of the initial days of transformation, the resistance against the change initiative will be high. There would be more bottlenecks found than anybody can imagine.

On the other hand, once the formal and informal organizations are synchronized, there is agreement on what, why, and how the goal would be achieved; how the tasks, roles, and people would be impacted; and how the performance would speed up and yield desired results.

This model highlights the importance of interplay of the four crucial components required for the success of a transformation.

6.5.1 Application for Semicron

- Involvement of employees (people) who collectively form the organization will be the key to success.
- How well the employees will perform will depend on factors such as how clearly the tasks are defined and what their interaction is with each other. In the case of Semicron, a lot of emphasis will be required in defining the tasks of the new department EICD and its interaction with the design houses. Subsequently, the passing on of requirements to manufacturing will be crucial for a successful transition to the transformed process.
- Semicron will have to mobilize the power of both formal and informal organizations to maximize the benefits of change.

6.6 Kübler-Ross Model for Dealing with Change

While change occurs at the organizational level, the pattern that individuals tend to follow can be explained by Dr. Elisabeth Kübler-Ross's model for dealing with change (Kübler-Ross 1969). Though based on her observations on patterns of terminally ill patients, it can well be applied for understanding the phases that individuals may go through while dealing with transformational change. Since an organization is composed of individuals, an understanding of how they deal with change can be helpful to formulate strategies for smooth transition.

The stages that an individual goes through are shock, denial, anger, depression, and acceptance. These do not necessarily occur in the same order, nor is there a guarantee that once they have occurred, they will not occur again.

There are many variations and adaptations of this model in the name of change curve. The basic underlying message is that people require hand-holding to sail through a disruptive change. The important difference from the stages of people who face death is that the end objective of a transformation is not a tragedy but rather a genesis of an organization which is alive and kicking.

People need to be told repeatedly about the end goals, sometimes at a high level and at other times at a level that impacts their day-to-day working. They need to know how to find their way through the fear of the unknown.

The performance can be expected to dip in the initial phases; however, as people establish for themselves that a particular change initiative is not an eyewash but an endeavor that is real and is happening, they tend to assess the impact on themselves, minimize the damage, and gradually start moving with some reluctance. As the inertia decreases, the learning curve for the new ways of working takes over. This is the time to start maximizing the benefits of change.

It is important for the change team and management to be consistent in the message and support the employees throughout the transformation. Support does not imply agreement and allowance on each voice of dissent but in making people aware of the benefits, seeking out possibilities for maximizing benefits, and minimizing pain. In case where other solutions are not available, allow and facilitate a smooth exit. An environment of trust and honesty should be created.

Ron realizes that while he can learn a lot from the theories, there is a need to go into greater detail to understand resistance to change.

6.7 Resistance to Change

Resistance can be "the" mega-blocker to change yet is a necessary evil. If there is little or no resistance to a change effort, another look is required on the "what," "why," and "how" of the change effort. Resistance can hold back a well-planned change with few discernible reasons. It requires insight and effort to identify and assess resistance, bring it to surface, and address it in a proactive or reactive manner (Jones and Recardo 2013).

Changing involves getting out of comfort zones, fear of the unknown, risk of fitment, and so on.

Consider John, the head of the design team in Semicron. He has had aspirations of being Ron's successor as and when Ron decides to hang its boots. Although the succession plan has never been public, there has been implicit understanding about John being the "chosen one."

In the changed scenario, John is apprehensive of his future. He realizes that the importance of his division is going to diminish as the primary focus of Semicron would move from design to fabrication. The move from being an integrated facility to a fabless manufacturer is unsettling for his division yet transformational in nature for Semicron.

He feels an internal conflict as on one hand he has been a strong ally to Ron in the Semicron journey, while on the other hand, he has a feeling of letting down his team from the design side. He fears that his position in Semicron may be compromised. He is actually contemplating if he should mobilize the design team to outmaneuver Ron's plan of moving to a fabless manufacturing setup. He needs to rationalize his emotions to think sensibly.

All is not hunky-dory in the manufacturing division as well. They fear that they will be suddenly exposed to comparison to market benchmarks. They are used to working under the fatherlike guidance of Ron, but the changed scenario will expose them to multiple speaking partners. This is truly overwhelming for them as they are only used to dealing with John's team. They are a capable lot but they don't know the impact of the change on their career path. They have heard through the grapevine that the implementation of Ron's plan may take years, making them unsure if they are going to pull it through.

6.7.1 Dealing with Resistance at Individual Level

Resistance at the individual level is a result of many factors and they are to some extent unique to every employee. These factors can however be grouped into social, psychological, economic, fitment, and fatigue factors as shown in Fig. 6.6.

Social Factors Man, being a social animal, associates a lot of importance to the environment they are in. With most employees in the current times stretching themselves far more than earlier, the workplace is almost like a second home. People tend to associate their life with their work. They often find friends in their col-

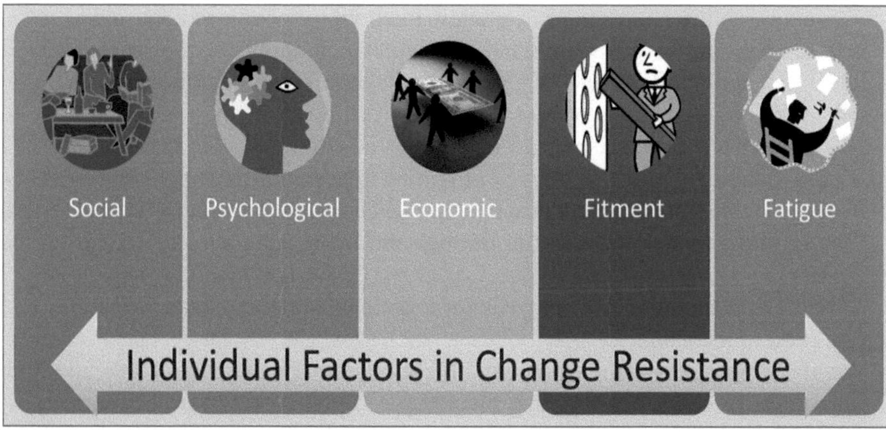

Fig. 6.6 Individual factors to change resistance

leagues and tend to feel a part of group. The position in the group, division, etc., is connected to the self-esteem and self-image to some extent. When people fear that the social scenario around them, including their own position, is in a limbo, it is a natural reaction to resist. This resistance can be visible in many forms such as withdrawal behaviors, conflict, and absenteeism.

Psychological Factors Each person is unique in attitude, aptitude, characteristics, and temperament. The requirements of one person in terms of engagement, involvement, influence, rewards, and motivation differ from another.

Economic Factors Economic factors also influence a person's willingness to remain at status quo. A new role may bring in a decrease in current and future emoluments which is never welcome. In such a scenario, it is common to go slow and delay so as to "drag it on" or till the initiative dies.

In other cases, the market situation in terms of other avenues outside of the organization may make a difference. People who may be placed well in terms of other opportunities may put up an open resistance as compared to people with a lower chance.

Fitment Factors Most employees look for congruence between their perceived and actual capabilities, current roles, aspirations, and future roles. It is important to realize that there is often a gap between the manager's assessment of current and future roles as compared to that of an employee. A software analyst may not deem himself fit for a leadership position while his manager may find it a perfect fit.

Fatigue Factors The fact that 70 % of change initiatives meet little success pumps in an innate skepticism in employees about the change initiative being yet another initiative that will drain energy yet bring in paltry results.

Some of the ways to deal with these individual factors are listed below:

– Create an environment of trust and honesty.

- Sometimes it is best to suggest yet allow freedom for people to choose new roles. These roles can be advertised and employees can apply for the same. Make it clear that application does not guarantee selection to a particular role.
- Be swift with exits as the rumor mills run overtime on them.
- If salaries need to be slashed, do it across cadres and ranks.
- Enable people in their new roles by providing opportunities to upgrade their skills.
- Communicate through every possible avenue about the intent of the change effort.
- Try to find avenues to have fun through the tiring schedules and keep up the spirits.
- Provide opportunity for employees for individual support as and when they feel the need of the same.
- Involve employees to the extent possible. Remember that many people find such initiatives so overwhelming that involving everyone can turn to be counterproductive. This does not mean that they should not be informed or active feedback should not be taken.

6.7.2 Dealing with Resistance at Organizational Level

At the organizational level, resistance often manifests itself in the form of unions. In other cases, it can occur on the basis of divisions or departments. The impact of change on the organization structure and thereby the associated ranks, power centers, etc., can stir up a mighty resistance which on the surface may be concealed. Employees tend to look up to their union leaders/division heads/managers to show the path to be taken.

The division leaders, managers, and union leaders should be convinced and taken along. Their concerns should be taken cognizance of and should be addressed. After all, they represent the employees and their concerns would be representative of employees. In cases where the reaction seems to be more of a power struggle than logic, one should not shy away from disciplinary action, rotation, etc. In no case, confusing signals should be allowed to percolate down the organization. It is important to recognize though that people need time to imbibe and internalize change and understand its implications. Some aspects therefore will not require intervention and would settle down on their own without extra effort. Communication is of paramount importance to facilitate the same. Understanding of the purpose of change at the level of leaders is required to align the thoughts of people. If the manager of a particular division is not convinced of the purpose and implication of the change, buy-in would be difficult.

The commitment of management is a powerful way of communicating the underlying importance of a particular change. The leaders should be actively prepared for cascading the message down the line. It cannot be assumed that if they have understood the purpose of the change, they would automatically be able to disseminate it down the line. Helping them with the means to pass on the message of not only the purpose but also the impact of the change is an effective mechanism. They need to be equipped to answer the questions. Answers should be palatable.

Suppose employees who are indifferent to technology are filled up with all the details of the technical solution that ensues the change, they would end up being confused about what is coming. In such a scenario, more than the technical details, an overview of the technical solution, why the solution is required, and what will change for the employees would make more difference. The harbinger of change should spread the notes of positivity.

Signs of resistance can be seen through the hallways, presence in meetings, delay in adoption, and so on. They would also be visible in open forms such as snide remarks, sarcasm, arguments, and sometimes even sabotage. These are not unexpected and should not deter the change managers from pursuing their goals. The trick is to understand where the shoe pinches and try to ease it out as far as possible.

6.8 Role of Change Manager

The traditional role of a change manager fits in the process team as well as the facilitator role in the team structure of the process Tangram. This role is crucial in ensuring the adoption of change and meeting the transformation objectives in time, budget, and quality. The role of the change manager is broad and encompasses an understanding of business processes, technology, systems, people, roles, structures, and program management.

The change manager has the ability to create, plan, and execute change management strategies. He or she is able to address resistance and drive the adoption of change.

The change manager is able to engage across the levels of organization whether it is the CXO level or the people down the lines. He or she is a coach for management facilitating the integration and transition of change into the ways of working. Additionally, support in training, change management assessment, and risk and resistance management is his or her forte. Stakeholder management, coordination, progress monitoring, and control are a must for someone undertaking this role.

The change manager is person who can work in a structured manner despite ambiguity in an environment. Exceptional verbal and written skills along with the ability to articulate are required to mobilize people towards the change objective. Flexibility, tenacity, and perseverance are required along with good knowledge of project and program management methodologies to work effectively. The change manager is experienced in carrying out large-scale change management initiatives.

6.9 Change Agent

Change agents are the extended arms of the transformation team. These form a force which does not have a formal form and setup, however, is a brigade that makes a big difference. These could be employees across the ranks and cadres who share the goals of the change and are willing to walk the extra mile.

Change agents are among the visible early adopters of the change and are not a part of the nominated change team but participate in the change out of choice and interest. They seem to be the antidote to the resisting forces prevailing in the organization.

These agents remain in the organization even when the change team is disbanded. They facilitate in institutionalizing the change not because of personal incentives but primarily because they believe in "the change" and its associated benefits.

Being a change agent is not anybody's cup of tea, as this category has to be the smug contented type who are not intimidated if people suspect them to be the "management's men." They just get along with anyone and everyone and are secretly admired by many.

Change agents have an understanding of what drives the business and have an aptitude of building up the momentum. They can see the opportunities and threats. They are trusted by the employees who reach out to them for understanding the "personal impact" of change. By virtue of their knowledge and the trust they create, change agents are very powerful in spreading the message of change.

6.10 Managing and Sustaining Change

Change should not be underestimated as it is a tedious, time-consuming, and continuously evolving proposition. The planning for change should be realistic and practical. A lot of commitment from leaders and the teams is required to sustain a change effort.

No change can happen without experiencing resistance. Change causes discomfort and collective wisdom helps in overcoming about individual and organizational resistance. Emotion and attachment to current ways of working often raise barriers of change.

The vision for change should be aligned with stakeholders and should be clearly articulated. The change team has to be available and accessible to employees. The core values of the organization should be taken into consideration while articulating the vision.

Communication is the key to be able to reach out to people, to listen to their concerns, and to ensure their participation. Communication is two way and involves observing and listening to verbal and nonverbal communication. It is about informing people and allaying their fears of the unknown. It is about having a perspective that is focused on the objective and is not directed personally to any particular individual.

Change will involve laying out bridges to connect to people and get them to buy in. Depending on the type of work, the needs and requirements may differ. The needs of the workers in a car manufacturing facility will differ from the needs of engineers in a software development unit. What appeals to one may not appeal to another. The measures to achieve an alliance with people are to be customized and tailor made to suit the requirement.

Employees are not motivated by rewards alone. A lot of other factors such as understanding, empathy, and recognition should be built in the change program to spread around good cheer and motivation. Having a sense of fun and enjoyment and starting with a clean slate facilitate the change effort.

Seeing is believing; when people see for themselves that change is reaping benefits, resistance decreases and involvement increases. Deploy metrics to track and showcase the benefits of change. Continue to innovate and evolve through the change. Through the change, retain the essence of the organization but add new flavors.

The attitudes and behavior of employees can be an enabler as well as a disabler, depending upon which way they move. The outcome of a change initiative is influenced by perception of the employees on the benefits of change. These benefits of change can be positioned from an outside-in or inside-out perspective. A hotel may want to transform itself to provide unparalleled service (inside out) or do the same thing to beat the competition head on (outside in). There should be a sense of honesty in the intent and plan of execution for people to buy in. For people to believe and feel motivated, the value of a positive scenario may be higher, though establishing urgency may be easier for a negative scenario. Once people participate along the change, there is some sense of commitment towards a cause. Participation facilitates engagement and adds to motivation to achieve. Coaching and on-the-job trainings, workshops, and open houses are all mechanisms to elicit participation and retention of the transformed ways of working.

In cases where automation is part of transformation, it should be utilized to track progress and to ensure that people remain at transformed levels. If at the time of implementation it is observed that despite all efforts the desired results are not coming in, it is time to take a deep dive to unearth the real obstacles.

When senior executives, sponsors, and change team take effort to visibly committing themselves, they pass on the message of change to the employees.

Semicron has now carefully drawn its change management plan as given below:

6.10.1 Context

Semicron will make foundry its core business while the vertical facilities will continue to exist for at least 5 years. As a wafer foundry, it will target high-reliability applications across industries. It will provide a testing facility with desired service levels to provide optimal benefit to design houses (Fig. 6.7).

Besides a tie-up with design houses, extensive tie-up with material suppliers will enable cost-effective, high-quality, big-volume manufacturing.

6.10.2 Offerings

- Digital catalog.
- Flawless foundry services.
- New process capabilities.
- Process platform specifications.
- Testing services.
- Technical support and reduced time to market by anticipating demands and preparing for demand peaks.
- Alliances for research and development.

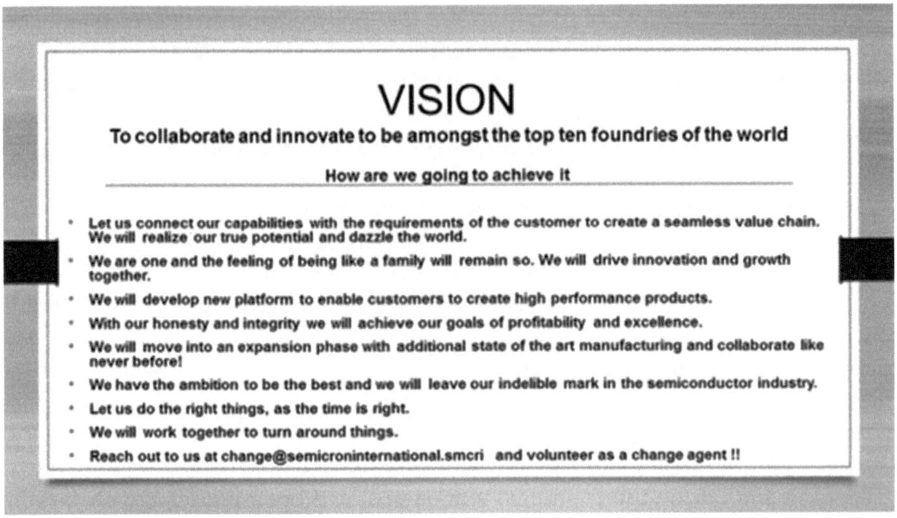

Fig. 6.7 Semicron's vision

- Develop an extensive portfolio of libraries for customers and offerings on third-party libraries as well. Together these facilitate the development of new designs on advanced process platforms.
- Build long-term relationships with customers and align Semicron's growth with the growth of their customers.

6.10.3 Timeline

Two foundries will be set up in a phased manner taking around 18 months each. This will result in addition of 800+ permanent staff. Processes would have to be redesigned to optimally utilize the new facilities.

6.10.4 Process

The interfaces between the following divisions would be (re)defined:

Sales and distribution to design houses: Sales and distribution would have to realign their functioning as now they would have customers with different requirements. Earlier, Semicron was only selling products designed and fabricated by them. Now they will fabricate products designed by design houses. The sales force would have to significantly upgrade their knowledge to understand the language of customers.

Sales and distribution (S&D) to economic interface collaboration and design (EICD): EICD is the new department that has been created. This department will not only design Semicron products but will interface with the design houses to operationalize the implementation of their designs through Semicron foundry services. S&D will benefit from their knowledge when closing deals and customer management.

Sales and distribution to operations: S&D would constantly interact with operations to get real-time information on the status. Certain items such as lead-time information, prototype development, and percentage completion would be updated on a regular basis and made available online. Distribution of finished products would be tracked through workflow to optimize delivery times.

EICD to operations and design houses: With their deep knowledge of design engineering, EICD will be ideally placed in understanding customer requirements and ensuring their delivery. Clearly, laid-down processes for prototype development and approval, change management, acceptance of products, incident management, and root cause analysis would need to be established.

Operations to P&O: Operations will scale up and down its temporary staff as per demand. In order to ensure the same, operational level agreements would have to be inked between operations and P&O to provide the timely information on the requirement of resources. Similarly, learning and development needs would also be an important point for consideration to ensure that the talent and skills are honed, retained, and developed. For new hiring, P&O will facilitate their coming up to productive levels in a short span of time.

Manufacturing engineering to internal and external clients: The design engineering, which is now a part of EICD, will be treated like an internal customer, while design houses will be external customers. Operational level agreements would have to be inked to ensure that business as usual can continue without disruption for the existing facility.

6.10.5 Change Team

Semicron is not a very big organization. All the department heads will be a part of the change advisory board which will review the progress of the change program on a regular basis. Ron will be the sponsor. The change program will involve ample automation.

All the nominated heads have been asked to free up some of their best resources, initially for 50 % of the time and subsequently full time to be a part of the change team. Department heads have been asked to delegate part of their work, so that they can free up time for the change program.

A senior change consultant has been hired to guide Semicron through the change program. He will also function as the change manager. He understands how the program will lead to change in culture as the current staff will have to embrace new people and new thoughts. They will have to believe in the segregation of work beyond their own facilities. Teams would have to wipe out history and start looking afresh to the forward outlook of collaboration. He knows that resistance would have to be surfaced to manage it properly. Being in this profession for a long time, he knows that conflicts would have to be resolved, fears would have to be allayed, and focus would have to be maintained before any results would start coming in.

A senior process consultant from the quality team has been freed up as well to (re)design and facilitate the deployment of processes. The movement of pure design engineering out of Semicron will take a while, and the new process would not be streamlined in a day. It will take various iterations before the final shape arrives.

As per requirement, more resources can be pulled out from mainstream to support the change program. The main focus is to get as many volunteers as possible as change agents to provide additional support and to galvanize the people on the floor to make the change program a success.

Ron has had a few coffee meetings with John, the design engineering head. John is concerned that staff engaged in the design side may feel sidelined and could lead to the formation of formal and informal groups. He feels that the processes would have to be aligned/defined to fit the new scenario. John has been assured that he and his department should in no way feel insecure as they have a chance to move to a strategic role. John has decided that he will support the initiative, and 3 years down the line, when the change is fully implemented, he will decide on his future plans.

Agnes, the P&O head, has been asked to look for a new operations head at the earliest. Besides this, she has also been asked to look after the communications, through the span of the change program.

Oscar, the S&D head, has been entrusted with the responsibility that these changes do not have any adverse effect on the existing customers of the vertical facility. He needs to scout for new customers as Semicron gears up to enter a new domain. A tie-up would have to be done with fabless customers which follow design best practices, so that Semicron can cater to multiple fabless customers and optimally utilize its capacity.

Peter, the head of finance, has agreed to release funds once the program is approved. He has even provided an internal cost center for the pre-study, required to prepare for the change program. To fund the cost of new foundries, Semicron will be going to the market which is on a bullish run at the moment. This way, his current facilities would continue to work efficiently and avoid additional financial burden. True to his profession, he is resolved to ensure that the financials do not take a hit while other things happen at Semicron.

Semicron's typical family-oriented setup and style of management is set to change. With plans of expansion and greater interaction with design houses, it would need to move to a more market-oriented style of functioning. He has decided to vest more decision-making authority in his subordinates to allow them to swiftly react to market demands.

Ron has a passion for operations and has promised the operations team that he is there for them. Though it may feel a little distant, he is not far away.

Armed with his understanding of the various change models, he hopes that he and his organization will be able to achieve its goal and capture a substantial market share.

Fig. 6.8 Change

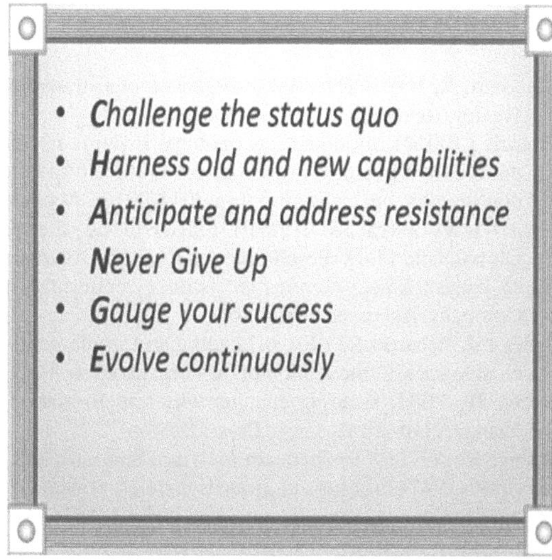

6.10.6 Communication

Visual cues of change such as posters, slogans, and images make people mentally attached to the change story. A series of sessions and meetings have been planned to inform people and to involve and engage them. If the staff will not be behind the change, chances of making a successful transition to the next level would be considerably low. The team needs to understand why the shift to a foundry setup is required and the difference it will make to them. A campaign has been planned to reassure the teams that objectives of change are going to benefit everyone.

If employees, especially from the design engineering team, would like to change their current roles, opportunity would be provided to look for an appropriate fitment. Positions would be advertised and employees would be eligible to apply against them.

Mailers would be sent out on a regular basis to update and reiterate on the change program and Semicron will have to mobilize the power of both formal and informal organizations to mobilize people and maximize the benefits of change.

6.10.7 Celebrations

The change manager is clear that the program would have to be given structure around milestones. Achievement of milestones would be celebrated to fill employees with enthusiasm. Individuals who make excellent contributions would be rewarded and recognized. These will not necessarily be people from the change team but could be the change agents or for that matter employees who make a noteworthy contribution.

Ron has thought of an acronym which he plans to put on a wall in his room (Fig. 6.8).

References

Beckhard R, Harris RT (1987) Organizational transitions: managing complex change. Addison-Wesley, Reading

Dorsch J (2014) Solid state technology, insights for electronics manufacturing, SEMI forecasts double-digit business growth in 2014, 2015. http://electroiq.com/blog/2014/07/semi-forecasts-double-digit-business-growthin-2014-2015/. Accessed 1 Aug 2014

http://www.cata.ca/files/PDF/Resource_Centres/hightech/reports/indepstudies/GlobalizationTaiwaneseSemiconductor.pdf. Accessed 1 Aug 2014

http://www.mckinsey.com/insights/strategy/enduring_ideas_the_7-s_framework, Mckinsey & Company. Accessed 1 Aug 2014

Jones DJ, Recardo RJ (2013) Leading and implementing business change management: making change stick in the contemporary organization. Routledge, Abingdon

Kotter JP (2007) Leading change: why transformation efforts fail, Harvard business review on change. Harvard Business Press, Boston

Kübler-Ross E (1969) On death & dying. Simon & Schuster/Touchstone, New York

Lewin K (1947) Frontiers in group dynamics: concept, method and reality in social science; social equilibria and social change. Hum Relat 1(2):143–153

Nadler DA, Tushman MA (1982) A model for diagnosing organizational behavior: applying a congruence perspective. In: Nadler DA, Tushman MA, Hatvany NG (eds) Managing organizations, readings and cases. Little Brown and Company, Boston

7 Managed Services: A Case of Business Process Transformation?

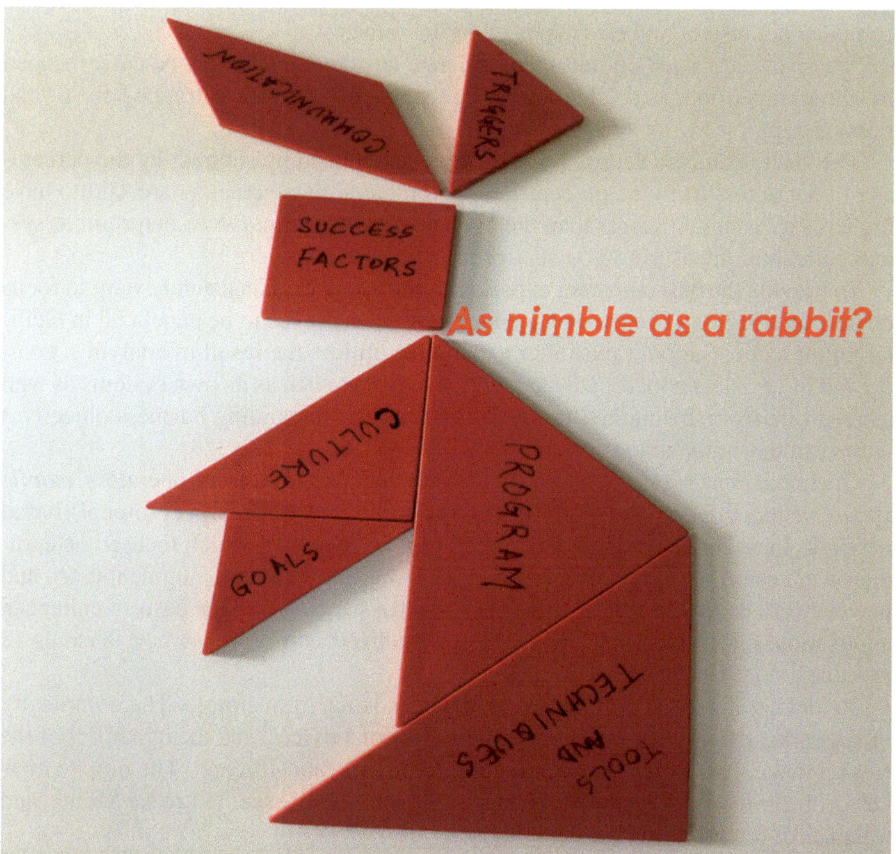

C. Sharma, *Business Process Transformation*, Management for Professionals,
DOI 10.1007/978-81-322-2349-8_7

7.1 Managed Services in Telecom

Managed services, which started with the information and technology sector, has spread its wings across industries. Today, telecom is one of the key sectors where managed services has evolved, witnessing a shift from traditional business models and enabling the operator to focus on other core areas. Managed services now also involves outsourcing of network, which was once considered a core business area.

The reshaping of roles and functions has brought about a paradigm shift in the way the given industry functions, thereby creating new business opportunities, while simultaneously serving the customer in the fastest and simplest way possible.

Operators focus more and more towards the voice of the customer. The "Net Promoter Score" is measured based on the analysis of the promoters, the "passives," and the "detractors" – which is increasingly utilized to measure customer loyalty.

"Promoters" are loyal enthusiastic customers who not only keep buying from a company but also urge their friends to do the same.

"Passives" are satisfied but unenthusiastic customers, who can be easily wooed by the competition, and "detractors" are unhappy customers trapped in a "bad relationship."

The "Net Promoter Score" is the difference obtained by subtracting the percentage of detractors from the percentage of promoters. Value creators are said to have higher Net Promoter Scores than the average company http://www.netpromotersystem.com/about/measuring-your-net-promoter-score.aspx.

To provide the best customer experience, the operators consistently want to focus on new offerings, and hence managed services have proved to be beneficial in facilitating the same. Superior customer experience utilizes the result of analytics, coming out of vast data pool drawn from various sources such as its own systems as well as feedback from the market. Every effort goes into integrating business objectives with customer satisfaction.

Operators continuously combat challenges posed by traditional operators, *mobile virtual network operators* (MVNOs), and new entrants. IP (Internet protocol)-based networks have challenged the older paradigms of operators, which focused on earning revenues on the basis of optimizing existing infrastructure, augmentation, and new network deployment. The differentiation has happened on the basis of enhanced application services, which are more personalized and serve as new sources of revenue.

Achieving this even with managed services is far from simple. The complexity of networks, the number of devices, the variety of services, and the dynamics of the market make it necessary for the operator to be agile and efficient. The time to market of a service is expected to be short; the service is expected to be secure and reliable for it to be ready for the end user.

The end users could be in a business-to-business (B2B) or business-to-customer (B2C) setup. All this comes at a cost. Thus, operators naturally require a transformation proposition to be able to offer such services, while still retaining their viability.

Managed service providers (MSPs), i.e., vendors, may have their own specific requirements, when it comes to managed services. With its roots in the IT industry, there are some areas that have been considered essential.

They are:

- Goals and objectives of the MSP
- Professional services automation tools
- Remote monitoring and management tools
- Financial tools and processes and procedures (Palachuk 2013)

Goals and objectives of the vendor are based on the mission and vision of the vendor. They act as guiding factors in their pursuit of offering services.

Professional services automation tools are necessary for the MSP to run its own functions, such as handling service requests, recording billable hours, etc.

Remote monitoring and management tools enable the vendor to reach out to the operator's network to deliver required services.

Financial tools are required to keep control over profitability.

Processes and procedures ensure that the service delivery is not person dependent and consistently meets operator's requirement.

In order to show the operator the plethora of possibilities, the MSPs should have a service catalog ready that fulfills generic as well as the specific requirements. Service catalogs can be based on business models.

7.1.1 Business Models

There are several business models that can be worked upon. Some of them are listed below:

- *Strategic Outsourcing* – This is a combination of strategic and business consulting. It involves activities across the network, ranging from planning and design, deployment, configuration, management and its network monitoring, and life-cycle maintenance.
- *Selective Outsourcing* – In this model, only a part of the network is outsourced to an MSP, so as to make it more efficient and effective. For the MSP to be able to fulfill this requirement, it may have to bring in transformational changes in the business process, so that the desired service levels can be achieved at a lower cost. This is beneficial for the operator, as this arrangement can help them achieve world-class processes utilizing vendor know-how and knowledge base, thereby maximizing benefits.

  This is a flexible arrangement where, initially, only a small portion of the network is given out for managed services. Once results are in line with expectations, it may be expanded to other, more elaborate models. Many a time, operators

repeat the cycle of selective outsourcing and then insourcing, again and again, in their search for the most effective and efficient business processes.
- *Managed and Hosted Applications* – In this arrangement, network-based services are hosted at the MSP site or are colocated/located at the customer premises. This arrangement enables the operators to offer application-based services at a rapid speed, without compromising on performance. At the same time, the reliability across legacy as well as state-of-the-art systems and devices is maintained. It also reduces the time to market and provides opportunities for new sources of revenue.

Certain aspects that may be considered before finalizing the managed and hosted application's master service agreement are:

- Who owns the hardware and the assets?
- Who is responsible for monitoring the hardware?
- Who is responsible for upgrades?
- Should the hardware be exclusively used for particular applications, or can it be shared across applications?
- Who takes responsibility of application life-cycle management?
- What kind of facilities are to be made available to the operator to monitor the quality of service delivered? In some cases, it may go to the extent of installation of remote cameras which enable the operator to monitor the alarms, should they wish to do so.

- *Operational Outsourcing* – This involves end-to-end network management by the MSP, to ensure seamless functioning of varied network elements. The endeavor is to make sure that the performance parameters are met at all levels and under all conditions. This includes redundancies at node level, at transport level, and even at resource management level. To achieve this, extensive monitoring and proactive maintenance are required.
- *Managed Capacity* – This arrangement involves planning and design, augmentation, and new rollout of network by the MSP. Besides this, it also involves traffic reshaping. As an example, a node that serves New York may be actually serviced through Newark. Depending on the scope, the MSP may be actively remote monitoring the utilization of the hardware, to prevent any kind of choking at any interface.
- *Build Model* – In this model, the operator is involved in the complete planning and design of the network, while the vendor not only provides the equipment but also deploys the same.
- *Time and Material (Labor Arbitrage)* – In this model, the operator takes advantage of lower wage rates in outsourcing locations, such as India. Very often, this happens via an arrangement with an onshore company, who has an offshore setup in the outsourcing location.

7.1.2 Pricing Models

These business models are backed by a variety of pricing models (http://blog.spc-intl.com/different-managed-services-pricing-models/).

- *Value pricing model*
  In the value pricing model, the focus is on "potential savings." The client (operator) gets an understanding of the saving possibilities, and the service provider (MSP), in turn, is able to maximize the return on the services offered. The pricing is a monthly, flat fee for agreed service components.
- *Per-device pricing model*
  When the pricing proposition is tilted towards price, rather than the value delivered, it makes sense to create a pricing model that offers device-based pricing. In simple words, it is a predecided, flat fee for each type of device supported by the managed service provider in the client environment.
- *Tiered pricing model*
  In this pricing model, tiers or levels of service offerings are available. Different names associated with good, better, or best levels of services are on the service catalog. With each level, there is a list of services which are offered as a "bundle" or package for a fixed price. The price is commensurate to the service offered. Services which are required by the customer, but are not covered by the tiered model, are handled as an add-on, through a different pricing model such as the a la carte model.
- *"Pick 5" pricing model*
  This pricing model allows the operator to choose a specific number of services, typically 5, from the tiered model. As an example, if there are 9 services available in each tier (good, better, best), then the client can pick up any 5 from any of the chosen tiers. The master service agreement is then built around that.
- This model offers flexibility, in terms of being a fit between what a client requires and the readily available services that the MSP can offer.
- *À la carte pricing model*
  This is a time-consuming model to implement, wherein the client chooses the requisite services from a complete service catalog offered by the service provider. This model also runs the risk of incorrect service selection. Unless the client knows exactly what they want, they may end up choosing services they may not really require and miss out on other important services. The a la carte nature implies that the master service agreement is also tailor made and hence costs time to negotiate and finalize.
- *Monitoring-only pricing model*
  This pricing model offers services which cover the monitoring of the network and alerting/creating tickets for the in-house or other managed service provider teams. This type of service stands on the lowest rung of the complexity scale, yet it could be a stepping stone for a more comprehensive association with the client in future.

7.1.3 Managed Service Offerings

A competent MSP will present itself in the market, well armed with a bouquet of services and a taut business plan that will bring in long-term partnerships and collaborations. It entails various steps crucial to ensure success.

For an MSP to offer managed services, the following steps are necessary:

- Formalize the goals and line of business.
- Categorize the service(s), which are often termed as "offerings."
- Map services to pricing model(s).
- Garner the know-how, resources, and tools to deliver the services.
- Close the master service agreement (MSA).
- Transition the services, tools, platforms, etc., to the MSP.
- Transform (if applicable).
- Create new opportunities for services. These services are delivered as add-on sales within an existing master service agreement or under a new contract.
- Deliver agreed services till end of contract. The services may continue or be amended if contract is renewed.

An overview of offerings from some of the leading telecom managed service providers is shown in Fig. 7.1.

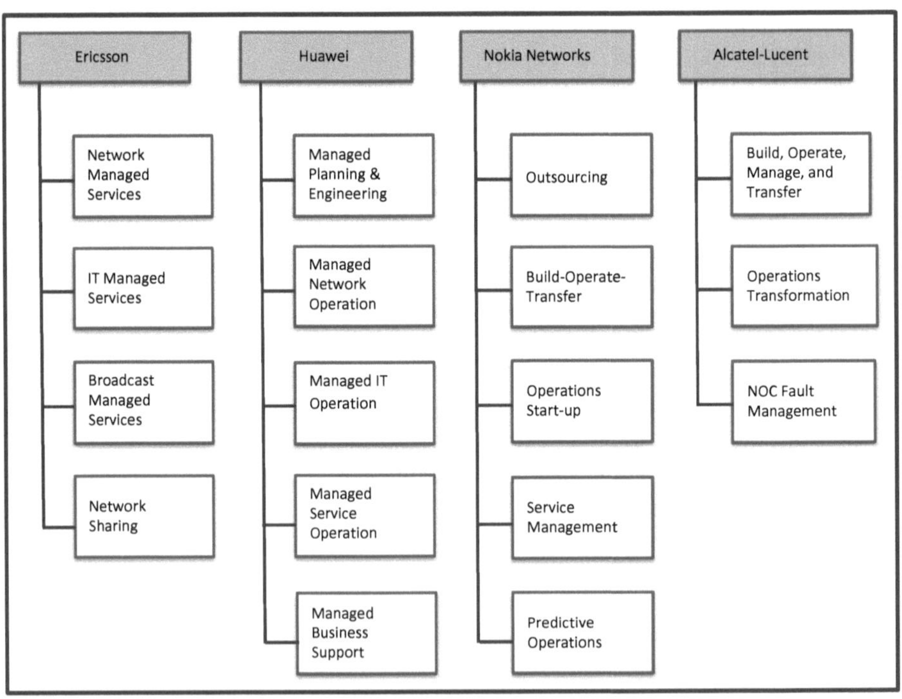

Fig. 7.1 Overview of managed service offerings

Disclaimer Scope can vary from the understanding of the content available on their official Websites (available in References section), accessed on 28 Oct 2014. There are other MSPs in the market which provide customized scope and offerings.

The details of managed service offerings of these four vendors along with their benefits, as proposed by them, are listed below (Table 7.1).

It is clear from the table above that there are many variations available, ranging from end-to-end network operations management and transformation to startup services. The vendors do not explicitly position themselves in supporting mobile-based applications and machine-to-machine-based innovation and support. However, in the coming times with a vibrant market scenario, this positioning may be more visible.

Since the a la carte offer is always possible to suit the service provider's requirement, it is actually the apt midway choice between the requirement of the operator and the vendor offerings. This makes managed services a viable and successful proposition.

Today managed services has moved on, from offering efficiency-centric solutions to customer-centric, differentiating solutions. One of the very important levers to managed services is information technology. In a scenario of changing roles, the MSP has become increasingly dependent on IT for more and more solutions and services.

7.1.4 Role of Information Technology

Information technology (IT) has started to play a very important role in telecom managed services. It is no longer just a support function but an integral part of core value proposition and transformation. So far, information technology has essentially been an enabler, which facilitates the telecom operator by providing tools and technology. With more and more telecom offerings expected to be on the creative side, IT now also provides analytical abilities which can pinpoint the aspects to be leveraged and how they can be improved.

In order to reap the true benefits of IT, the IT team should be multidisciplinary and should have a good understanding of how the telecom operators run their business. It should be able to gauge the operator's needs and challenges well in advance, in order to design apt solutions.

When the IT department is agile and responsive to the operator's requirements, it is able to provide critical service delivery and stay ahead in the game. It also leverages its own position as a market leader.

There are many offerings in various domains that rely strongly on IT. These are referred to mobile value-added-services (MVAS).

Table 7.1 Comparison of managed services offerings

Company name	Offerings	Description	Proposed benefits
Ericsson (http://www.ericsson.com/ourportfolio/services/managed-services-1)	Network managed services	Day-to-day operation and management of the entire network infrastructure	Network managed services can enable achieving desired quality at a foreseeable cost
		Management of end-customer problems escalated from your customer care function	By letting Ericsson handle the network operation, the operator can focus on business strategy, services, and customers
		Corrective and preventive field maintenance	With a focus on improving operational efficiency, network quality, and asset utilization, Ericsson can help in improving profitability and customer experience
		Optimization of systems and services to ensure performance is maintained at or above agreed quality levels	
		Management of changes to the network	
		Installation and upgrades of equipment	
		Multi-vendor support	
	IT managed services	IT and business operation	IT managed services can enable improved operational efficiency and reduce opex and capex, increasing overall profitability
		Managed cloud services	With a managed service agreement, Ericsson can bring telecom expertise straight to the operator's IT environment, delivering the highest possible reliability and availability
			Ericsson's methods embrace multi-vendor environments, providing the flexibility to develop and deploy services and infrastructure using any chosen vendor

	Broadcast managed services	Responsibility for technical platforms and operational services related to the content management, playout, and service provisioning of a broadcaster's business, like content logistics, library management, quality control, playout services, WebTV, and mobile services	When broadcasters are facing increasing competition and need to focus on customers and content, Ericsson can manage the day-to-day operations, so the broadcaster can devote attention to customers, program and content acquisition, and strategic planning
			Through economies of scale, Ericsson can create cost efficiencies and at the same time improve quality of the operations
			Partnering with Ericsson enables broadcaster to meet the increasing commercial and technological complexity and competition in the TV market
	Network sharing	Roaming, site sharing, and active network sharing	Network sharing brings financial benefits such as cash release from existing assets and cash flow improvements by linking costs to revenues. It also brings operational benefits in the form of increased specialization and flexibility, reduced technology risk, and reduced barriers related to culture and governance
		Wholesale network sharing for RAN, backhaul, and core networks	
		Small cell capacity/sharing offering connected venue	
		Managed rural coverage	
Huawei (http://www.huawei.com/en/services/hw-u_256556.htm)	Managed planning and engineering	Planning and design: customized network and service planning and service design to help operators achieve business objectives. This solution takes into consideration factors such as technical standards, management process, ROI, etc.	Enable operators to share Huawei's professional expertise and best global practice to reduce service innovation cost and increase network quality competitiveness
		Engineering management: includes network design management, project group management, acceptance, and testing service. This solution helps the client to achieve simplified operation through establishing a service-centric end-to-end organization and optimizing process to accelerate supply and service commercialization	Customized network planning and spare parts management solution to accelerate time to market
			Primer integration as the only customer access point to reduce opex
	Managed network operation	Network operations center (NOC)	Provide unified multi-vendor, multi-technology management and reduce complexity

(continued)

Table 7.1 (continued)

Company name	Offerings	Description	Proposed benefits
		Provide 7*24 remote network assurances for multi-vendor network and enable secure and smooth network operations for high performance and efficiency	Support rapid deployment of new technologies (MBB, FBB, FMC) enabling fast time to market
		NOC provides service fulfillment and remote complaint handling as well; thus it helps operators to reduce fulfillment duration and improve complaint handling efficiency	Improve network quality and operation efficiency
		Field maintenance	Enhance enterprise customer satisfaction
		Manage corrective maintenance, preventive maintenance, and planned maintenance tasks of sites and transmission network, enabling intelligent, visible, and efficient field operations	
		Network performance management	
		Proactively monitor, diagnose, and manage multi-vendor network performance and capacity. This will exploit the potential network performance and assure higher network resource utilization	
		Spare parts management	
		Provide complete professional services of integrated service delivery management, spare parts supply, planning, storage and warehousing, logistics, and spare parts repair. By effectively managing multiple vendors, technologies, and networks, the Huawei spare parts service eliminates the need for operator investment, reduces opex and operational risks	
		Enterprise account management	

		Provide dedicated enterprise customer assurance through technical hotline, proactive monitoring, remote and on-site problem handling, solution design, and service fulfillment. This helps to improve enterprise customer satisfaction	
		Home connect management	
		Provide on-site services including installation, relocation, and maintenance of fixed network last mile. This enables efficient on-site services and customer satisfaction enhancement	
	Managed IT operation	Infrastructure management: includes cloud resource management, IT infrastructure management, and data center facility management. As an enabler, E-iNOC provides automated cloud service provisioning, efficient cloud resource scheduling, and unified O&M management	Improve operational efficiency and quality
		Application management: offers a full range of application management services, including application operations and application development from design to testing. It helps operators to free up resources, focus on core business, and respond quickly to the competitive telecom markets	Maximize resource utilization and improve ROI
		E2E service management: based on eTOM/ITIL and our best practices, Huawei has developed an IT and CT converged operations model which provides a single point of contact for operators and an end-to-end service assurance across IT and CT	Support cloud business development
			End-to-end service assurance
			Reduce risk and address technology evolution challenges

(continued)

Table 7.1 (continued)

Company name	Offerings	Description	Proposed benefits
	Managed service operation	Complaints handling: effectively manage customer complaints on service issues leveraging on rich experience in service data analysis and problem processing method	Fast service problem demarcation and closed-loop operations
		Service quality monitoring: proactively identify service performance problem through service quality monitoring and reporting	Improved service quality through proactive monitoring and management
		Service analysis and demarcation: through a service quality problem database and analysis platform/tools, we realize fast service quality problem demarcation and drive the resolution of service problems including voice service and data services like Web and streaming	Improved end user experience and reduced churn
		Valued customer care: proactive service quality management for valued customer especially for VIP customer and enterprise	
		Recommendation and readiness support: provide service development recommendation and service readiness suggestion	
		Huawei is now the leading managed service provider with its own service operations center (SOC) and provides service-oriented platform and processes, with per-service per-user (PSPU) capability on service quality management. We utilize our matured methodologies to help operators transform to service-centric operations, create operation synergy by SOC and NOC closed-loop operations, and increase overall customer satisfaction	

	Managed business support	CP/SP aggregation: our unified platform and automated tools help operators to introduce global CP/SPs through faster contracting, onboarding, and performance management. Huawei has partnered with 500+ content and service providers to support operator's growth. Huawei's standardized processes and agreements with these providers enable operators to roll out services faster and more efficiently. Our SDP ensures services operate as designed with no revenue leakage	Faster CP/SP aggregation with and reduce TTM
		Advanced VAS business operations: help operators to enhance revenue by focusing on the full-cycle business management which covers business consulting, product design, and operations by leveraging on Huawei's global practice and experience. Utilizing user behavior insights through data mining and analysis, operators can do more personalized marketing and brand enhancement	Improve VAS operational efficiency by leveraging on our professional business platform and infrastructure
		VAS hosting services: Huawei's hosting service help operators bring new services to their end users quickly and cost-effectively. It offers a simplified business model that allows operators to test new services or host existing value-added services (VAS) with a lower cost entry and reduced risk. Using Huawei's hosted service delivery platform, operators have reduced the time to launch new services and most importantly increase ARPU	Enhance revenue through segment marketing enablement, service penetration increase, and customer base growth Flexible business model and reduced business risk

(continued)

Table 7.1 (continued)

Company name	Offerings	Description	Proposed benefits
Nokia Networks (http://networks.nokia.com/portfolio/services/professional-services/managed-services)	Outsourcing	Enabling you to outsource all or part of your network-related activities	Freeing you to focus on differentiating activities
		Responsibility for providing high-quality and efficient network-related services	Improved operational efficiency and EBITDA
		Ensures efficient service delivery through economies of scale, centralized and automated processes, and globally tested, shared best practices that only a global service organization can deliver	Higher-quality services and operations
			Better management of technology and operational complexity
			Efficient use of capex
			Visible and predictable opex
			Single point of contact for multi-vendor operations
	Build-operate-transfer	Service products from across the project life cycle, such as design services, build services (network implementation and operations setup), operations services, the transfer of operations to you (or we could continue operations in a managed service approach), and related project management and consultancy services	BOT ensures faster time-to-market, with guaranteed service performance from day one. At the same time, it builds operation and maintenance competencies within your organization
		Delivers ongoing services that are designed to develop and grow your competence. Together, these services support an effective handover of network operations and optimization from us to you	
	Operations startup	Introducing new technologies swiftly and without problems. Our services support your operational team in understanding and implementing new technologies	Three key benefits of our operations startup solution are faster time to market, problem-free launches of new services, and competence transfer to your personnel

	Service management	Monitor service performance and make use of all the latest tools to optimize your services	Boost your revenue through increased service usage and improved service quality
		Help in planning, designing, and launching new services quickly and smoothly, so you can offer differentiated services to your customers and develop new revenue streams	Improve your customer experience with excellent service performance
		Design new service launches, looking at the service capability requirements and monitoring their performance	Build stronger customer loyalty with differentiated service offerings
		LTE service management is the latest innovation from our Service Management Capability Center and helps you to ensure excellent quality mobile broadband services running over LTE networks. It reduces restoration time by 21 % and churn by approximately 5 %. Besides LTE, the solution is also available for 2G and 3G networks	Reduce customer care costs by up to 70 %
			Restore service quality by up to 21 % faster and reduce churn by 5 %
			Cover the entire life cycle of mobile broadband services running on the LTE network, including service design, launch, and monitoring
			Gain an integrated view of all services across the evolved packet core (EPC), transmission, and radio networks.
			Improve overall availability, accessibility, retaining ability, and mobility of all services on LTE
	Predictive operations	Based on big data and a self-learning predictive analysis engine, which monitors and correlates a multitude of data including KPIs, KQIs, social media data, weather, location, and CEM data	Get accurate forecasts of network and service degradations up to 48 h before customers are affected with 95 % accuracy
			Improve your overall service quality levels by 15 %
			Significant reduction of customer complaints due to higher overall availability of the network and related services

(continued)

Table 7.1 (continued)

Company name	Offerings	Description	Proposed benefits
Alcatel-Lucent (http://www.alcatel-lucent.com/services/managed-services)	Build, operate, manage, and transfer (BOM/T)	Build: network planning and deployment, which includes business and operations analysis, network design and integration, and planning, as well as deployment packages from the Alcatel-Lucent service suite	Alcatel-Lucent as the single vendor and strategic partner provides this complete solution, leveraging its years of experience, its unique blueprint delivery model, and expertise in networks, operations, and customer experience management
		Operate: operational execution, providing full operations support, billing, fulfillment, assurance, and field support from the Alcatel-Lucent service suite	
		Manage: continued operational execution and business management to meet and exceed customer expectations and delivery of a superior end-user customer experience using Alcatel-Lucent's three-tiered governance model	
		Transfer: transfer back of the operations ownership to the carrier customer at the end of the contract with options to license Alcatel-Lucent intellectual property supporting standard network operations processes and tools	

	Operations transformation	Analyze the customer network and operations using Alcatel-Lucent's consultancy framework	Alcatel-Lucent improves the telecom service provider's network operations efficiencies and quality through transformation to our standard delivery model, also known as the managed service blueprint. Additional benefits include migrating to new technologies and enabling more rapid service introduction on customer networks, leading to an overall TCO reduction while also improving the end-user customer experience
		Identify clear areas of improvement and agree on a operations and technology transformation scope with the customer	
		Move the customer's existing network operations under Alcatel-Lucent control	
		Transform the customer's multi-vendor network operation functions by applying the Alcatel-Lucent standard delivery model	
		Manage, when applicable, the legacy infrastructure and adapt the transformation pace to customer constraints	
		Transfer back the operations ownership to the customer at the end of the contract, with options to license Alcatel-Lucent intellectual property on standard network operations processes and tools	
	NOC fault management	Cost-efficient solution for service providers looking to further decrease operations costs while maintaining network performance. The service is ideal for customers who no longer want to invest capital in their own operations infrastructure	*Reduces operational expenses and risks*
			No need for customer to set up and manage their own 24/7 NOC organization
			Service is provided by standard Alcatel-Lucent toolset (possible interfaces to customer)
			Alcatel-Lucent blueprint delivery model and service suite model provides cost-efficient operations
			Reduces capital expenses
			Have access to a fully established tool infrastructure; there is no need to acquire tools

(continued)

Table 7.1 (continued)

Company name	Offerings	Description	Proposed benefits
			Can take advantage of experienced and competent Alcatel-Lucent staff
			No need to make additional investments with Alcatel-Lucent infrastructure and organizations already in place
			Able to leverage innovative Alcatel-Lucent processes and work methods
			Can remain flexible with a variable cost-structure model
			Reduced time to market
			Significant time-to-market savings by using current Alcatel-Lucent delivery organization and standardized tools platform
			Operational efficiency
			Increased number of filtering and correlation rules by leveraging from experience in similar technology
			Processes and work instructions in place
			Processes and toolset in place
			Continuous measurement of internal network and service performance
			Three-tiered governance method in place
			Customer interfaces are defined according to customer needs and Alcatel-Lucent processes and working methods in the service suite

			Alcatel-Lucent experience in technologies and working methods can be leveraged
			Scalable state-of-the-art OSS platforms
			Engineered to operate with third-party network element management systems (EMS)
			Includes Bell Labs-developed support tools as well as other leading OSS vendor platforms
			Delivers superior end-user customer experience
			Incorporates proven remedy-based ticketing system

7.1.4.1 Mobile Value-Added Services

By penetrating the everyday life of the average consumer, MVAS have become an inherent part of the telecom services provided via smartphones across the globe. It has created a free-market space where the common person can access humongous amounts of data for learning, communicating, and gathering information and even for commerce.

The MSP is touching lives in an everyday manner and simplifying systems for everyone across demographics of age, location, or financial situation.

These services allow operators to add new sources of revenue, which are directly or indirectly paid by the consumer. Some of them are listed below.

Education

Nowadays, mobile networks can allow students to access content and collaborate on the go. They do not have to be necessarily in a classroom to participate in a session. There are a lot of open online schools, which are made available to students at a nominal cost. Such sessions can be attended by students through their mobile phones, which are becoming smarter every day. Ready-made as well as custom-made tutorials for hundreds of subjects, including music and art, are also available for free.

Students can not only avail of the online content, but they can also create and share content in this age of collaboration. E-books and e-tutoring are some other applications in this domain. All of these are already in use, in varying degrees across continents. A working professional, for example, can take a certified online course in management from a university abroad, without having to leave the job or the country.

Financial Sector

The end user, i.e., customer, is no longer dependent on paid professionals for money-related services.

There are lots of possibilities, in what is often termed as M-commerce. Right from transferring funds to authorizing payments, mobiles are making banking facilities available on the screen of smartphones. An intricately designed network, which connects the mobile phone to other services, allows one to consult professionals, pay taxes, and receive confirmations, just with access to a basic Internet connection. Even the customer help desk which had traditionally been available as a voice call has now evolved to a face-to-face conversation through mobiles. Senior citizens for example can pay their electricity or phone bills online and are saved from the cumbersome effort of physically going and queuing up in different departments of organizations.

Governance

These kinds of applications are built around the interaction of citizens with the government. Right from licensing to payment of bills, everything is possible through a click on the mobile. Government agencies have a dedicated response team attending to the same, making processes simpler and faster than ever before. It is common to check the status of one's passport application through mobile applications.

Healthcare

There are many possibilities in the healthcare sector as well. A patient can make an appointment and have a face-to-face conversation with a doctor through a smartphone. Smartphones can either store and forward information to the health center though mobiles or have an interactive session with a doctor. Health-related applications are able to store relevant data of a person's medical records and information coming out of smartphone interactions for future reference. Medical institutions can even send regular reminders for appointments to patients via a preprogrammed SMS.

Energy and Utilities

Networked machines can communicate with each other even without human intervention. Product and usage information can be sent via uplink of data and software update, and equipment monitoring can happen remotely via downlink. This opens up possibilities for continuous monitoring and preventative maintenance. As an example, a machine that reaches a certain threshold and requires attention can send an alarm to the relevant system.

Transport

Today, a large number of people use their smartphone for location information using the global positioning system (GPS). In some cars, there are applications built around the location information, which create a service request if there is a failure in the important parts of the vehicle. In such a situation, the application can guide them to the nearest service center. Fleet management, traffic information, road tolling, and traffic optimization/steering are some other applications.

All this brings in additional responsibilities for the IT team to bring in platforms that are application agnostic and therefore have the capability to support a wide range of services. Security aspects assume greater importance with the risks of tampering, destruction, and theft of information being high in a connected world.

Unauthorized access to the network, spoofing, denial of service, interception of data, and unauthorized usage of data are all real threats that the IT department has to deal with. Therefore, vulnerability assessment and corrective action is a continuous activity that IT needs to perform to support the success of their offerings. A lax approach can not only lead to loss of reputation and revenue but also invite regulatory action and penalties.

7.1.5 Transformation of Telecom Operator TX

The managed service provider is expected to play a vital role in taking over some or most of the operator's functions and ensuring a smooth flow of services for the consumer. It operates in a mutually beneficial way, thereby sustaining the growth of both entities.

Consider the case of telecom X, hereafter called TX, an operator operating in Western Europe, offering mobile and fixed-line telephony. Through this case, light is shed on the factors considered by the operator while evaluating the MSP, role of IT, factors considered by the MSP before getting into a master service agreement, and transition of services.

Further, with reference to TX's case, it is finally evaluated if managed services can be classified as a case of business process transformation.

7.1.5.1 Background

TX's mobile division currently offers services on 2G and 3G. With the decline in user percentage of its 2G services, the network is skewed in favor of 3G services. TX expects its 3G users to continue to increase steadily to 50 % of its total revenue in the coming 2 years. The average revenue per user (ARPU) is currently 30 euros per month, averaged over voice and data usage. The voice ARPU continues to decline while data ARPU is showing a consistent increase.

TX has seen a steady decline in revenue in the last three quarters. The decline is under 5 % per quarter but it is a trend that needs to be reversed. The overall market share in the mobile market is 40 %. TX operates in three market segments: individuals, small and medium businesses, and enterprise customers. All this loosely totals to around three million subscribers, thus having an average monthly revenue of around 90 million euros.

TX wants to roll out a long-term evolution (LTE) standard, as it expects 20 % of its revenue in the coming years to come from LTE. TX is exploring options on how it can achieve this goal, without losing focus on bringing out new offerings. It needs to find newer avenues of revenue which continue to satisfy its customers so that market share can be increased and can offset the reduction in ARPU.

Since the deployment of LTE sites can take a lot of time, managed services seems to be a viable option. TX wants to let a managed service provider handle the operational aspects, while it can focus solely on a service-centric approach.

TX is concerned about the total cost of ownership of the current and proposed network. Although it has provisions for rollout, the operational expenses have been rising. It suffers from the classic situation, where revenues are decreasing, while the cost of running the networks is increasing. At the same time, the demand, especially for data services, is increasing as well. The revenue-to-cost gap needs to decrease for TX to remain viable.

TX has floated a request for proposal (RFP) which lays down the terms and conditions and the requirements that must be fulfilled for the end-to-end management of its network operations and deployment of LTE network. From its current network architecture comprising 2G and 3G, it wants to move on to LTE and eventually to the 5G standard. The current and proposed network architecture[1] is shown in Figs. 7.2 and 7.3, respectively.

---

[1] The current and proposed network diagrams are based on the author's knowledge and understanding of telecom networks.

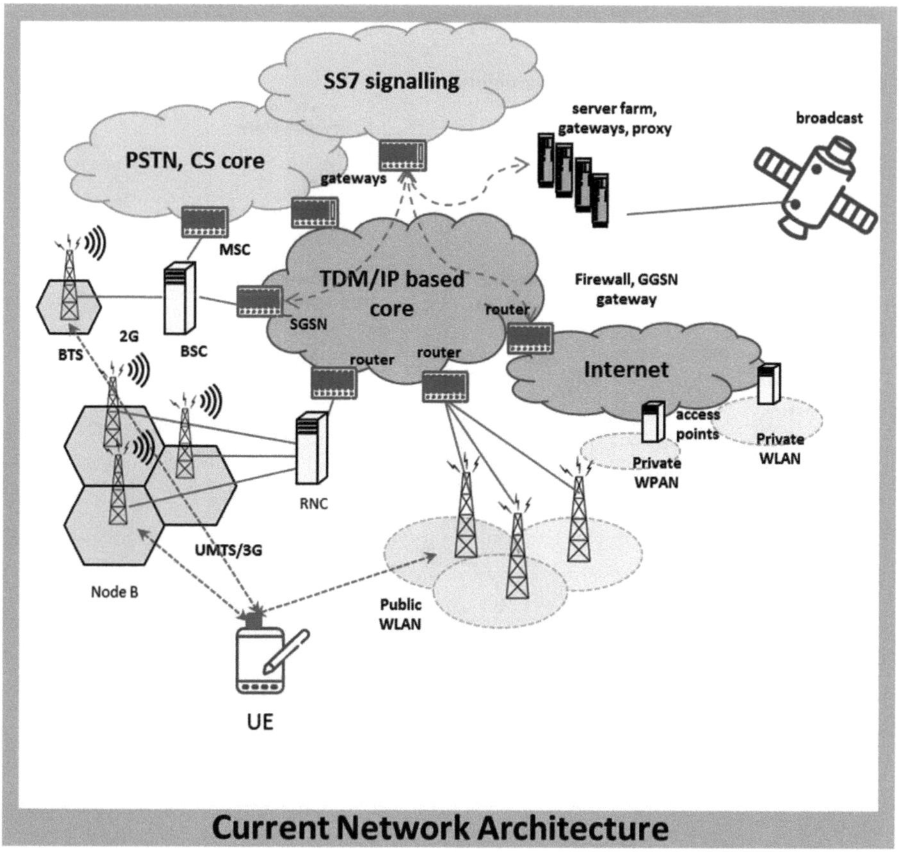

Fig. 7.2 Current network architecture TX

Although the details would have to be further defined, the primary requirement in RAN (radio access network) is to replace the 3G node B network elements with LTE/4G network elements. LTE/4G promises to be a simpler architecture. On the core network side, the entire infrastructure would have to be replaced, as it is an overlay network based on the asynchronous transfer mode (ATM) technology, as compared to the simplified, all-flat Internet protocol (IP) network technology.

While in 3G, there is a distinct equipment for voice and data, and in LTE voice, video and data would run over a common IP network. Radio access network (RAN) backhaul technology would also require an upgrade to a technology such as a carrier Ethernet.

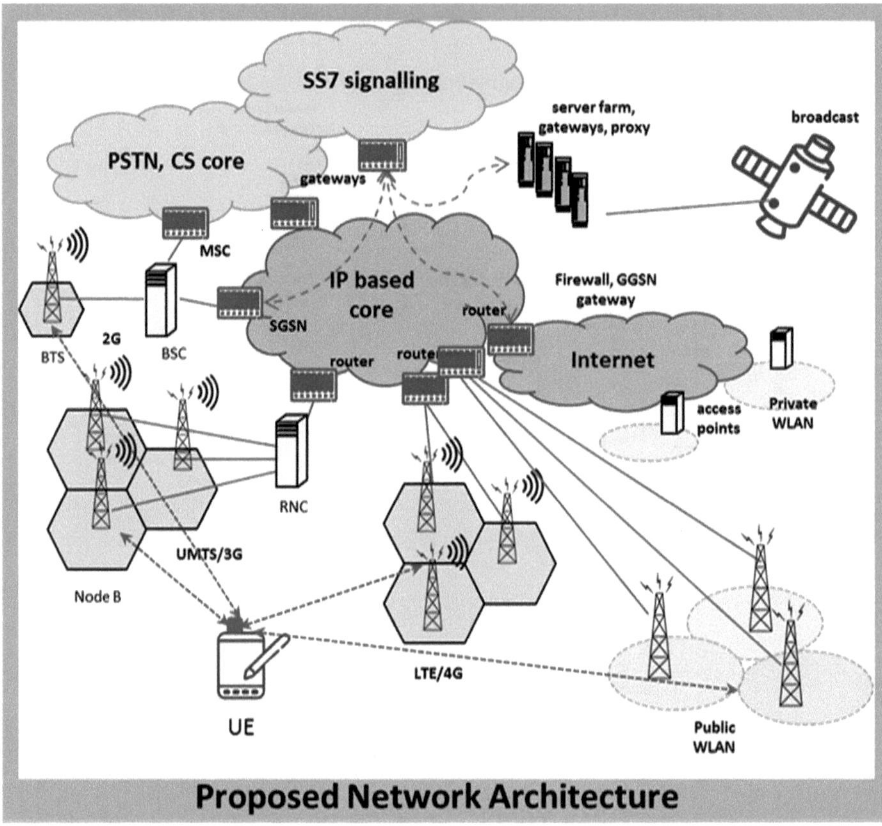

Fig. 7.3 Proposed network architecture TX

7.1.5.2 In-Scope Processes

In a nutshell, substantial changes in the network are required. From a process perspective, the processes shown in Fig. 7.4 fall in the scope of RFP.

7.1.5.3 TX's Vendor Evaluation Criteria

The vendors responding to the RFP will be evaluated by the TX based on the criteria given in Fig. 7.5. Based on these criteria, vendors will be evaluated on a scale of 1–10, and an aggregated result will decide the winner.

Certain criteria will have a higher weightage for the operator and will be given greater importance. Among all the RFPs submitted, the operators may shortlist the top three and then rank them as per the number of criteria they fulfill.

Let's assume vendor Y, hereafter referred to as VY, was chosen as the managed service provider for the network management process.

VY in turn had its own considerations while deciding to go ahead with TX. A successful relationship requires due diligence from the vendor/MSP's perspective. It is as important for the operator/client as for the MSP/vendor to assess if the scope,

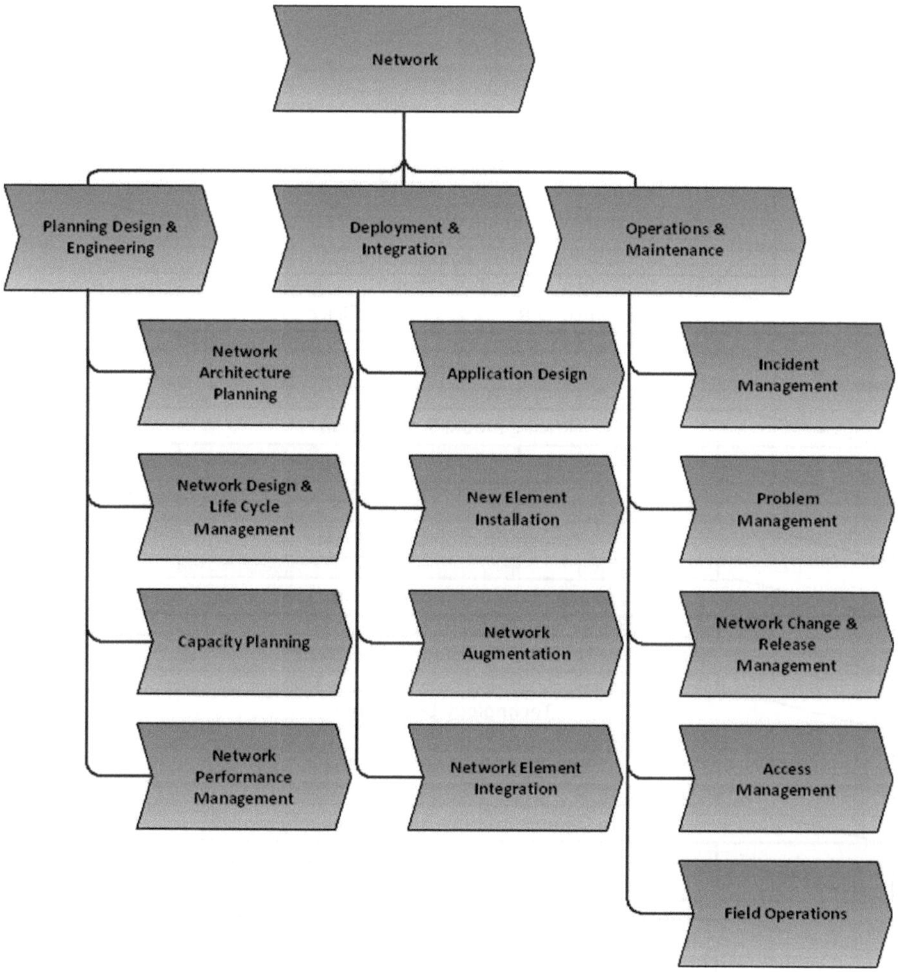

Fig. 7.4 In-scope processes for RFP

size, expected performance levels, and timelines are feasible for delivery. This has a direct impact on the success of the MSP business case. Hence VY would have also evaluated the RFP to assess its attractiveness and viability.

7.1.5.4 VY's Assessment Criteria

Realistic Goals

The cost to VY for a simple outsourcing deal designed for cost reduction is quite different from the costs associated with a complex value-adding managed service. In both cases, the expectation is that the costs for the client would be reduced, but the latter arrangement is likely to cost the MSP more than the former. This cost should be built-in in the MSP business case.

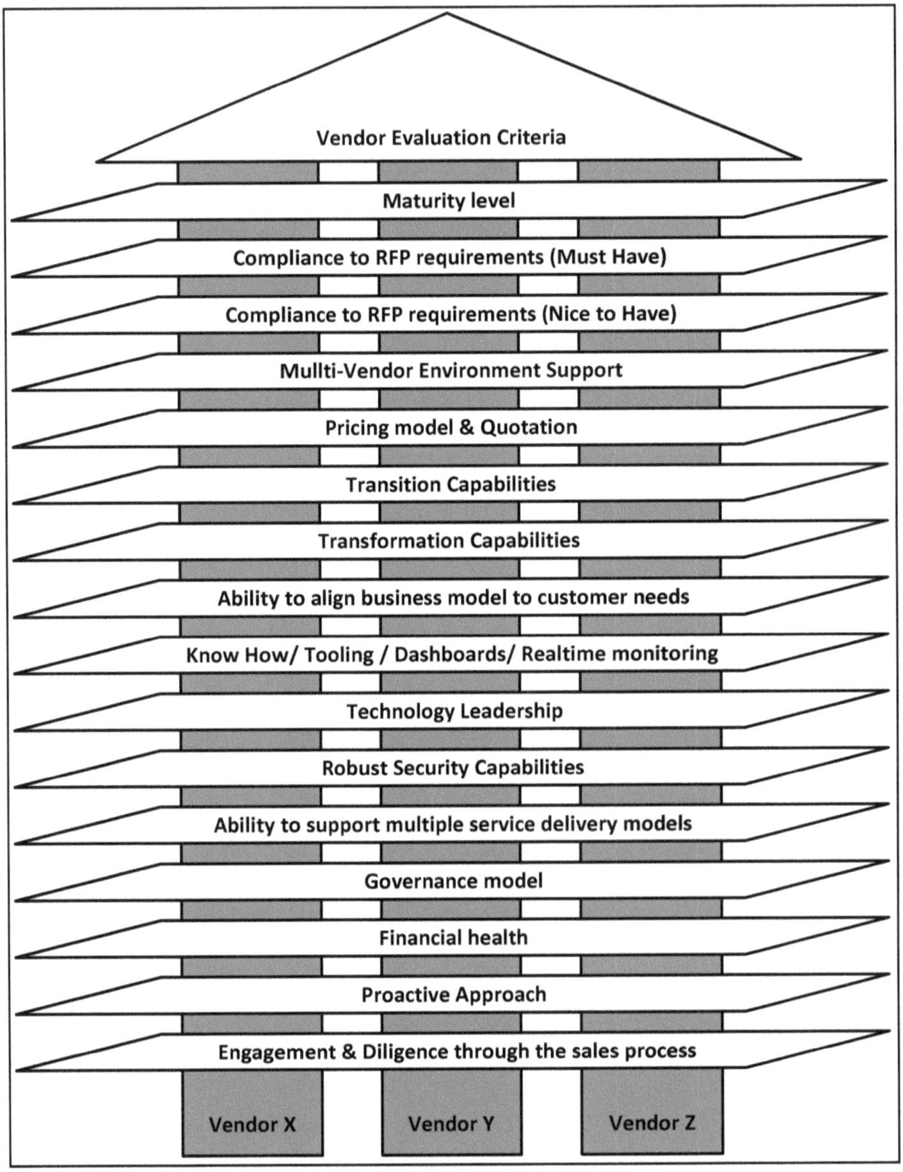

Fig. 7.5 Vendor evaluation criteria

In-Scope and Out-Scope Processes

In the initial stages, the roles, the processes, and their boundaries falling in scope may not be clearly demarcated. Additional processes are often required to provide the client a feeling of control and manage a healthy managed service relationship. The MSP should strive to get clarity on the "in-scope" processes as soon as possible.

This enables the creation of accurate business case and realistic expectations between the client and MSP. It also prevents conflict on basic issues and creates a harmonious working relationship.

Multi-vendor or Single-Vendor Environment

It is the order of the day to maximize and optimize. This leads to operators being very specific on the selection of the vendor for their network elements. One vendor may be superior in one functionality while others may score on other functionalities. In current telecom scenarios, most operators have equipment of multiple vendors deployed in their networks. So, for example, a TX may select VY for a specific role, product, and number of services but a VX (vendor X) and VZ (vendor Z) for other product or preferred services that may be more cost-effective.

The complexity of multi-vendor networks is higher and more difficult to manage as compared to single vendor networks. Supporting multi-vendor networks implies that the MSP should have the competence to handle their own equipment, other vendor's equipment, and the integration of equipment and network elements to let the network run smoothly.

Multi-vendor scenarios also impact the capability to deliver as per service level agreement (SLA). There should be back-to-back SLAs with other vendors to cover the MSP in cases where the fault lies with their equipment. Typically, a single point of contact (SPOC) is made available at the client's end to facilitate and mediate in such circumstances.

Environmental Factors

Consider a scenario of fiber deployment, where the fiber rollout is dependent on right-of-way permission from the government. If the service provider has an SLA of 48 days to provide the right of way, then the MSP responsible for the rollout cannot delay the same, by delivering in 50 days. These loose ends need to be checked and tied up; otherwise they become classic "pain points."

Economies of Scale

To ensure a profitable run and to viably sustain their running costs, the MSP may choose to provide some generic services to other operators as well. This helps to provide economies of scale, allowing for the substitution of resources and sharing of knowledge and expertise. This possibility should be leveraged to provide optimal solutions to the operator it serves. By passing on benefits to their clients, the vendor strengthens its position in the market as a reliable and ethical contender.

Governance

Governance is the foundation and key to the functioning of a successful partnership. It helps in clearly laying down the responsibilities and accountabilities, before and after transition of service. With due emphasis on reporting, feedback, guidance, collaboration, and communication, governance provides a structure around which a managed service arrangement remains healthy. An MSP looks for a balance in responsibilities and accountabilities, so that the business and functional requirements of the managed service agreement can be met.

Transition

Transition should be carefully planned, preferably in phases to meet agreed acceptance criteria. It is required to ensure continuation of service.

Transformation

It is akin to the restructuring of an existing building where one has to first study the structure; point out the places which need to be repaired, renewed, or replaced; and then find the appropriate solutions' providers to do the job. At times, it may even go a step further, creating a totally new building and moving on to it.

In cases where the network operator wants to transform its processes, the first step is very often, to align with the best practices and processes of the MSP. Subsequently, operator-specific initiatives are taken. An assessment of the ease of alignment provides an estimation of the effort required.

Transformation does not involve processes alone; it involves a careful look at the current technical architecture of the operator and its aspirations as well. Technical transformation such as IP transformation or any other form of transformation will have commercial considerations, resource requirement, etc.

In cases where the transformation aspirations are not clear, then a provision should be made to assess and consider it as a change request, over and above the agreed contract. This is required because changes accompanying the clarified requirements have financial and commercial implications, and therefore amendment to the existing terms and conditions would be required.

In case there are requests which go beyond the scope of the contract and cannot be handled through change requests, renegotiation of contract may be required. It is never possible to have a watertight contract as a lot of items are a matter of interpretation, as they arise. To ensure that such items are sorted out smoothly, guidelines and guiding principles should be established well in advance.

Besides this, location, time zones, local language and culture, and local laws and their implications should be considered before the finalization of contract. This holds especially true for MSPs located in different cities or countries, as words/sentences can be misinterpreted and many laws may or may not be applicable.

Financial and any other tax implications should be taken into consideration. A partnership is worth entering into, only if it is mutually attractive. Government and any other regulatory compliance requirements should always be cross-checked by professionals.

Exit Mechanism

It is possible that either of the parties want to exit the relationship. The exit mechanism should be clearly laid out.

7.1.5.5 Master Service Agreement and Readiness Assessment

After evaluation and assessment from both the sides, a managed service arrangement between TX and VY, the master service agreement (MSA), was finalized and signed. The MSA is an agreement of terms and conditions of future business.

Subsequently, the necessary steps in the form of a program were initiated for the transition and transformation of services.

Milestone Evaluation by the Program Manager

The program manager Ms. ABC conducted a "milestone evaluation." This was to assess her readiness to move to the tollgate of transition. Milestone evaluation by the program manager included the following aspects:

Contract Management

Consideration

Are there any third-party contracts that still need to be transferred?
Has the service rate card been finalized?
Are the on-site visits and travel allowance covered by TX?
What are the efficiencies that can be brought in, with respect to TX?
Can some synergies be derived with respect to other master service agreements?

Assessment

The third-party contracts for tools and platform are pending for three processes: network design and life-cycle management and network performance management. The on-site visits and travel allowance are not relevant at the process level but are covered under the overall master service agreement.

Finance

Consideration

Is the invoicing process clear?
Are the payment terms acceptable?
Is it transaction based or volume based?
Are there clear guidelines for the acceptance of service deliverables?

Assessment

There are clear guidelines for the acceptance of service deliverables. Payment terms are based as per the line items of the master service agreement.

Human Resources

Consideration

Have the affected employees been informed of the transition to managed services?
Are there any employees who are moving over to the managed service provider?
If so, have they received and accepted new employment offers?
Can the transitioned employees be housed in an existing space?
What is the level of competence of the employees taking handover?
Has necessary action been undertaken to retain critical resources?
Has necessary hiring been done at the MSP end to ensure business continuity?

Assessment

The affected employees have been informed. Some employees of TX would be moving to VY. They have received and accepted new employment offers. Office space for transitioned employees is not ready right now but would be ready by the time of movement.

The competence of the MSP employees has been evaluated. Competence gap exists in network design and life-cycle management process. Necessary trainings are in progress and would be concluded in time. Hands-on training will continue in the initial months to bring the competence to necessary levels.

Key resources have been retained. Retention bonus has been offered to some of the critical resources.

Process

Consideration

Have the processes been assessed, to establish if they are mature enough (not broken and fragmented) to be transitioned?

Is the documentation of current processes available? If not, how soon can it be created? What are the SLAs for the process?

Have the processes been prioritized, such as core and support processes?

Are there any key performance indicators (KPIs) that are required for legal regulatory requirements?

Are there any processes which fall in the category of "shift and fix" and would require immediate action post-transition?

Are there any workflows that still need to be modified, to enable MSP to work?

Assessment

The network design and life-cycle management is broken and will be fixed subsequent to transition. A special project would be required to fix and transform the process. Other processes are mature.

Network performance management process is streamlined with respect to rollout and managed services. Documentation for network design and life-cycle management process is not available. It has been gathered on the basis of process discovery.

Process SLAs have been defined and prioritization has been done. KPIs required for regulatory authorities are clearly defined and currently being complied to.

Network design and life-cycle management process would need immediate action post-transition.

Tools and Technology

Consideration

Have arrangements been made for their laptops, software, user accounts, etc., to be shifted or assigned?

Is the technical environment ready for transition?

Are technical assets being transferred?
Have the warranty, annual maintenance contract, etc., been checked?
What is the health of these assets?
Will spare parts and additional inventory be transferred?
Have necessary network security measures been undertaken?

Assessment
Arrangements have been made for laptops, software, etc., and they would be ready as per schedule. Technical environment readiness is a work in progress and covered under a tools and platform transfer program.
Spare parts and inventory would be transferred. These assets have been verified and are in good condition. The warranty and annual maintenance contract transfer is a work in progress.
Network security measures are being covered under the tools and platform transfer program.

Transition Management
Consideration
How long will the operator team shadow (support and oversee) the MSP team?
Have internal operational level agreements (OLAs) been secured in MSP organization to support customer SLA?
Are robust measurement systems to monitor performance (activities and outcomes) and to deliver necessary reports?
Are there any rewards and penalties associated with any KPIs?
Is the format and frequency of reporting established?
Is the escalation mechanism established?
Have the parameters to quantify resultant benefits against the business case been finalized?
Has *relevant* knowledge transfer happened?
Have people been trained to take on new jobs in a live environment?
Are the transition and shadow period costs fully covered and recoverable from the customer?
Have the risks and controls been identified and necessary action taken?
Is there an on-site requirement for a longer period?
Are there any visa requirement?
Is there a setup for support to employees during and post-transition such as help desk, intranet site, and line manager support?
Is the transition scheduled in "waves" or is it a "big bang?" That is, will it happen in installments or at one go?
Is there sufficient communication to generate awareness about transition?

Assessment
Shadowing will be required for 4–6 weeks, based on the activity, to ensure there is minimum disruption in service. Internal OLAs are a work in progress.

Measurement systems are being covered under the tools and platform transfer program.

Rewards and penalties are there; setup (format, frequency) is being covered under the "tools and platform transfer" program.

Escalation mechanism has been established. Transfer and shadow costs are being covered via contract management.

On-site requirements may be there for two resources. Visa requirements are being taken care of by HR.

Risk management is being done on an ongoing basis.

Transition is scheduled in waves. The operation and maintenance wave was the first, while planning design and engineering is covered in the second wave.

Overall Assessment

Third-party tool transfer can be a "showstopper" as work cannot be done without the availability of requisite licenses and therefore should be addressed *as* high priority.

The "network design and life-cycle management" process is broken and will require attention post-transition.

There is a dependency with a "tools and platform transfer" program.

Once these points are covered, the program manager can seek approval on tollgate for transition.

7.1.5.6 TX-VY Interface

TX is also aware that VY has an offshore setup, which would be undertaking most of the managed services' work. For its convenience, it has requested the mode of interaction as shown in Fig. 7.6.

It will enable TX to have face-to-face contact with the onshore team. The onshore team will work in tandem with the offshore team to deliver world-class services to TX.

Having made a thorough analysis of this arrangement, TX and VY enter into a mutually beneficial collaboration. The requisite actions are taken as per the program manager's assessment. Both parties have clarity when they sign the contract.

7.1.5.7 Benefits to TX (Post-MSA)

TX's customers have taken very well to the higher speed offered by the 3G networks and stand to benefit from LTE. 3G is no longer a service available only for the high-end customer. Rather, with the reduced prices and high penetration, it has become a service for the mass markets. The range of devices such as laptops, tablets, and smartphones have played an important role in the acceptance of 3G, and their capabilities have led to a decline in the need for data cards and dongles. TX has the vision to offer a new level of customer experience, with improved efficiency, quality, and flexibility. It will also ensure that the data traffic surge in smart devices is handled smoothly. It expects to be benefitted in a number of ways:

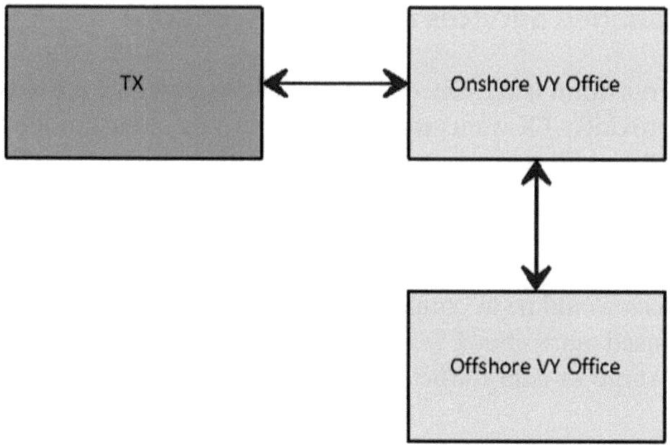

Fig. 7.6 TX-VY interface

- The minimizing of capital expenditure (capex) and operational expenditure (opex), leading to the reduction in total cost of ownership.
- Solid experience of VY consultants can help in balancing the goals, expectations through their neutral views, and global experience. This will ensure that the agreement is mutually beneficial.
- Significant reduction in time to market of new services.
- Improved business productivity by leveraging vendor platforms and know-how.
- Agility and improved responsiveness to the customers by streamlining existing ways of working and adding efficiencies.
- Optimal utilization of internal resources by redesigning their technical and process architecture.
- Enhanced quality of services by utilization of business, data, and network analytics available with the MSP.
- 24 × 7 service availability capitalizing on different time zones.
- CXO-level executives will be able to see dashboards of real-time network performance and ARPU impact of any disruption.
- Reduction in unplanned down time.
- Savings on account of physical space.
- Savings on account of data center setup and maintenance.
- Savings on account of cost of compliance.
- Savings on account of manpower learning and development requirements.
- Access to MSP knowledge and know-how.
- Focus on building the business and transfer the day-to-day operational responsibilities into the able hands of the MSP.
- Leveraging MSP expertise to reduce risk.
- Transformation of processes to align with vendors' "global best practices and frameworks."
- Differentiation in business value brings in the best of both worlds.

7.1.6 Is Managed Services a Win-Win Scenario?

TX wishes to transform itself. Once the network processes are passed on to the managed service provider, TX wants to focus on offerings in the mobile-based application domain. To begin with, it wants to transform itself by making inroads into *M*-commerce and *M*-health. This will not be possible unless VY rolls out the LTE network in the shortest possible time and takes over the running of TX's network.

This will then enable TX to become a virtual service provider. On the network side, 2G services would be at "sunset," implying that it will no longer be supported and will be phased out within 2 years and systems would be initiated to bring in 5G services. The surge in data traffic will continue and LTE network would be fully leveraged.

As per the contract, VY will have an assured source of revenue for the next 5 years. Chances are that, besides services, it will be able to sell its equipment as well. It will have to guard against "scope creep" so that it does not miss on additional sources of revenue for "out-of-scope" requests. This will ensure that its business case remains viable.

Managed services can be win-win, when things are kept as simple as possible but are able to accommodate the complexity of the business environment. The agreement should have the flexibility to adjust targets to account for changes within the frame of MSA. The processes should be standardized with the ability deal with handling exceptions. There should be built-in scope to accommodate business and economic changes.

A balance between price and service delivery is required for the operator as well as the MSP. Reduced costs, combined with effective and efficient delivery, are what the operator wants. However, the cheapest vendor may not always be the one which offers the desired service levels. Selecting and working with an MSP differs from case-to-case basis.

At times, it is a win-win to opt for a new MSP, as the existing MSP may offer synergies but may not have the best solution for all requirements. Evaluation based on weighted criteria is utilized in many organizations to objectively identify the most suitable vendor. In many cases, a multi-vendor strategy may be desirable.

Besides the technical performance, other parameters should be fulfilled. Factors such as language, culture, and trust need to be aligned between both entities in order to achieve a smooth transition and service delivery.

The nature of the tasks executed by the MSP has moved from simple to fairly complex. A transformational MSP goes beyond simplified standardized outsourcing to provide customized strategic solutions that enable the client to create value propositions. For a win-win scenario to exist, the MSP should have such capabilities.

In their model on strategic advantage of offshoring, Gupta et al. (2007) proposed that an integrated "24-hour knowledge factory" is a preferred sustainable, global model rather than a short-term fiscal model.

The relationship between both the partners goes beyond the financial equation with each other. The mutual respect, coordinated efforts to ensure profitability, and the effort to nurture a long-term relationship (which is usually conceived for 3–5 years) go a long way in making this collaboration successful.

The perceived value of the MSP lends itself to clues which go beyond the remuneration of tasks executed. The client looks for more than what they are paying for. What is quantifiable in the SLA is a prerequisite for a successful relationship, but the extras in the form of strategic advice, thought leadership on the part of the MSP, ability to visualize client's business scenario, and thinking along with client pave the road for a lasting relationship.

Another factor that plays a pivotal role is the technological leadership and reputation of the MSP. Nobody wants to pay to make the MSP employees learn at their expense. Operators are on the lookout for knowledge transfer from the MSP to their own workforce. The expectation is that the MSP employees are competent enough to respond to the requirements in very little time. This evaluation starts through the transition and finds ground through the life of the contract.

In case the MSP is very reputed, there may be some positive bias. However, if it is a first-time relationship and the MSP is new, the client is covertly and overtly evaluating if the decision to enter the relationship is correct. Once a level of trust is achieved, the client feels assured and confident of the competence. The relationship smoothens and perceived value increases.

It is important to note that the SLAs are the primary criteria for the value addition of the MSP, while other factors are the add-ons. The speed and time to market, global knowledge gain, and pool of more resources are relevant as well.

It is the add-ons though which help the MSP to provide innovative offerings to the customer. Following an SLA does not add to the innovation and differentiation. In some cases, however, if the SLAs are way ahead of the market norms, it may act as a differentiator. In other cases, the client looks to the MSP as its innovation partner.

The greater the possibilities offered through collaboration, the better the result.

It can be concluded that managed services is a win-win scenario when benefits are not one sided. The MSA allows the MSP to build its business while maximizing the benefits to the operator.

The pillars on which the verdict of win-win scenario stands are:

- Structured governance
- Technological and thought leadership
- Beating the KPIs instead of meeting them
- Ongoing collaboration and support to operator to enable it to come up with innovative service offerings

7.1.7 Is Managed Services a Case of Business Process Transformation?

In many cases, a managed service arrangement allows the operator to achieve one or more of the following goals as covered under the goals' "tan" of process Tangram:

- Dramatic improvement in performance
- Optimal advantage of technological advancements
- Achieve/retain market leadership
- Virtualization of enterprise
- Customer delight through customer experience management
- Enterprise as a network
- New revenue streams
- Economies of scale
- Increase in competence
- Increase in productivity
- Revenue growth
- Cost reduction
- Competitive advantage on the basis of cost or differentiation
- Regulatory compliance
- Plug revenue leakage
- Consolidation
- Standardization
- Improved measurement and control

These goals are very difficult to achieve under a transactional approach, typically associated with a delivery of a service purchase order. In the complexity of today's world, only a MSP with a "transformational approach" can anticipate the problems and to be ready with the solutions.

Managed services can be considered a case of business process transformation. This is only if it allows and enables the operator to evolve to a level, which is a big leap from small improvements. A simple case of labor arbitrage may free up resources and bring in cost efficiencies. However, it will perhaps be classified as a business process transformation if the impact is transformational.

What may be transformational for one may be ordinary for another, so it is the customized scenario of each operator, its expectations, its current state, and similar factors that decide the transformational nature of managed services.

References

6 different managed services pricing models, Erick Simpson, posted by MSP University. http://blog.spc-intl.com/different-managed-services-pricing-models/. Accessed 12 Aug 2014.
http://www.ericsson.com/ourportfolio/services/managed-services-1. Accessed 28 Oct 2014.
http://www.huawei.com/en/services/hw-u_256556.htm. Accessed 28 Oct 2014.

http://networks.nokia.com/portfolio/services/professional-services/managed-services. Accessed 28 Oct 2014. http://www.alcatel-lucent.com/services/managed-services. Accessed 28 Oct 2014

Gupta AS, Mukherji S, Ganguly A (2007) Offshoring: the transition from economic drivers toward strategic global partnership and 24- hour knowledge factory. J Electron Commer Organ 5(2):1–23

http://www.netpromotersystem.com/about/measuring-your-net-promoter-score.aspx. Net Promoter® and NPS® are registered trademarks and Net Promoter Score and Net Promoter System are trademarks of Bain & Company, Satmetrix Systems and Fred Reichheld © 1996–2013. Bain & Company. Accessed 28 Oct 2014

Palachuk KW (2013) Managed services in a month. Great Little Book Publishing, Sacramento

8 Recapitulation and Application of "The Process Tangram"

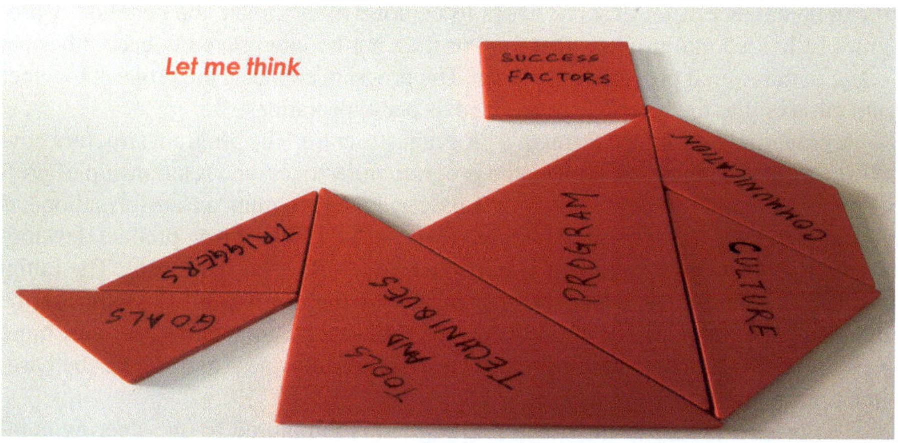

8.1 Process Tangram

Process Tangram is a framework defined to provide professionals at all levels a way to identify the important tenets of a business process transformation through the "tans" of the Process Tangram. This chapter is an attempt to recapitulate what was covered through the book from the perspective of applying the framework to actual business situations.

8.1.1 Transformation Program

Business process transformation is strategic in nature and comes into existence to achieve the identified goals. With its timelines spanning over years, it is easy for the

C. Sharma, *Business Process Transformation*, Management for Professionals,
DOI 10.1007/978-81-322-2349-8_8

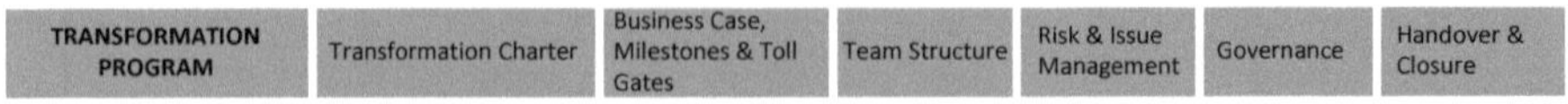

Fig. 8.1 Transformation program

objective to get lost in day-to-day mundane issues that projects frequently face. Given the scope of transformation, the complexity, the change involved, and the resource requirements, Process Tangram Framework proposes to undertake business process transformation as a program (Fig. 8.1).

Very often the goals are still fuzzy when the organization is triggered into a transformation. This usually results in a pre-feasibility study to give a form to the goals of the program, the associated risks, and a very rough estimation of resource requirement and its relationship with overall organization vision. Based on the results of the feasibility studies, a transformation program gets initiated.

A program comes into existence to achieve the identified goals; however, before it can commence, a lot of work needs to be done to maximize the benefits. A program is divided into projects that may or may not be interrelated to each other but relate to the overall program objectives. The program connects the projects together and ensures that the benefits are realized as per expectations.

A program is organized through a program structure. The program structure covers the projects, important project and program milestones, and relationship of projects to each other and to the program. Like any other program, a transformation has associated costs which must be justified by benefits. Unlike a new product development or service development, it is not so easy to build a business case. The initial business case takes its cues from the results of the pre-feasibility study. As the details of the program are worked out, the program business case becomes more realistic and is based on assumptions. The approved business case forms the baseline for the program.

The progress of the transformation program is monitored by the steering committee through review moments called tollgates or stage gates. Before going to the steering committee, the program manager conducts a review for himself called the milestone review, many a times with the important members of his team.

The transformation team and its composition are crucial for the program. The steering committee provides approvals, resources, guidance, and necessary authority to roll out the "to be" processes. The cross-functional process team comprises of people who actually get the work done through activities such as gap analysis, "to be" process modeling, and process rollout. The process team cannot achieve this mammoth task without the help of line managers, facilitators who could be internal or external, and a select group of super-users. Super-users are sometimes subject matter experts or policy experts and, at other times, people with a lot of practical common sense and understanding of the working of the organization. They are the internal resonating board for a realty test of any process or decision, for this group understands the organization and how the organization thinks.

Like any other program, transformation comes with risks and issues which need to be managed. At the program level, these are a combination of important issues and risks for projects that may affect the program or the ones existing at the program level itself. As an example, the possibility of a delay in the delivery of a project on critical path would impact the delivery of the program as well and would be thus included as a high priority risk at the project as well as program level. Depending on the likelihood and impact, risks should be monitored, managed, or escalated. As such the standard risk mitigation strategies of acceptance, avoidance, transfer, contingency, and reduction are valid at project as well as program level.

Depending on the organizational setup, the frequency and setup of governance is established. Irrespective of the setup, governance is critical. This enables time-to-time evaluation of progress and performance of the program. It is a juncture to receive guidance, identify opportunities, and seek alignment with stakeholders. The effectiveness of governance impacts the realization of proposed benefits of a program. Dashboards and established formats are used as the basis for weekly, monthly, or bimonthly governance with different stakeholder groups. Besides the interaction with stakeholders during governance, the program manager should reach out to the stakeholders as and when appropriate.

Since some of the projects may be running in parallel, others in sequence, the deliverables would be transitioned and handed over through the life of the program. When all the deliverables have been transitioned, approval is sought for closure of the program. Handover and closure should be properly documented as they are a rich source of information for future programs.

Undertaking process transformation as a program has the benefit of providing a structural mechanism to ensure that the benefits are realized. The institutionalization of the benefits may be supported by retaining some of the core members of the process team usually for a period of 1–3 months. All the other "tans" contribute to the development and realization of program benefits.

8.1.2 Triggers

The program initiation could be triggered by many reasons. "Triggers" form one of the "tans" of the Process Tangram (Fig. 8.2).

Identification of these triggers facilitates in assessing if one or more of these triggers are pointing toward the need of a transformation. There can be many internal or external triggers that necessitate a transformation. Within the Process Tangram, a comprehensive list of triggers has been drawn to form the elements of this "tan." It goes without saying there could be many other variations. The triggers identified

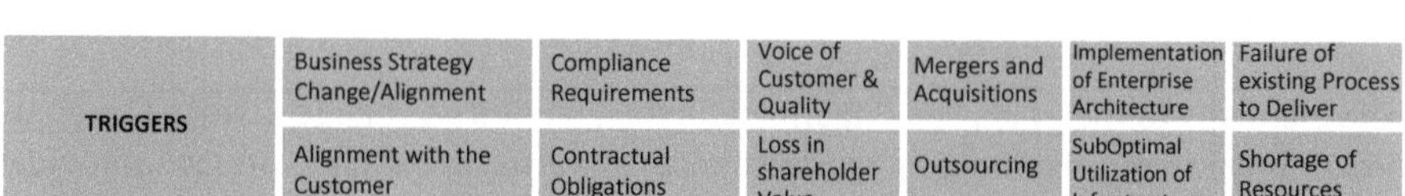

Fig. 8.2 Triggers

here, based on the author's experience and research of available material, stand a high chance on being one of the triggers that get the transformation started.

In the dynamic world where organizations need to be agile, business strategies undergo change and require the processes to be aligned to the strategy. Sometimes strategy is in place, but the processes are archaic and not aligned with the strategy. In both the situations, an incremental improvement may not suffice and require a fundamental change.

The customer has always been the king, and in the current times, the processes are no longer confined to the boundaries of the organization. A strategic partnership with a customer may require alignment with the customer processes.

Compliance requirements from regulators, tax agencies, and stock markets may trigger a transformation as well. There may be a contractual obligation to transform processes, for example, to remain a preferred supplier.

Voice of the customer or voice of quality can indicate a need to transform. Voice of the customer is captured through feedback from customers. This applies to capturing the requirements of internal and external customers. Voice of quality trigger pertains to the situation where the parameters that are critical to quality are not being met. This could also be due to change in input parameters and not necessarily a case of a broken process.

If the organization realizes that it is losing shareholder value, action may be required on the processes. When organizations merge or when acquisitions happen, the processes need to align with each other and lead to a transformation. Similar is the case of outsourcing where both the client and the outsourcing vendor may need to transform their processes in order to maximize the benefits.

Enterprise architecture involves looking at the organization from a holistic perspective, taking into account business, standards, and information technology. Enterprise architecture leads to better decision making and adaptability to market requirements but requires the processes to be efficient and in sync with the chosen standards and technology. The existing processes of the organization may not be aligned to the enterprise architecture, thereby necessitating a transformation.

In the scenario where an organization is unable to optimally utilize its human resources and IT infrastructure or there is shortage of resources, innovative transformation comes into picture. Finally if the processes are totally broken and fail to deliver, a transformation may be the solution.

These triggers lead to goals that must be fulfilled. Goals form the third "tan" of the Process Tangram.

8.1.3 Goals

The elements of the goals "tan" facilitate in the creation of change vision. The goals are dramatic improvement in performance, optimal advantage of technological advancements, achievement or retention of market leadership, customer delight,

GOALS	Dramatic Improvement in Performance	Achieve/Retain Market Leadership	Customer Delight	New revenue streams	Increase in Competence	Revenue Growth
	Optimal Advantage of Technological Advancements	Virtualization of Enterprise	Enterprise as a Network	Economies of Scale	Increase in Productivity	Cost Reduction

Fig. 8.3 Goals

TOOLS & TECHNIQUES	Process Analysis	Functional Analysis	Best Practice Analysis	Lessons Learnt logs	Performance Metrics	Quality Tools
	Productivity Analysis	Business Process Modeling	Competitive analysis	Life Cycle Analysis	Financial Metrics	Data Analytics
	Customer Analysis	Value Stream Mapping	Market Trends	Organization Analysis	Investment Analysis	Cost Analysis

Fig. 8.4 Tools and techniques

new revenue streams, economies of scale, enterprise as a network, increase in competence, increase in productivity, revenue growth, and cost reduction (Fig. 8.3).

Goals are the objective which a business process transformation wants to achieve. Clarity in visualization of goals goes a long way in crystallizing the deliverables and their subsequent achievement. It is upon the organization to decide on the scope and scale of change. The elements of the "goals" tan are a source for examining if there are more goals that can be included in the transformation vision.

8.1.4 Tools and Techniques

In order to achieve the goals, a lot of disciplined, systematic hard work is required. Tools and techniques come in handy for the same. While there are many tools, the important ones from a process transformation perspective have been taken in the "tools and techniques" tan. This book is intended to provide basic awareness of the relevant tools and techniques and their possible utilization. For deployment, a deeper understanding of these tools will be required (Fig. 8.4).

Tools and techniques can be deployed in many innovative ways. Some of the suggested clusters for their utilization are analysis of process, analysis of performance, learning, understanding of environment, and program business case.

8.1.4.1 Cluster 1: Analysis of Process

Process analysis, functional analysis, and values stream mapping help in analyzing the current process (Fig. 8.5).

Process analysis provides insight into the current process and expected end objectives. Commonly available as flow charts, this provides information on scope and boundaries. In cases where FMEA is available, the process functions with high risk priority number can be analyzed for suitable action. In case of new process design, rigorous FMEA should be done to ensure the service levels are maintained.

Functional analysis with its roots in system engineering can be used for analysis of current and "to be" process. Functional flow covers activation, control points, and termination of a flow with decomposition of functions. It can be utilized to define

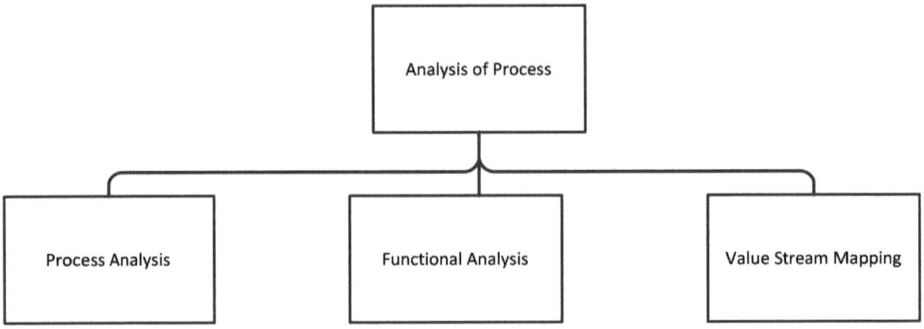

Fig. 8.5 Cluster 1: Analysis of process

functional, performance, and interface requirements along with the identification of constraints.

Value stream mapping enables high-level identification of process flow from the perspective of customer. It classifies activities into value-adding, business value-adding, and non-value-adding activities. Non-value-adding and business value-adding activities are critically evaluated to establish their requirement. Alternatives are considered for value-adding activities. Since values stream mapping occurs at a high level, it can also be utilized for transformation planning.

8.1.4.2 Cluster 2: Analysis of Performance

Analysis of performance can be done through utilizing productivity analysis, performance, and financial metrics. Productivity analysis helps in understanding the gaps in process performance, while gap analysis of current productivity with respect to future goals. It involves finding ways to minimize input and maximize output. Not only does it concern itself with the efficiency but also the effectiveness of a process (Fig. 8.6).

Each organization may have its own version of performance metrics. Some might have the customer perspective based on customer's opinion and feedback of process performance, while others may be based on key performance indicators. Care should be taken while utilizing these metrics as sometimes these are dated and may not be a correct measure of performance.

Financial metrics capture the current financial performance of the organization. These can be linked to the process performance as well. Processes should be designed to increase revenue and decrease the cost of goods sold. These metrics help in measuring the operational efficiency. They also measure the liquidity and working capital situation of the company. Processes should be designed to free up as much capital as possible, help in shorter cash conversion cycles, and maximize return on equity.

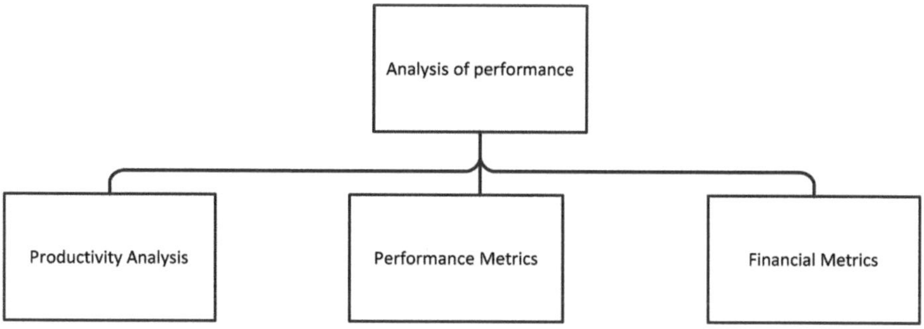

Fig. 8.6 Cluster 2: Analysis of performance

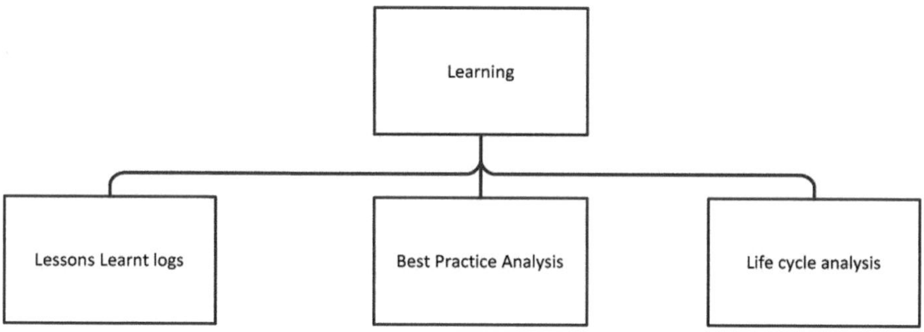

Fig. 8.7 Cluster 3: Learning

8.1.4.3 Cluster 3: Learning

Learning from inside and outside the organization can be incorporated in the "to be" designed processes. Lesson learned logs, best practice analysis, and life-cycle analysis can be utilized for the same. Lessons learned logs are rich sources of information, especially because they are in the context of the organization, and not only contain information on what has worked but also on what has not worked (Fig. 8.7).

Best practice analysis also known as benchmarking helps in learning from the best performing comparable functions in the organization and best performing comparable functions outside the organization and looking across industries for best practices in different sectors and industries. This could also involve looking at frameworks, databases, etc.

The stage of product or service in its life cycle should be taken into consideration to design processes that are appropriate and fit to use. This helps in the logical planning and introduction of processes of higher level of maturity.

Learning cluster helps in creating superior processes by learning from inside and outside.

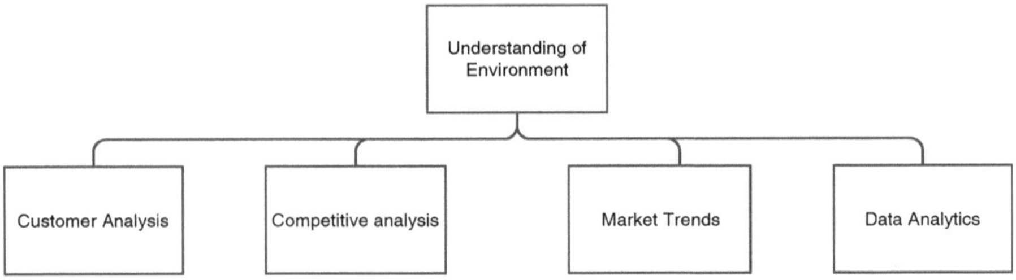

Fig. 8.8 Cluster 4: Understanding of environment

8.1.4.4 Cluster 4: Understanding of Environment

Customer analysis, competitive analysis, market trends, and data analytics can be utilized to facilitate the understanding of the environment. An understanding of environment helps in creating processes that are in sync with the environment in which they operate (Fig. 8.8).

Customer analysis is concerned with aligning the process to the customer to ensure value maximization to them. Customer preferences, demographic factors, and spending capacity can all have an influence on the design of the "to be" process.

Competitive analysis involves looking at competitors in and beyond the addressable market. The intent is to consider the strategic moves of the competitors, and it is helpful in identifying where the real boundaries of the end-to-end process lie. This analysis can be gathered from various sources such as market research.

Market trends provide organizations an opportunity to align their processes to market moods and movements. This enables the creation of a fit between the collective corpus of customers and their wishes and needs which can be catered through transformed processes.

Data analytics guides in process design by uncovering information based on synthesis and analysis of internal and external data. This information could not only involve the prediction of future scenarios but also provide information of performance from different perspectives.

Taking environment into consideration enables making informed decisions while selecting between alternatives and can be useful in aligning processes to changing business paradigms.

8.1.4.5 Cluster 5: Program Business Case

The business case for transformation program can be tested for financial soundness using investment analysis and cost analysis. Investment analysis helps in assessing if the costs involved are outweighed by the benefits. Investment analysis can be done using techniques like cost benefit analysis based on criteria such as benefit cost ratio, net present value, internal rate of return, and payback period. While net present value and internal rate of return take time value of money into picture, payback period ignores the same (Fig. 8.9).

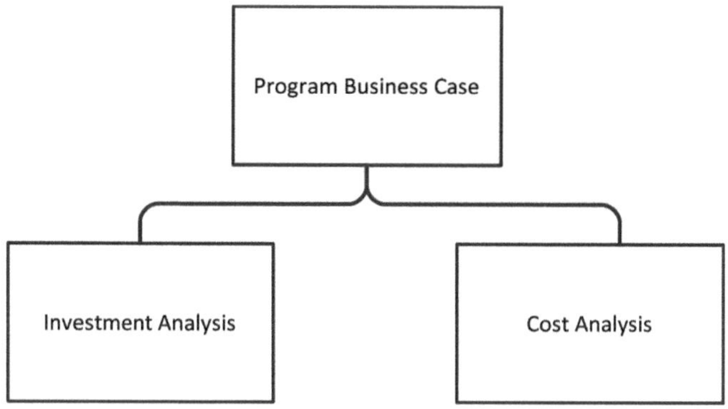

Fig. 8.9 Cluster 5: Program business case

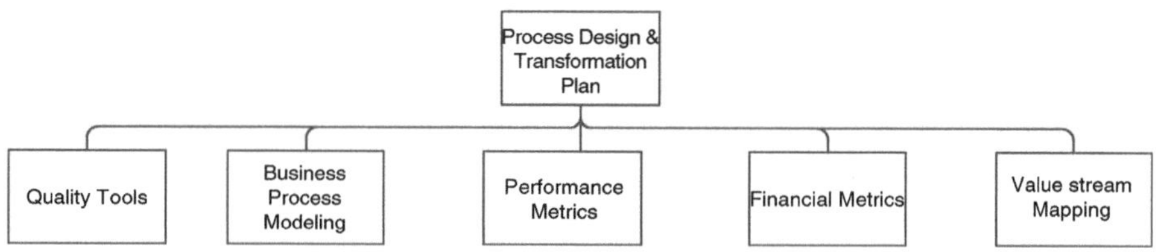

Fig. 8.10 Cluster 6: Process design and transformation plan

Cost analysis focuses on costs that will be incurred through the transformation program. Direct and indirect, opportunity, sunk, variable, fixed and mixed, and incremental/differential and marginal costs analyses are ways to understand the costs. Time-based activity approach is a costing approach which relies on capacity cost rate and capacity usage and offers insight in unused capacity which can be used to find new avenues for transformation.

8.1.4.6 Cluster 6: Process Design and Transformation Plan

Process design and transformation plan are facilitated by quality tools, business process modeling, performance metrics, financial metrics, and value stream mapping. Quality tools can be helpful in process design. Brainstorming helps in collectively generating ideas in a group setting of 7–8 participants. Root cause analysis can be used to analysis the reasons a particular level (transformed process level) cannot be reached. Cause and effect diagrams and Why-Why diagrams are common techniques utilized for root cause analysis (Fig. 8.10).

In case of transformation, business process modeling plays a very important role. It enables having meaningful discussions, analysis, design, and optimization of processes by comprehending and conceptualizing complex processes around us.

Before a process can be modeled, the approach and perspective should be finalized. While some frameworks point to abstract conceptualization and taking the internal external viewpoint into consideration (Franken and Weger 1997), others emphasize linking the core processes to realize strategic objectives (Kaplan and Murdock 1991). Business processes can also be seen as deterministic machines, complex dynamic systems, interactive feedback loops, and social constructs (Melão and Pidd 2000). Output requirements linked to customer requirements (Ramias and Rummler 2009) as well as linkage of IT and process redesign (Davenport and Short 1990) provide some other perspectives.

A process model should be complete, realistic, and partitioned when it becomes too complex. The elements within the process and their interactions lead to complexity (Mohapatra 2013). Structured models which are correct, clear, and consistent are necessary for process deployment.

For the purpose of process modeling, many notations can be utilized such as event procedure code (EPC) and business process modeling notation (BPMN). Within the scope of this book, BPMN 2.0 has been used to explain how process modeling can be done. Irrespective of the notation, a process model is a means of presenting information in a way that the users can understand it and capture the desired viewpoint necessary for design and deployment of process.

Performance metrics and financial metrics help in measuring and designing performance parameters for the process, and value stream mapping helps in creating high-level transformation plan.

On the whole, tools and techniques are necessary to bridge the gap between strategy and operations and to realize the potential of an organization to transform.

8.1.5 Culture

An understanding of culture can help in uncovering the value system of the organization and in understanding the relationships that exist. When we know what motivates people, we can channelize and mobilize energetic forces for the benefit of transformation. Change management also forms an integral part of transformation. No transformation happens without conflicts, and they are not necessarily negative when managed properly. Besides this, in order to ensure that the results of transformation are sustained, capabilities should be developed. Scoping is very important with respect to the culture, as cultural transformation is a complete field in itself and should not be undertaken as a part of process transformation. Value systems, organization structure, motivation, change management, conflict management, and capability development are the elements that need to be taken into consideration to place the culture "tan" correctly (Fig. 8.11).

Value systems are an interaction of individual values, organizational values, and the environment in which they operate. Individual values are formed through factors such as upbringing, education, and national values. Organizational values are

Fig. 8.11 Culture

affected by factors such as founding fathers and organization history. Environment is where the organization operates.

Information on organizational culture can be gathered from artifacts, philosophies, and principles of the organization and the basic assumptions that impact the understanding and coherence of the world around people. Organizations can have different culture types in terms of their values and maturity. Every culture has its own unique characteristics; however, culture is not static. It is influenced by new entrants, the information passed on by older employees, leadership, diversity, and sub-cultures.

The knowledge of value systems can help the transformation team in positioning the processes in a manner that the "new" way of doing things becomes a part of the organizational values. This is a tedious process and it is unreal to expect though that this happens overnight.

Changes in organization structure may be utilized to facilitate change in processes. Often changes in the span of control and degree of centralization are made to create an optimal environment for the "to be" process.

In order to ensure that employees wholeheartedly engage themselves in the transformation, they need to be motivated. Although the motivating factors may vary from person to person, expectancy theory and equity theory of motivation can be applied during the transformation. In other words, people should feel that the objectives and targets are real and their completion will make them feel satisfied by their performance. It is important that they feel that the evaluation of their performance in comparison to others is fair. Rewards and recognition are often utilized to motivate people. In rare cases, penalties may be used to force a certain behavior.

Change management is an indispensable part of business process transformation. Change management is complex and ambiguous and requires agility like never before. There is no one rule for success, yet there are models that can be looked upon for guidance while embarking on a change initiative.

In this book a case was worked out to understand the application of change models. It was clear that it is necessary to surface the driving and resisting forces. Once the desired state is visualized, the creation of dissatisfaction with the current state acts as a motivator for achieving the desired state. Change agents along with reward mechanisms help in moving and remaining at the desired state.

A change has to be placed in the context of organization vision. The change vision has the power to provide direction to the change initiative. Momentum is achieved when a group of committed individuals are willing to relentlessly support the leadership. The benefits of change should be visible to everyone and should outweigh the costs. Strategy links the vision to its realization. People perform well when their tasks are clearly defined and the change goals are incorporated in them. People need to be told repeatedly about the end goals, sometimes at a high level and at other times at a level that impacts their day-to-day working. They require the know-how to find their way through the fear of the unknown.

Resistance can very easily become "the" mega-blocker for change; however, the absence of resistance can indicate that people are either not affected by the change or they are indifferent. Resistance can exist at the level of individuals, groups, or organization.

A change manager role which can be vested in any person of the transformation team can facilitate change management with the support of change agents. People need time to imbibe and internalize change and to understand its implications. While some aspects in internalization require intervention, others settle down on their own without extra effort.

It is important for the change team and management to communicate continuously and be consistent in the message. They should support the employees throughout the transformation. Support does not imply agreement and allowance on each voice of dissent but in making people aware of the benefits, seeking out possibilities for maximizing benefits and minimizing pain.

Change management is not an easy task, where even a lot of personal sacrifices are required. Celebrating achievements helps in keeping the element of fun alive. Transformation programs must give change management its due importance to facilitate achievement of transformation goals.

Interaction of groups and individuals gives rise to conflicts. Conflict is sometimes introduced to create a competitive environment and may not be necessarily detrimental to transformation. Within acceptable levels, conflict aids in meeting challenges, looking out for alternative options, decision making and creativity. Care should be taken that conflict does not become disruptive.

Capability development impacts the performance of people and enables them in believing that they can perform at the transformed levels. Unless the capabilities are built in line with the expectations of the transformed process, it will leave employees demotivated. In order to design and execute a training for capability development, a stepwise approach can be taken. The steps to training design and execution are inventorize, prioritize, define, specify qualitative and quantitative requirements, conduct gap assessment, finalize approach, and design and execute training, followed by evaluation and feedback which acts as an input for future training design and execution.

Culture is a significant "tan" of the Process Tangram, and its power to make or break the transformation program should not be underestimated.

8.1.6 Communication

Within the "Process Tangram," communication is divided into engagement strategy, stakeholder analysis, communication plan, identification of barriers to communication, communication package, and feedback and evaluation (Fig. 8.12).

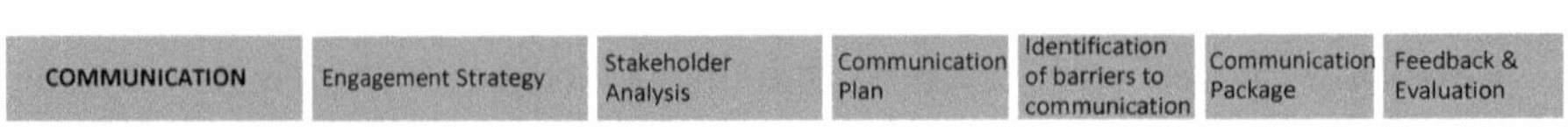

Fig. 8.12 Communication

Defining the engagement strategy is complex as engagement is not something tangible and is difficult to measure. The way an individual receives a communication is dependent on the message, the sender, and the receiver, yet engagement drivers can be selected which then become the key drivers along which the engagement strategy can be framed. There are various techniques that can be deployed to engage employees such as appreciative inquiry, message maps, and storytelling. The important aspect to consider while chalking out the engagement strategy is to ensure that core message is developed and validated in a manner that it becomes compelling. Employees need to understand why things around them are being transformed and how the transformation affects them.

Stakeholder analysis concerns itself with identification of stakeholders and the impact of transformation on them as well as their impact on transformation. Stakeholders can be internal and external. Their role, influence, position, knowledge, associations, issues, and means to address any identified issues enable chalking a strategy to engage with them and garner their support for transformation.

Communication plan is a live document and helps in creating a context for transformation and simplifying complex ideas. This is required to ensure that the stakeholders can link the transformation to themselves. The communication plan ensures that stakeholders get information on an ongoing basis. The communication plan is linked to the overall project plan and may involve coaching the leadership on effective storytelling.

Barriers to communication should be identified so that they can be dealt with in an effective manner. Communication barriers are detrimental to effective communication as they create difficulties in proper understanding of the conveyed message. The sender, message, receiver, and the environment can create barriers to communication in a transformation program. Barriers to communication can be overcome by designing the message carefully and involving direct reports along with respectable and influential leaders in the communication plan. The key messages should be validated before they are communicated. Optimal utilization of existing and new channels without introducing redundancies, visual theme, and message creation and repeating communication are mechanisms to overcome communication barriers.

The communication package is the actual artifacts, supporting material, training, and instructions of their deployment. This helps the communication team and leadership in communicating to the target groups.

Feedback and evaluation are activities that measure the outcomes of success and run through the life of the transformation program. It is necessary to do so to ensure that the overall communication objectives are met and if required corrective action can be taken. The approach to the feedback and evaluation should be pragmatic to ensure that the money spent in the evaluation exercise is commensurate to the expected result.

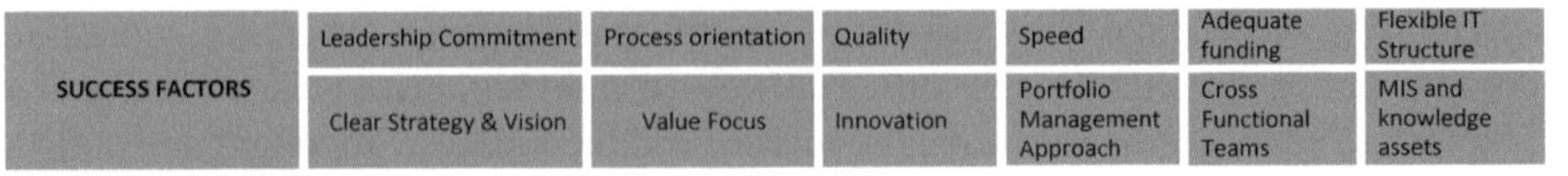

Fig. 8.13 Success factors

8.1.7 Success Factors

Success factors are the factors that increase the chances of success of a transformation program. Organizations which pay attention to these factors will be more likely to achieve their transformation objectives (Fig. 8.13).

The success factors that are relevant for transformation are leadership commitment, clear strategy and vision, process orientation, value focus, quality, innovation, speed, portfolio management approach, adequate funding, cross-functional teams, and MIS and knowledge assets.

Leadership commitment helps in the transformation by inspiring, guiding, and supporting the organization. A committed leadership helps in identification of key challenge, supporting the program from external pressures, challenging norms, conflict resolution and empowering the program to achieve its objectives. It strikes a balance between the running business and the changes that the program demands. While funding is seen as a form of leadership commitment, leaders should be an integral part of communication plans so that they can reach out to people and influence them to fully participate in the transformation initiative.

Vision refers to a visualization of the future, provides direction, motivates people to take action in the right direction, and helps in coordinating actions of different people (Kotter 1996). Strategy lays down the path to be taken to achieve the goals set out in the vision. The vision should be clear so that it can provide direction. The overall end objective could be picked up from the goals mentioned in the "goals" tan of the Process Tangram, yet a certain level of quantification would be required to make it real for the organization. The "do-ability" of the vision is established through the strategy. Transformation strategy could also include a guideline on the rollout of transformation program, such as projects in parallel or sequence, phased rollout, or a big bang approach.

A clear transformation vision and strategy serve as the guiding principles in how the transformation should be carried out and are very important for a successful transformation.

Value focus enables aligning processes with business strategy. This is achieved by aligning the transformation to the value proposition of the organization. Value proposition is the offering that the organization has for its customers and the reason that customers are able to differentiate between their products and services with respect to the competitors. When value enhancement and creation are central themes of a transformation, the organization visualizes the associated benefits. It also enables prioritizing and decision making when multiple courses of action are available. A value focus ensures that the transformation program remains connected to the business and eventually contributes to the achievement of the value proposition.

Quality should be a key criterion inherent in the work that is delivered as a part of the transformation. Quality ensures that the expected results are as per specifications. It also results in reducing the unnecessary costs that are incurred due to poor quality. Quality should be ingrained not only in the transformation team but also in the people who ultimately run the transformed process. For only then can the end objectives be achieved, be free of deficiencies, and satisfy the acceptance criteria.

Innovation is very important for the success of transformation. With the same resources, an innovative team can achieve far more than its expectation. Innovation can take many forms in a transformation program. It could range from innovative ways of sourcing funding to innovative ways of process redesign. Since innovation has such prime importance, it should be approached in a systematic manner such that new ideas are not a matter of chance. With the budgets ranging from frugal to substantial, innovation rejuvenates current offerings, setting the direction of the future. Innovation increases the competitiveness of a transformation through creative generation and adoption of ideas.

Speed is vital while designing the "to be" processes. Transformations which are designed to anticipate can speedily respond to customer requirements. The ability to reconfigure continuously is required to enable handling of disruptive changes. In the times of global enterprises, provisions are required for a mix of standard global processes with local flavors. Besides being able to deliver with speed, processes should also be able to create a perception of high-speed delivery.

Process orientation has been defined in various ways. The emphasis ranges from customer focus, strategic business process based oriented (Hammer and Champy 1993) to process culture (McCormack 1999) (www.drkresearch.org/research/kmpaper.doc). A process-oriented organization may or may not have a process-oriented structure. Process orientation ensures that the number of interfaces is limited. It also ensures that there is greater cooperation around the process irrespective of departments, products, or divisions. It would be easier to streamline and deploy processes in an organization which is process oriented.

A portfolio management approach to transformation implies the ability to have a holistic view so that functional silos do not jeopardize the benefits of transformation. In other words, it implies focusing on end-to-end process instead of departmental subsets. It helps in ensuring that all the participants of the process come on the same page. It also helps in providing end-to-end visibility. Portfolio management approach to transformation broadens the horizon and brings in universal benefits. It opens up possibilities of analytics and benchmarking that can drive overall performance.

Adequate funding is essential for a successful completion of a transformation program. Careful planning of costs and firm commitment for the release of funds through the life of the program should be taken. At the onset, acceptable overlay of funds should be established. Opportunities for consolidation of existing programs should be looked into so that returns can be maximized and duplication is avoided.

Keeping control on costs right from the beginning is essential for the program success. Funding is a form of management commitment to the program. Insufficient funds scuttle the achievement of complete program benefits.

Cross-functional teams offer an opportunity to take advantage of the diverse views and perspectives of its team members. Collectively a diverse group has the ability to generate ideas as different perspectives push the boundaries of thinking beyond the sets of vertical thinking. When members of such teams interact, they bring in their knowledge for the benefit of the transformation program.

A flexible IT structure enables dealing with changes and is able to accommodate changes. Flexible architecture can play a significant role in the success of a business process transformation through offering opportunities of data analysis, data manipulation, control of process, and harnessing the most of new technologies.

Management information systems help in keeping a check on the impact of the activities of a transformation program while it is being carried out and subsequently in ensuring the benefits and ways of working become a way of working in the organization.

Knowledge is an intellectual asset that enables value creation. Knowledge assets can therefore be leveraged in ways that they can provide significant advantage to an organization undertaking business process transformation. Artifacts that represent prior experiences provide important inputs and aid in the prevention of repeatable mistakes and utilization of best practices. Knowledge that is not yet externalized is also as useful when looking out for new paradigms.

8.1.8 Managed Services as a Case of Business Process Transformation

An evaluation of managed services as a case of business process transformation was done in this book. Managed services is a form of outsourcing which allows the operator (service provider) to free themselves from operational running of the network and enables focusing on tactical and strategic aspects. The speed of change in business and technology coupled with the demands of the customer makes managed services very useful for operators. Managed services has moved on from client-vendor relationship to a thought and technical level partnership with the managed service provider (MSP) resulting in differentiating innovative revenue-generating offerings to the end customer.

The triggers for managed services in telecom may be business strategy change, business strategy alignment, alignment with customer, voice of the customer and quality, merger and acquisitions, outsourcing, failure of existing process to deliver, or shortage of resources.

There are various forms of managed service arrangements or models such as strategic outsourcing, selective outsourcing, managed and hosted applications, operational outsourcing, managed capacity, build model, or simply labor arbitrage. The choice of the arrangement is dependent on fit between the requirements and offerings.

The service arrangements can be backed by many innovative pricing models such as value pricing model, tiered pricing model, and customized a la carte model. Before being able to offer services, MSP should formalize its goals and lines of business, map its offerings to pricing models, and ensure resource and tool availability along with the necessary know-how. Once the master service agreement is closed, transition and transformation are carried out.

Managed services has moved on from offering efficiency-centric solutions to customer-centric differentiating solutions. Managed services is enabled by information technology. With more and more telecom offerings expected to be on the creative side, IT provides analytical abilities which can pinpoint the aspects to be leveraged and the aspects to be improved.

Managed services can be said to be a case of business process transformation if it allows and enables the operator to evolve to a level which is a big leap from small improvements. A simple case of labor arbitrage may free up resources and bring in cost efficiencies, but perhaps be classified as business process transformation only if on the operator's side the impact is transformational. What may be transformational for one may be ordinary for another, so it is the customized scenario of each operator, its expectations, its current state, and similar factors that decide the transformational nature of managed services.

References

Davenport TH, Short JE (1990) The new industrial engineering: information technology and business process redesign. Sloan Manag Rev 31:11–27

Franken HM, Weger MK (1997) A modelling framework for capturing Business process dynamics, Knowl Proc Manage 4:153–162

Hammer M, Champy J (1993) Reengineering the corporation: a manifesto for business revolution. HarperBusiness, New York

Kaplan RB, Murdock L (1991) Rethinking the corporation: core process redesign. The Mckinsey Q 2:27–43

Kotter JP (1996) Leading change. Harvard Business School Press, Boston

McCormack K (1999) The development of a measure of business process orientation and its link to the interdepartmental dynamics construct of market orientation. www.drkresearch.org/research/kmpaper.doc

Melão N, Pidd M (2000) A conceptual framework for understanding business processes and business process modelling. Inf Syst J 10(2):105–129

Mohapatra S (2013) Business process reengineering – automation decision points in process reengineering. Springer, New York

Ramias AJ, Rummler R (2009) The evolution of the effective process framework: a model for redesigning business processes. Perform Improv 48(10):25–32

MIX
Papier aus verantwortungsvollen Quellen
Paper from responsible sources
FSC® C105338

If you have any concerns about our products,
you can contact us on
ProductSafety@springernature.com

In case Publisher is established outside the EU,
the EU authorized representative is:
Springer Nature Customer Service Center GmbH
Europaplatz 3, 69115 Heidelberg, Germany

Printed by Libri Plureos GmbH
in Hamburg, Germany